To:

_____

From:

_____

Open Doors – A Year of Daily Devotions

Published by Purpose Driven Publishers
23182 Arroyo Vista
Rancho Santa Margarita, CA 92688

PB370901-20190828

RICK WARREN

A Year of Daily Devotions

January

OPEN DOORS

We Love Because God Loves Us

"If I do not have love, I am only a noisy bell or a crashing cymbal."

1 CORINTHIANS 13:1 (NCV)

Life is all about love. Without love, we are just adding to the noise.

Love is not just something God does, it's who he is. Love is God's character and we were created to be like him. *"God is love. Whoever lives in love lives in God, and God in them"* (1 John 4:16 NIV). God demonstrated his love by creating you. He sent his only Son to earth to die for you. Every good thing you have is a gift from him, given because he loves you.

In order to really love others, you first need to understand how much God loves you: *"We love because he first loved us"* (1 John 4:19 NIV). You can't just know about God's love, you need to personally experience it. It's not enough to simply give a definition of love, you have to have tasted it for yourself.

His love is perfect, you can't do anything to earn more of it. You can't do anything to lose it. You can't hide from it, and you can't outrun it. Don't ignore his love because his love includes forgiveness for everything we've ever done wrong. It replaces our guilt, shame, and resentment. When you fully understand that God loves you completely and unconditionally, you will become secure in the truth that you cannot make God stop loving you.

Once you're secure inside God's unconditional love, you'll be able to love others the way God loves you. You'll be more patient and less angry. You'll be more thoughtful and willing to serve others. When you are hurt, you'll be more forgiving and show grace. You cannot give to others what you have not received yourself.

As you learn how much God loves you, his love will overflow from your life into everyone you meet.

One Step at a Time
Leads to Maturity

"The LORD directs the steps of the godly. He delights in every detail of their lives. Though they stumble, they will never fall, for the LORD holds them by the hand."

PSALM 37:23-24 (NLT)

Do you feel like you aren't growing fast enough?

When you first become a Christian, you start growing quickly in your faith. After a while, the growth slows down. Your spiritual growth is like a baby; they double in size within their first year. However, that growth isn't sustained. If they grew that fast every year, they'd quickly be bigger than a house!

God isn't in a hurry for you to grow— he is never in a hurry! You might be, but he isn't. He wants you to have a life deeply rooted in Christ. He wants you to stand strong so when the rough winds of life hit you, you won't get blown over.

In seasons of slow spiritual growth, you may feel like God has stopped caring about you. This is never true because he "delights in every detail" of your life. Your spiritual growth is a process that will take your entire life. You won't finish growing in a week, a month, or even a year.

However, if you take one or two small steps every week, you'll be much further along at the end of the year than you would be otherwise. In fact, a slow walk with God allows you to focus and carefully take in all that he wants to teach you.

The spiritual growth of a believer isn't one big leap across the Grand Canyon. It's a steady journey of one step after another. God's plan for making you into the person he wants you to be is a lifetime commitment, one that you can be confident in, knowing God will direct your every step.

Overcoming Temptation

"Accept God's salvation as your helmet, and take the sword of the Spirit, which is the word of God."

EPHESIANS 6:17 (NCV)

You are in a constant battle for your mind. That's where temptation begins. When God gives you an idea, that's inspiration. But when the devil gives you an idea, that's temptation. Every day, you have to choose which ideas you're going to accept.

The Bible says if you want to overcome temptation you need to resist the devil. How can you do that? By replacing tempting thoughts with biblical truth.

There are two steps you can take to prepare for battle:

The first step is to *"accept God's salvation as your helmet."* What does a helmet do? It protects your mind. Your mind is where the battle against temptation is fought. Before you can say "no" to the devil, you have to say "yes" to Jesus Christ.

The second step is to *"take the sword of the Spirit, which is the word of God,"* and use it against the devil's temptations. This requires memorizing Scripture so you will know how to counter the devil's lies. He isn't afraid of your opinion, but he will flee from God's truth.

When you memorize Bible verses, you always have God's Word with you. If you only keep your Bible on a desk at home, what good will it be when you're tempted at work, at the movies, in traffic, or in the grocery store? Memorizing Scripture gets the Bible off your desk and into your heart. Once it's in your heart, the Holy Spirit can bring it back to your mind at the moment of temptation, so you can replace the devil's ideas with the truth of God's Word.

Tell God You Love Him

*"Sing out your thanks to him;
sing praises to our God."*

PSALM 147:7 (TLB)

You've probably noticed that music and love go together. That's because music comes from the heart. Listening to music is not something you do intellectually; it's something that penetrates your soul and your emotions.

That's why there are so many love songs. But did you know that more songs have been written about Jesus Christ than any other person in the world? Christianity is a singing faith. Why? Because it's not about religion. It's about a love relationship with God, who loves you so much that he sent his Son to die for you.

Nothing will make you more aware of God's love and presence in your life than singing praises to him. You may be thinking, "You don't understand.

I can't sing." But the Bible says to *"make a joyful noise to the Lord."* So just sing it out! You don't have to hit the right note. You just have to make a joyful noise.

Can you worship outside of church? Yes, because worship is simply expressing your love to God. That means you can worship in the shower. You can worship while you're mowing the lawn. You can worship washing dishes. You can worship driving to work or even playing golf! You can express your love to God anytime, anywhere, and everywhere. Always keep a worship song in your heart. God loves it when you worship and sing to him.

God Wants to Give You Freedom

"If the Son sets you free,
then you will be really free."

JOHN 8:36 (GNT)

We hear the word "freedom" a lot these days. But it isn't the freedom Jesus gives. Instead, this false freedom is built on a selfish way of living, where people believe they can live life without restraints. It's an attitude based on the false belief that it's okay to step on everybody else to get your own way.

But the freedom that comes from Jesus—true freedom—is about living the way God meant you to live. It's about the ability to make clear choices, free from the fear, guilt, worry, and bitterness that once kept you in chains. You're free to see life from God's point of view, and his perspective is the absolute opposite of a selfish freedom.

You will never find real freedom by insisting that you can do whatever you want. Freedom is not something you can demand or earn. It is a gift from God. He sent Jesus to proclaim and deliver freedom from the sin that keeps us trapped in a cycle of anger, envy, greed, sexual immorality, broken relationships, unforgiveness, and selfishness.

You can live this way because true freedom is rooted in the knowledge that God is with you and he is for you, which frees you from the need to demand your own way.

How to Overcome Fear

"They threw me into a pit and dropped stones on me.
The water rose over my head, and I cried out, 'This is the end!'
But I called on your name, LORD, from deep within the pit.
You heard me when I cried, 'Listen to my pleading! Hear my cry for help!'
Yes, you came when I called; you told me, 'Do not fear.'"

LAMENTATIONS 3:53-57 (NLT)

Fear is the number one problem most people face—fear that they're not going to make it, fear of the future, or fear of what others think of them. The prophet Jeremiah had a lot of reasons to be afraid. His job was to deliver a very unpopular message to his nation. He knew he was putting his life at risk. But in his fear, Jeremiah turned to God. What did God say to him? *"Do not fear!"*

You might be dealing with a circumstance right now that has made you fearful. You might even be feeling hopeless. But there are several ways you can overcome fear.

Fill your life with the truth. The more you fill your mind with God's Word, the more it will drive fear out of your life.

Fill your life with love. The more you get to know God, the more you will understand his unconditional love.

Fill your life with faith. As you begin to trust God and his perfect love for you, you will begin to overcome your fears.

No matter what you're going through, and no matter how bad your circumstances appear, turn away from your fear and expect Jesus to restore your life.

Nothing Surprises God

"Your eyes saw my unformed body; all the days ordained for me were written in your book before one of them came to be."

PSALM 139:16 (NIV)

God can see past, present, and future—all at once.

This part of God's character is something we can't fully understand, for God is not like us! However, we can take great comfort in God because he knows everything that has ever happened and will happen.

You trust a doctor with your health because s(he) has great knowledge. Greater still, you can confidently trust God because his knowledge is perfect. God has never learned anything new!

The future will surprise you because things don't always work out as planned—but God is never caught off guard. He is never baffled or bewildered by anything that happens. He is above it all!

The next time you face a crisis, you may want to ask, "What's happening, where is God?" The truth is, God is constantly aware of everything. He's with you now, and he knows what's coming around the corner. When times are difficult, he is still with you.

It is impossible for God to learn anything new because he already knows everything. God knows all of your "tomorrows," and therefore you need to ask him for help.

God knows everything that will ever happen to you, but he's not going to reveal it all to you all at once. Why not? Because you wouldn't be able to handle it. You'd get discouraged by all the difficulties you are going to face, and you'd get prideful over all of the successes. God gives you just enough for you to handle, just enough to draw you closer to him. God knows what you need.

Friendship with God

"For since our friendship with God was restored by the death of his Son while we were still his enemies, we will certainly be saved through the life of his Son. So now we can rejoice in our wonderful new relationship with God because our Lord Jesus Christ has made us friends of God."

ROMANS 5:10-11 (NLT)

Your relationship to God has many different aspects: God is your Creator, Lord, Master, Judge, Redeemer, Provider, Savior, and much more.

In Christ, God is also your friend.

In Eden we see God's ideal relationship with us: Adam and Eve enjoyed an intimate friendship with God. There were no rituals, ceremonies, or religion—just a simple, loving relationship between God and the people he created. Unhindered by guilt or fear, Adam and Eve delighted in God, and he delighted in them. We were made to live in God's continual presence, but after the Fall, that ideal relationship was lost.

In Old Testament times, we see friendship with God in the lives of Enoch, Noah, Abraham, Moses, and David. When Jesus paid for our sins on the cross, the veil in the temple that symbolized our separation from God was split from top to bottom, indicating that direct access to God was available.

As Creator, we know that nothing is bigger than God. As Provider, we can go to God for our needs. As Savior, God helps us with our biggest problem: our separation from him. Why does God call us his friend?

The answer is found in a single word: joy. Our relationship with God means that we can live with joy, no matter what is happening in our lives.

Today, is your joy rooted in Christ?

You Can Forgive Others

*"Be kind and compassionate to one another,
forgiving each other, just as in Christ God forgave you."*

EPHESIANS 4:32 (NIV)

God calls us to forgive others, but how do we do that? Here are four ways to help you let go of your pain, hurt, and bitterness.

Recognize that no one is perfect. When we've been hurt, we tend to lose our perspective about the person who offended us. But we need to remember that we are all imperfect people.

Relinquish your right to get even. Trust God to confront the person who hurt you and trust him to work things out for you. Choose compassion over your need to retaliate.

Respond to evil with good. Getting even only brings you down to the other person's level. Take the high road instead. The Bible says to treat your enemies with kindness. It's nearly impossible to do this on your own. That's why you need the love of Jesus to fill you up.

Refocus on God's plan for your life. When you are focused on the people who hurt you, you're actually letting them control your life. When you forgive them, you find the freedom to refocus on God's purpose for your life.

Don't go another day with resentment, bitterness, and unforgiveness in your heart. Start doing these steps, and move on to live the life God created you to live.

Why Faith Matters

"God looks down from heaven on the entire human race;
he looks to see if anyone is truly wise, if anyone seeks God."

PSALM 53:2 (NLT)

The Bible tells us three things about the importance of faith.

Faith matters because God is looking for people who seek him. God is physically, visibly, and actively looking for faithful people he can bless. If you make yourself usable, God will accomplish more than you ever dreamed possible. God is always looking for faithful people who he can use.

Faith matters because it stands out. Some people talk the talk of faith, but they don't live a life of faith. They say they believe in God, but they don't fully trust him when it comes to

specific things in their lives, such as their finances, health, or job. Faith is hard to find. When the challenges in life are causing you to doubt God's goodness, remember every test is an opportunity to trust.

Faith matters because it leads to blessing and victory. The Bible says, *"For every child of God defeats this evil world, and we achieve this victory through our faith. And who can win this battle against the world? Only those who believe that Jesus is the Son of God"* (1 John 5:4-5 NLT). God wants to fill your life with blessings. But in order for you to enjoy those blessings, you have to put your faith in Jesus.

Confess Your Mess to Jesus

"Everything that we have—right thinking and right living, a clean slate and a fresh start—comes from God by way of Jesus Christ."

1 CORINTHIANS 1:30 (THE MESSAGE)

Jesus is in the business of giving people a fresh start. You may think, "I've blown it; I've really made a mess of things in my life. I wish I could have a fresh start."

Here's some life-changing news: You don't have to stay the same! When you confess your mess to Jesus, he lovingly and graciously responds by giving you a fresh start.

Beneath all the sins, all the things you've done wrong in life, God sees you. He created you to love you. God's message is, "You can be what I made you to be—and start living in a whole new way."

God will show you how he sees you, and that will transform your life. When you commit your life to God, he will give you a fresh start. If you've never submitted your life to Jesus, do that now. Just say, "Jesus, I want you to be the Lord of my life." The Bible says, *"Anyone who belongs to Christ has become a new person. The old life is gone; a new life has begun!"* (2 Corinthians 5:17 NLT).

How's that for a fresh start? You get your past forgiven, a purpose for livin', and a home in heaven. What a deal!

The Son Reveals the Father

"Christ is the visible image of the invisible God. He existed before anything was created and is supreme over all creation."

COLOSSIANS 1:15 (NLT)

Our culture has no shortage of false ideas about God. Some people think God is powerless, distant, or uncaring. Others believe that God is like a vending machine, if you pay the right price, you can get whatever you want. Some people think God is angry all the time. Public opinion is a terrible way to discover what God is like.

You could look to nature to discover who God is. Actually, there's a lot you can learn about God from nature. The heavens and the earth reveal the glory of the Creator. The waves and the lightning demonstrate his power. When you notice the sheer variety of living things, you can see that God is creative. The complexity of it all—from a single cell to the entire cosmos—shows us that God is organized.

But, if you want the complete picture of who God is, you need to look at Jesus.

Nature won't reveal God's love, mercy, and grace. Nature can't tell you God's purpose for your life. The most important qualities of God can only be discovered by looking at Jesus and studying his life. God the Father is invisible; God the Son "is the visible image of the invisible God."

Jesus came to pay the price for our sins—a price we could never pay—but he also came to teach us who God is.

Where do your ideas about God come from? Are they based on Jesus and God's Word, or have you settled for something less?

The Resurrection Changed Everything

"I am the one who raises the dead and gives them life again. Anyone who believes in me, even though he dies like anyone else, shall live again. He is given eternal life for believing in me and shall never perish."

JOHN 11:25-26 (TLB)

The resurrection of Jesus changed everything. The resurrection of Jesus Christ is one of the most well-documented events in history. It would stand up in any court of law. In fact, it has—many, many times throughout the centuries.

The resurrection proves that Jesus is exactly who he claimed to be. He repeatedly said he was the Son of God who came to die for our sins so that we could have life.

The resurrection proves that there is life after death. Jesus paid the price we could never pay, so eternity in heaven with God is secure for everyone who believes.

The resurrection proves that Jesus keeps his promises. Jesus promised to defeat death and he did. Since Jesus kept that promise, you can trust in all of his promises.

Jesus promises eternal life for everyone who believes in him.

Where else are you going to get a promise like that? Nowhere! Who else can offer you eternal life? No one! If you don't get it from Jesus, you won't have it. That is an amazing benefit, and it's available to you today.

To help you understand how to begin a relationship with Jesus Christ and join God's family, go to: pastorrick.com/know-god

God Grieves with You

*"The Lord is close to the brokenhearted, and
he saves those whose spirits have been crushed."*

PSALM 34:18 (NCV)

When you grieve, you may feel like God is a million miles away. However, what you feel and what's real are not always the same thing. God isn't a million miles away. In fact, he's never been any closer.

Did you know that God grieves with you? The Bible tells us that Jesus was *"a man of sorrows, acquainted with deepest grief"* (Isaiah 53:3 NLT). When you come to Jesus with your grief, he knows what you're talking about, and he understands your pain. God is sympathetic, He's not aloof or apathetic. He's not standing on the sidelines of your life watching in, he's in the game and grieving with you.

God doesn't only give you himself, he gives you a church family for support. You were meant to grieve in community. Healing comes in groups. Healing comes in the church. Healing comes in community. We're better together!

On a practical level, what kind of grief support does a church family offer? They can bring meals, help with childcare, stock your pantry, and run errands—to name a few. But above all, they can just sit with you—*pray with you*—and simply be present like Jesus, who is called Immanuel, which means "God with us."

Martin Luther once wrote, "God is quick to catch the sigh of the heart." Are you sighing heavily these days? God hears even the faintest cry. Let him comfort you. He longs to be near.

Stay Hungry for God

"You must crave pure spiritual milk so that you will grow into a full experience of salvation. Cry out for this nourishment."

1 PETER 2:2 (NLT)

Your faith is a life-long process of growth that is nourished by spiritual food.

Several times in the Bible, God compares his Word to food. Jesus calls himself the living water, and anyone who drinks of it will never thirst again. When tempted by the devil, Jesus said that for a person to live, God's Word is just as important as bread!

What's the point? You were created to connect with God. He alone meets your deepest needs, and nothing this world offers will ever satisfy you.

There are countless "junk food" options. You might try filling your need for God by staying busy, achieving success, exercising power, pursuing popularity, constant amusement, chemical addictions, and the list goes on and on. These things will never satisfy your deepest needs because you cannot fill your need for eternal things with things that will never last. They stunt your spiritual growth and keep you from participating in the "full experience of salvation," which is God's best for your life.

God provides the perfect spiritual banquet; our responsibility is to sit down to the table and eat. Peter tells us to *"crave pure spiritual milk"* because this a choice you must make.

Will you let God feed your soul? Or will you settle for something that will never satisfy?

Make it your goal to spend time with God every day—you can't survive on one meal a week! Pick a time and a place where you are less likely to be interrupted. Talk to God about the important things in your life. Read his Word and consider what it means for your life. You need a daily quiet time with God so he can nourish and grow your spiritual life.

Be Wise: Look Ahead and Face Reality

"The wise man looks ahead.
The fool attempts to fool himself and won't face facts."

PROVERBS 14:8 (TLB)

Many people start life well but progress poorly because they don't plan for the pitfalls. The Bible says the wise man looks ahead and faces reality.

Even though we make plans for our future, we still face pitfalls—voices of doubt, tempting shortcuts, cultural distractions, and discouraging delays. Just look at Noah: He faced many pitfalls after God told him to build the ark, but he overcame them—and you can too.

Now, this doesn't mean God will give you a goal as audacious as building an ark! But he will give you a big goal—even an audacious one—if you'll ask him to.

By looking ahead, you'll not only be prepared to spot the pitfalls when they come into your life, but you'll also be equipped to make plans that help you become the man or woman God wants you to be.

So go ahead. Ask God to help you establish goals for the next season. Pray, "God, what do you want to do in my life over the next five years?" Then move forward in faith. God will show you how to handle the pitfalls.

And remember, it's his plan, you're his child, and he will finish what he started.

Empathy Is an Antidote to Loneliness

"The first time I was brought before the judge, no one came with me. Everyone abandoned me. May it not be counted against them. But the Lord stood with me and gave me strength so that I might preach the Good News in its entirety for all the Gentiles to hear."

2 TIMOTHY 4:16-17 (NIV)

Eventually, everyone feels loneliness.

Isolation isn't fixed by beauty, wealth, fame, or success. Even marriage isn't proof against being alone. Many people marry out of loneliness and divorce a few years later for the same reason.

Paul's life goal to the end, even when he was dying in loneliness, was that he wanted other people to know about Jesus. He focused on others because he knew everyone needed to hear about God's love. He could have focused on his own problems, but instead he looked at what he could do to help others.

When you're lonely, quit having a pity party and stop saying, "I'm alone. Nobody loves me, nobody even likes me." That's focusing on yourself.

Instead, turn the focus outward and build bridges to others. There are a lot of lonely people who are also looking for a connection.

Build bridges by empathizing with other people's needs. Ask God to help you connect with others by praying, "Father, help me be a friend to people who need a friend."

What's causing the loneliness in your life? Extreme seasons of transition, separation, rejection, or opposition can lead to devastating feelings of loneliness. Don't let the difficult times keep you from reaching out to others. Look beyond your own problems to build bridges to others by considering their needs.

Defeating Your Destructive Thoughts

"When [the devil] tells a lie, he is only doing what is natural to him, because he is a liar and the father of all lies."

JOHN 8:44 (GNT)

You need a game plan to overcome destructive thoughts. At the root of every one of these thoughts is a lie. Where do these lies come from?

Satan told the first lie. He sold it to Adam and Eve by wrapping it up in false promises, and he's been telling lies ever since. Satan can't force you to do anything, but he tells great lies. He knows exactly what we want to hear which makes his suggestions extremely powerful. Satan has set the trap, and he knows what bait to use. Once he gets one person to believe his lies, he'll work through that person to influence others, creating a domino effect. Satan is constantly working to plant destructive thoughts in your mind. Here's the truth: You can't stand up to Satan on your own.

Jesus was tempted by Satan with three different lies. Each time, Jesus responded with Scripture. God's Word has the truth you need!

The person you lie to the most is yourself. Lies also come from your old nature. This is the part of you that is broken and sinful. Through faith in Jesus, we have the gift of God's grace. He erases the guilt in our hearts and the debt we owe him. While we are no longer under the power of our old nature, it still influences our lives. The old desires say, "You deserve this; it won't hurt you; it will be good for you." However, the more we indulge our old desires, the more we lie to ourselves. Without divine interruption, it becomes a never-ending cycle.

Overcoming destructive thoughts goes far beyond positive thinking. God's game plan for destructive thoughts is to counter them with truth. You need daily appointments with God to remain connected to his power and his Word.

The Path Back to God

*"When you get serious about finding me and want it more
than anything else, I'll make sure you won't be disappointed."*

JEREMIAH 29:13 (THE MESSAGE)

When you've drifted away from God, how do you get back to him? What does it look like to "get serious about finding God" again?

Be honest with yourself because nothing is going to change until you admit that things aren't working as they should. Finding God requires your full commitment—half measures won't work here! You will need to want it "more than anything else."

God wants to be first in your life; if you are distant from him, something else has taken the number one spot in your heart. You will need to do some significant soul searching to discover what has taken God's place. Then you need to confess your sins to God. He loves you unconditionally, just as you are! But you need to ask for his forgiveness for the things you've done that have taken you away from him.

Once you've said "yes" to Jesus, you'll never lose your relationship with him. However, when God isn't your top priority, a distance begins to develop. At first, you will feel a sense of guilt. God gave you these feelings to draw you closer to him. It's like the "check engine" light on your car's dashboard, telling you it's time to get the car fixed. When you ignore your guilt, over time, you will feel a wall go up between you and God. Bad things happen to your car when you ignore the "check engine" light, and the same is true with your relationship with God.

When you trust in God more than anything else in your life, you will never be disappointed. Take the path back to God because he will never let you down.

Why God Tests You

"Fire tests the purity of silver and gold, but the LORD tests the heart."

PROVERBS 17:3 (NLT)

The stress you're feeling may be a test from God.

When the prophet Daniel was still a teenager, the Babylonians put down a rebellion in Judah and took some of the Israelites into captivity. One of those Israelites was Daniel.

God had big plans for Daniel, he wanted him to tell people what the end of the world would be like. Before he could trust Daniel with this message, God gave him a stress test.

In Daniel's case, the Babylonian king, Nebuchadnezzar, wanted to secularize Daniel by teaching him a new language, a new culture, a new religion, and new habits.

When the king tried to change Daniel's diet, he found unexpected opposition because Daniel ate in obedience to God's commands. In essence, the king told Daniel to forget God and the spiritual values he'd followed his whole life. Daniel wouldn't do that, and so he passed God's test.

In the same way, God will often test your inward integrity before giving you outward influence. He wants to be sure you're ready to handle the power, the blessing, the influence, or whatever else he wants to give you.

Here's the good news: God is testing you because he wants you to succeed, and he's right there with you, cheering you on along the way.

Learn to Control Your Anger

"A person without self-control is as defenseless as a city with broken-down walls."

PROVERBS 25:28 (NLT96)

Anything that's uncontrolled will eventually destroy you.

In today's society, it's obvious we don't know how to handle anger. We live in a fast-paced, hectic world where people get stressed out. We're always on the go and trying to burn the candle at both ends.

Anger is not a sin; if you read the gospels you will see that Jesus got angry. What's important is how you express your anger. If you don't learn how to use it wisely, it will destroy you and your relationships. If you use it in the correct way, managed anger actually becomes an asset. There are some situations where the only proper response is to get angry. For example, when you see someone being taken advantage of, or when you see an injustice, anger is an appropriate response.

If you're going to learn how to control your anger, you have to stop making excuses and start accepting responsibility for your reactions. Anger is a choice, just like every other emotion.

When you realize that anger has a cost, you're more likely to control it. You always lose when you lose your temper. You may lose your reputation, your children, the love of your husband or wife, or your job.

You've got to think before you speak because anger control is mouth control. If you are slow to speak and quick to listen, then inevitably you'll be slow to get angry.

When you practice self-control and evaluate the cost of your reactions, you're going to manage your anger instead of it managing you.

Prepare Your Heart to Receive

"Faith comes from hearing the message, and the message is heard through the word about Christ."

ROMANS 10:17 (NIV)

Let's say you're a gardener. You've learned that you can take the exact same seed, plant it in three different locations, and get three different results. In one spot, you'll get giant tomatoes. In another, you'll get small tomatoes. And in a third, you'll get nothing. What's the difference? It's not the seed; it's the soil. The soil must be prepared for the seed.

The same is true when you hear God's Word. It's the reason you can take two people to church, seat them side-by-side, and one will walk out thinking God really spoke to him while the other won't get anything out of the service. The heart of one person was prepared; the other's heart wasn't.

Many people heard Jesus teach during his time on earth, but they didn't understand him. Their hearts weren't prepared.

Some people were amazed by Jesus' teaching, others got angry. What made the difference?

If you want to grow in your faith, you need to hear God's message for you. It's your responsibility to prepare your heart to receive the seed of his Word. This means cultivating the right attitude before you show up to church every week and expecting God to speak to you when you spend time alone with him every day.

Learn to Be Content

"Isn't everything you have and everything you are sheer gifts from God? So what's the point of all this comparing and competing? You already have all you need."

1 CORINTHIANS 4:7-8 (THE MESSAGE)

Instead of focusing on what you don't have, be grateful for what you do have. Rather than focus on what didn't happen, be thankful for what has happened. This doesn't come naturally, not even for the apostle Paul, who said, *"I have learned to be content"* (Philippians 4:11 NIV). Developing contentment is a learning process.

It's difficult to admit you struggle with envy because it's such an ugly emotion. When you're envious of others, you can't be content because you are consumed with the object of your envy. You may even want them to fail because you think it'll make you feel better. That's ugly, isn't it?

If you learn to be grateful for what you have, the chains of envy will be broken.

It's important to understand that envy is not about having a desire or a dream or a goal. It's good to have those. Envy is not about wanting something to happen in your life—or even wondering if you should have something. Desire can be healthy! It's actually an important marker of spiritual maturity when you want what God wants.

Envy resents somebody who has what you desire or has reached a goal you have yet to obtain.

The Bible tells us that we already have more than we need and far more than we deserve. Every good thing in our lives is a gift from God, and it is up to him to decide when and how he blesses us. It's up to us to choose to be grateful and make the most of what we've been given.

Trust God with Your Worry and Pain

"I am suffering here in prison. But I am not ashamed of it,
for I know the one in whom I trust, and I am sure that he is able to guard
what I have entrusted to him until the day of his return."

2 TIMOTHY 1:12 (NLT)

When something is precious to you—a rare coin, an expensive piece of jewelry, or an irreplaceable heirloom—you take it to the bank and entrust it to the protection of a safe deposit box. You trust that it won't be stolen, broken, or burned up.

What do you need to entrust to God today? How about these two things: whatever you're worried about and whatever is causing you pain. God promises to take care of them.

Worry is practical atheism. It's acting like you don't believe you have a Father in heaven who loves you. Worry is saying you don't believe God can be trusted to take care of the things that matter to you.

The most difficult thing to put in God's safe deposit box is your pain. But God is your Comforter, and he can be trusted with your deepest hurts. That's why Paul tested God when he was suffering in prison.

God wants you to entrust your worries and your pain to the safe deposit box of his love. You can rest assured that he will take care of them. God is infinitely more trustworthy than any bank!

Make Peace with Others

"If it is possible, as far as it depends on you, live at peace with everyone."

ROMANS 12:18 (NIV)

Is there someone you need to make peace with? Take the initiative and make the first move.

Peacemaking is a priority, whether you are the offender or the offended —either way, the ball is in your court. This is a hard step but the longer you wait to make peace, the more difficult it will become.

Unresolved conflict hinders your fellowship with God. When you're in conflict with others, you can't have a clear connection with God. The Bible even says that your prayers are hindered. When you need to make peace with someone, your happiness suffers. You can't be happy and in conflict at the same time. When conflict comes in the front door, happiness goes out the back door.

Take the initiative, reach out and schedule a time to meet face to face. Don't do it when you're hurried, tired,

or pressured. Find a time that works for both of you, and choose a place where you've got enough privacy to talk.

Reserve time to pray before you meet. Ask God for the wisdom and patience you need to bring glory to him in the peacemaking process. Remember God is your biggest fan, and he'll be right beside you cheering you on.

Once you sit down with the person you're having a problem with—your husband, your wife, a parent, a teenager, a colleague at work, or a neighbor—be the listener. Listening shows you care. Let them speak first and don't cut them off to get your point across. If you want to make peace with somebody, you've got to focus on the other person's hurts, needs, and fears.

When you need to make the peace, do everything in your power to bring restoration.

The Power of Self-Control

"A person without self-control is like a city with broken-down walls."

PROVERBS 25:28 (NLT)

Where do you lack self-control in your life? When you live according to our impulses, you open the door to pain and heartache. Self-control protects you from harm and allows you to fulfill God's purpose for our lives.

Without self-control, you will be mastered by your moods, which wildly swing back and forth. God gave you emotions, but you can't be mastered by them. It is better to live by your values and commitments, which means doing the right thing even when you don't feel like it.

When you develop self-control, you are able to restrain your reactions. You won't be careless with your words because you'll think before you speak. When others gossip, your self-control will keep you from joining in. When the little league umpire makes a bad call, you won't yell at him like it's the last game in the World Series.

Without self-control, your schedule will be managed by your opportunities and not your priorities. If you don't determine how your time is spent, other people will decide for you. Your time is important because once it's gone, you'll never get it back.

Managing your finances with self-control is critical for a life well-lived. When you are disciplined enough to live on less than what you earn, you can invest the difference. The power of your budget is that you get to tell your money where you want it to go rather than wondering where it went.

These aren't the only areas of life where self-control is needed. Take some time to talk to God about this issue and ask him to reveal where you need to develop greater self-discipline.

A city without walls is defenseless against enemies. Self-control will protect your life.

Waiting on God

"I will bless the Lord and not forget the glorious things he does for me."

PSALM 103:2 (TLB)

Your blessing is powerful because it reveals your priorities.

To bless someone or something is to call it good. When parents bless a marriage, they are saying it's good for the couple to get married. What motivates the parents to give their blessing? In a word, thankfulness. The parents are thankful for their new son or daughter-in-law, so they bless the marriage. Since the early stages of the relationship were good, it stands to reason that things will only get better over time.

Blessing and thankfulness go hand in hand. This is why David says he won't *"forget the glorious things"* God has done for him. Here are a few he includes in his psalm: God has forgiven sin, saved him from death, shows love and compassion, gave good gifts, and he is slow to anger and abounding in love.

That's quite a list! No wonder David was able to bless God. What would make your list? What has God done in your life to help you?

You need to make it a habit to bless God every day.

Here's the truth: You will always bless something with your life. You may not use that word, but the choices you make reveal your priorities. Do you bless business, physical beauty, or material success? What do you call "good" with your life? While many of these things are important, none of them are as important as God.

How would your life change if you really believed God was good?

Who Will Be in Heaven Because of You?

"The most important thing is that I complete my mission, the work that the Lord Jesus gave me—to tell people the Good News about God's grace."

ACTS 20:24 (NCV)

The most important thing in life is not to get married, fund your retirement, travel the world, become famous, or pay off your mortgage. The Bible says the most important thing in life is to fulfill your mission.

Jesus died on the cross for you so that you can fulfill your mission. If you don't do it, you are wasting your life.

God put you on earth for a purpose. He has a mission that only you can fulfill. Part of that mission is to tell other people the Good News of God's grace. You know Christ because somebody told you about him. Now, who are you going to tell?

If somebody died for you, wouldn't you want to know about it? Jesus died for every single person in the world. God wants to bring everybody into his family—and because God cares, we need to care too.

Ask God to open your eyes so you can see people around you who need to hear the Good News. Then show gratitude for the grace God has given you by doing *"the most important thing"*—telling as many people as you can about the Good News.

Take Advantage of Wasted Moments

"You can make many plans, but the Lord's purpose will prevail."

PROVERBS 19:21 (NIV)

Wasted moments are those transition times of life when you're driving, getting ready, or waiting in a doctor's office. During such times, instead of mindlessly scrolling through trivial information on your mobile device, you could be thinking, praying, reading, memorizing Scripture, or listening to audiobooks or podcasts.

The Bible says that one of the ways we demonstrate that we know the meaning of life, that we're living life on purpose, is by making the best use of our time. In those transitional times, you can read books that you never thought you had time to read.

You can use your transitional time to go deeper in your study of Scripture. Perhaps you could study the life of Moses, David, or Paul. What if you did a study of the parables of Jesus or the Psalms?

In fact, you can even take online courses in accounting, creative arts, public speaking, and business management during these potentially "wasted moments"—while taking a lunch break at work or waiting in the carpool line at your kid's school.

However, the Bible talks about people who are always learning without ever coming to the realization of who God is and what his will is for their lives. This is ineffective learning. No matter what you choose to learn, remember everything must be filtered through the truth of God's Word and the character of Christ.

Take an inventory of how you spend your time each week. Is God calling you to learn something new during your "wasted moments"? Whether it's learning a new skill or developing your prayer life, what might you be able to accomplish for the glory of God?

Focus on Pleasing God, Not People

"Our purpose is to please God, not people.
He alone examines the motives of our hearts."

1 THESSALONIANS 2:4 (NLT)

God did not make you to be the person somebody else wants you to be. God didn't make you who your parents want you to be, who your girlfriend or boyfriend wants you to be, who your spouse wants you to be, or who your boss or your friends want you to be.

God made you to be you. He has a plan for your life, and it's a perfect plan. If you're going to become all you can be, you have to refuse to be defined by others.

Moses had an identity crisis. He was born a Hebrew slave but raised as Egyptian royalty, the grandson of Pharaoh. When he grew up, he faced two options: He could pretend to be Pharaoh's grandson and live a life of luxury, fame, and power. Or he could admit to be who he really was—a Jew—and live a life of pain and drudgery as a slave.

Which would you choose?

Many people today are trying to be people they're not. But Moses insisted on being who God made him to be, despite all kinds of peer pressure.

A resolution you need to make is this: "I resolve to no longer let other people press me into their molds. I'm going to be who God wants me to be. I'm going to do what God wants me to do. And I'm going to fulfill the plan God has for my life."

God Is a Caring Father

*"As a father has compassion on his children,
so the LORD has compassion on those who fear him."*

PSALM 103:13 (NIV)

You matter to God. He loves you and cares about every detail of your life. God's compassion is one of his most outstanding characteristics. Why? Because the world often lacks compassion.

In Mark 4, Jesus' disciples were in their boat on the Sea of Galilee, when out of nowhere a furious storm came up. They started taking on water and the boat began to sink. They cried out to Jesus, "Don't you care if we drown?"

Isn't that the ultimate question: "Lord, don't you care?" Have you ever felt like that? "I'm going under Lord! Don't you care if I drown?"

Does God care if you are drowning in debt? Does he care if your business is about to go under? Does he care if your marriage is on the rocks or your kid's future is about to be shipwrecked? The answer to all of these questions is simply "yes."

God cares about your big problems and your small problems—the truth is, they are all small to him.

God is a good Father; he has compassion on us. This is good news! Every parent loves to see their kids succeed. Your heavenly Father takes delight in taking care of you.

February

OPEN DOORS

Memorizing Scripture Leads to a Blessed Life

"Whoever looks intently into the perfect law that gives freedom, and continues in it—not forgetting what they have heard, but doing it—they will be blessed in what they do."

JAMES 1:25 (NIV)

If you're serious about being spiritually strong and mature, the greatest habit you can develop is to put James 1:25 into practice. It gives us four steps that lead to a blessed life.

Read the Bible: *"Whoever looks intently into the perfect law that gives freedom"*

Review the Bible: *"and continues in it"*

Remember the Bible: *"not forgetting what they have heard"*

Respond to the Bible: *"but doing it"*

James is telling us that the key to a blessed life is to memorize Scripture—read it, review it, remember it, and respond to it. You may not think you have a good memory, but you remember what's important to you. You remember phone numbers and dates that you care about. You can quote songs from your childhood and rattle off the statistics of your favorite athletes. Memory is a skill you can learn. It's like a muscle you can strengthen with practice.

If you memorize Scripture, you will always have God's Word with you. Choose a verse a week. In a year, you'll have memorized fifty-two verses. In two years, you'll have memorized more than one hundred verses. Don't wait any longer. Start memorizing Scripture today. Then watch how God blesses your life.

God's Remedy for Emotional Exhaustion

*"Elijah was afraid and ran for his life... The Lord said,
'Go out and stand on the mountain in the presence of the Lord,
for the Lord is about to pass by.'"*

1 KINGS 19:3, 11 (NIV)

When Elijah was emotionally exhausted, God led him to do three things to help him recover—things that will also help you recover when you're at the end of your rope.

Rest your body. Sometimes God makes you lie down because you're unwilling to do it on your own. You can't be spiritually and emotionally strong while you're physically depleted.

That's what happened to Elijah. God did not scold Elijah. God didn't say, "Come on, man. You're just having a pity party." He simply let Elijah sleep.

Release your frustrations. Revealing your feeling is the beginning of healing. Elijah didn't hold anything back. He didn't filter his feelings. He told God his frustrations.

God isn't shocked when you complain to him. He'll listen to you until you run out of words. Let them all out. God can handle anything you throw at him.

Refocus on God. Elijah was focused on the wrong things; he needed to trust God. When you're struggling with burnout, it's often because you're trying to play God and control everything. When you refocus on God, you realize he is in control. You can stop exerting your own control.

If you're emotionally exhausted, God hasn't forgotten you. Just like he did with Elijah, God is ready and willing to help.

Faith in Action

"Suppose a brother or sister is without clothes and daily food. If one of you says to him, 'Go, I wish you well; keep warm and well fed,' but does nothing about his physical needs, what good is it?"

JAMES 2:15-16 (NIV84)

Faith is more than a feeling. Many people confuse emotions and feelings with faith. They come to church and are moved emotionally; they're inspired and stimulated. But that doesn't mean they're walking in faith.

Faith is something you do, not just something you feel. In other words, faith is not mere sentimentality. If you saw someone who is homeless, destitute, hungry, cold, and in need of clothing, would you be showing great faith if you walked up and said, "Cheer up! Don't worry; be happy! Feel good! Put on a happy face"?

This is not faith, it's wishful thinking. It's easy to have wishes, it's difficult to have faith. Wishes are passive, and cost you nothing. Faith is active and requires sacrifice.

Real faith produces compassion, and compassion produces action. Throughout the gospels, Jesus was often moved with compassion for people. Jesus showed us that faith is practical.

Faith says, "I'll do anything I can to soothe your hurt."

When you see a need, do something about it. Don't just toss out a quick "Well, I'll pray for you." Ask God how he wants you to help and think of ways to show your faith by putting it into action.

Stay out of Arguments

"Any fool can start arguments; the honorable thing is to stay out of them."

PROVERBS 20:3 (GNT)

Wise people are peacemakers, not troublemakers. Wise people don't carry a chip on their shoulders, looking for a fight. They don't intentionally antagonize other people.

The fact is, if you're around anybody for any length of time, you'll figure out what irritates that person. You'll file away that information in case you can use it against them in the future. When you get in an argument, and that person says something that hurts, then you push their hot button. And the argument ratchets up as the other person does the same.

You know what the Bible calls that? Foolish! You're not getting any closer to the resolution. You're not helping the relationship. In fact, you're hurting it. It is not wise.

Never compare your wife, your husband, your kids, your boss, or anybody else because everybody's unique. Comparing opens the door to anger.

When you start laying on the guilt in a relationship, all you're going to do is get the exact opposite of what you expect. It doesn't work. It's foolish to condemn others without expecting an argument.

William James, an influential psychologist in the early twentieth century, said, "Wisdom is the art of knowing what to overlook." Sometimes, it's best to hold back from calling someone out; you don't need to contradict them.

In the heat of the moment, your words can feel justified. But ultimately, they undermine your relationships. If you're wise, you will stop using hurtful words in a conflict.

Remembering What God Has Done

"Remember today what you have learned about the Lord through your experiences with him."

DEUTERONOMY 11:2 (GNT)

Moses led the Israelites out of slavery in Egypt and to the Promised Land. This journey across the wilderness should have only taken them a few weeks, even with the 200,000-plus people in tow—but it took them 40 years.

Why did their journey take so long? For 40 years, they were essentially walking around in a circle. God gave them seven tests, saying, "Will you trust me?" Every time they failed the test, he sent them on another lap around the wilderness.

But even in the wilderness, God had a purpose for Israel.

You may be in the wilderness right now. If you are, remember this: The way to the Promised Land is through the wilderness. You've got to go through the dry spell in the desert to receive the rich blessings of God. God does important things in your life during waiting periods. He is always at work!

While you're waiting, you need to keep a written record of your spiritual progress. Begin by journaling what you learn as you depend on Jesus, especially when it seems like you're getting nowhere. A journal is different from a diary. A diary is for everyday events; a journal is for lessons.

Some lessons God can only teach you in seasons of waiting. Remembering them will keep you from needing to be taught again.

Finding the Power to Change

*"I've tried everything and nothing helps. I'm at the end of my rope.
Is there no one who can do anything for me?
The answer, thank God, is that Jesus Christ can and does."*

ROMANS 7:24-25 (THE MESSAGE)

Have you figured out yet that a lot of times you are your own worst enemy? Left to yourself, without an outside power source, your fears and inadequacies will get the best of you. This will lead to you acting in foolish ways that are ultimately self-destructive.

You might reach a point where you think, "I need to be saved from myself because there are things I don't like about me—things I wish I had done differently, things I'd like to change. But I can't change them, not on my own power. I need someone greater than me."

Even the apostle Paul admitted he needed to be saved from himself, that he couldn't change on his own power. He needed someone to save him.

The truth is, if you didn't need a Savior, God wouldn't have sent one. He wouldn't have sacrificed Jesus for no reason.

People look for power in all the wrong places. Some look for it in self-help books, others in therapy or in the latest diet trend. Some look for it in a promotion and pay raise, others think getting married and having a baby will lead to personal salvation.

You won't find your answer in any of those places. The answer is not a place, a program, or a pill. The answer is a person: Jesus Christ.

The only way to experience lasting change is believing in Jesus as your Savior. He provides the power you need to become who God created you to be.

Love Your Enemies

"Love your enemies! Do good to those who hate you.
Bless those who curse you. Pray for those who hurt you.
If someone slaps you on one cheek, offer the other cheek also.
If someone demands your coat, offer your shirt also."

LUKE 6:27-29 (NLT)

When you're persecuted, harassed, or mistreated, Jesus expects you to respond by praying for and being generous toward your enemies.

It's tough enough to do all of this with your friends, let alone your enemies!

This is the example Jesus set for you. He isn't asking you to do anything he hasn't already done for you. When you treat your enemies with love, you stand apart from what's normal in the world. This is a powerful witness, and your loving actions speak louder than words.

Any fool can fight back. Any wimp can retaliate. Anyone with a critical heart can say something mean. Even parrots can be taught to curse. To love your enemies, you need to learn humility.

It's not easy, but it's the attitude that pleases God. The normal response is to hate your enemies and wish for their misfortune. You may even work actively against them.

Following Jesus will cost you your pride, but your reward in heaven is guaranteed.

How to Make a Case to Someone in Authority

"Daniel then said [to the king's official] . . . 'Please test your servants for ten days: Give us nothing but vegetables to eat and water to drink. Then compare our appearance with that of the young men who eat the royal food, and treat your servants in accordance with what you see.'"

DANIEL 1:11-13 (NIV)

As a believer, you will face situations in which you will need to make an appeal to an authority, asking them to change their minds.

In Daniel 1, we see five things that will help you make your case.

Develop a reputation for responsibility. People with great responsibility notice people who are responsible. The king's official had great respect for Daniel because he was dependable. That's why Daniel was able to make his appeal.

Be humble and not belligerent. Don't demand your way. Daniel asked the king's official to try a different way. Be humble or you'll stumble.

Don't be deceptive or manipulative. God does not honor dishonesty. Appeal to their goals and their interests. Start with what they want, not what you want. Daniel told the official, "We have the same goal. We both want me to eat food that makes me healthy. I just want to do it differently."

Choose the right place, time, and words. What's the right place? Always privately. Never confront authority in public. What's the right time? When the person is not frustrated, tired, or hungry. What are the right words? Be polite and pleasant.

Trust God if they reject your appeal. He is still in control when things don't go your way.

Don't Compare Yourself to Others

"Let everyone be sure that he is doing his very best,
for then he will have the personal satisfaction of work well
done and won't need to compare himself with someone else."

GALATIANS 6:4 (TLB)

It's impossible to be happy and envious at the same time. In fact, one way to experience true satisfaction in your life is by learning how to eliminate envy. Acknowledging your struggle with envy can be painful, but it is the first step toward a change of values and a more mature spiritual life.

Envy compares what you don't have with someone who has it. It could be a job, car, house, kids, spouse—even your lawn! But, any time you choose envy, you lose because you miss out on the satisfaction God has planned for you.

You challenge envy in your life by changing your perspective. Satisfaction doesn't come from gaining what others have; it comes from doing the work God has specifically prepared for you. If you can learn to accept this, you will escape the comparison trap.

Significance comes from doing your best. You have more important things to do than to compare yourself with others. You can't focus on your purpose while being preoccupied with what other people have. You can't be content with what you have while you're busy envying what everyone else has.

Do you want a more satisfying life? Be assured it doesn't come from comparison. Instead, it comes by becoming the person God made you to be. Don't pursue what others have, for comparison will always leave you feeling empty and frustrated.

God has a plan for your life, custom-tailored just for you. Do your best work, and you will find your satisfaction in him. Comparing yourself to others will quickly become a thing of the past.

Avoid Spiritual Drift

*"It's crucial that we keep a firm grip on what we've heard
so that we don't drift off."*

HEBREWS 2:1 (THE MESSAGE)

What are you doing to remember the lessons God has taught you?

As you grow into spiritual maturity, you will have to learn perseverance. This means believing God is working in your life, even when you don't feel it.

There are seasons in your spiritual life. Sometimes you will have a short, intense burst of growth (spring), followed by a period of stabilizing and testing (fall and winter).

What would it look like for you to keep a firm grip on your faith so that you don't drift?

Every day give your problems to God. It's fine to pray for a miracle, but don't be disappointed if the answer comes through a gradual change. Over time, a slow, steady stream of water will erode the hardest rock and turn giant boulders into pebbles. Over time, a little sprout can turn into a giant redwood tree.

Keep a notebook or journal of all the lessons you've learned. This is not a diary of events but a record of what you are learning. Write down the insights and life lessons God teaches you about himself, yourself, relationships, and everything else. Record these so you can review and remember them. If you don't remember, you'll have to relearn.

Reviewing your spiritual journal regularly can spare you a lot of unnecessary pain and heartache.

Prepare Yourself to Hear from God

"The seeds that fell on the footpath represent those who hear the message, only to have the devil come and take it away from their hearts and prevent them from believing and being saved."

LUKE 8:12 (NLT)

For the next four days, we are going to look at the Parable of the Sower found in Luke 8.

A major barrier to hearing God speak is resistance. Many people are closed off to the possibility that God might speak to them. If you don't think God can or will speak to you, guess what? He won't.

Jesus illustrated this resistance by comparing it to a seed falling on a footpath. As the farmer walks down the footpath between each row in his field, the soil is trampled down and becomes compacted. So, if a seed lands there, it lies on the surface until it is crushed or eaten by a passing bird.

There are two characteristics of a footpath: It's hardened, and it's narrow. Do you know any people like that? People who have a closed mind, a hard heart, and a narrow view of life? They don't even give God a chance. Their minds are made up; they're unwilling to listen.

The tragedy of a closed mind and a hard heart is that even if a little seed does happen to fall there, nothing can grow because it can't take root.

How can you prepare your mind and heart to hear from God? The Bible says, *"Get rid of all the filth and evil in your lives, and humbly accept the word God has planted in your hearts, for it has the power to save your souls"* (James 1:21 NLT). This means saying to God, "I won't resist anymore. I'm ready to listen. I'm opening my mind and heart so your Word can take root and bear fruit in my life."

Hurry Is a Barrier to Hearing God

"The seeds on the rocky soil represent those who hear the message and receive it with joy. But since they don't have deep roots, they believe for a while, then they fall away when they face temptation."

LUKE 8:13 (NLT)

When we live hurried lives, God gets shuffled to the sidelines. We say, "God, I want to hear from you. But hurry up! I've only got five minutes!"

Hurry is a barrier to hearing from God. He wants more than your leftover time and spare moments. He wants to be the center of your life, and that requires taking the time to listen to him.

Otherwise, we develop a superficial faith. Jesus compares this to when a seed falls on rocky soil. The seed sprouts but doesn't develop deep roots, so the plant withers and dies. The shallow, rocky soil represents a superficial mind.

In a similar way, we can react superficially to God's Word. We get excited. We get emotional. We're moved impulsively. But we don't let God's Word sink into the bedrock of our personality, so there's no real change.

Without roots, we fall into temptation.

How do you develop spiritual roots? Start by scheduling a daily quiet time with God. It can be 10 or 15 minutes. Just sit, be quiet, listen to God, and ask him, "Is there anything you want to say to me through your Word?" Nothing will build spiritual roots faster than a daily quiet time with God.

This requires you to be intentional with your time. When you allocate part of your day for a quiet time, you are showing God that you want him at the center of your life and that you want to hear from him.

Uprooting the Weeds of Distraction

"The seed that fell among thorns stands for those who hear, but as they go on their way they are choked by life's worries, riches and pleasures, and they do not mature."

LUKE 8:14 (NIV)

God wants to speak to you. But first, you must eliminate distractions so you can hear him. You can't hear God when your mind is crowded with worries, plans, and activities. You can't hear God when you're preoccupied with TV, the Internet, or your cell phone. These distractions are like weeds that keep a plant from growing to its full potential. When a seed lands among weeds, it will sprout and start to grow, but then the weeds will choke it, preventing it from bearing fruit.

Today's verse describes three common weeds that can choke God out of your life—worry, riches, and pleasure.

The word "worry" really means "pulled in different directions."

You can also be so busy making a living that you're not making a life with God.

What's wrong with pleasure? Nothing—except when you're so busy pursuing pleasure that you forget God.

There are other weeds besides these three. A weed is anything you allow to take first place in your life instead of God. A weed is anything you allow to choke God out of your schedule. How much effort does it take to grow weeds? None. Weeds are a sign of neglect. If you don't eliminate them, they can strangle the spiritual life out of you.

God is trying to speak to you. Is his Word sinking in? Be proactive and eliminate the weeds so that God can speak to you and produce fruit in your life.

Decide in Advance to Obey God's Word

"The seeds that fell in good soil stand for those who hear the message and retain it in a good and obedient heart, and they persist until they bear fruit."

LUKE 8:15 (GNT)

God speaks to the person who decides in advance to do whatever God says to do.

God doesn't speak to the person who says, "God, tell me what you want me to do, and I'll decide if it's a good idea or not." No. God's not going to waste his time on that. You have to say in advance, "God, I'm willing to cooperate with whatever you want me to do. I'm signing a blank check; you fill it in."

Jesus says people who listen to God with an obedient heart are like rich soil where a seed can grow into a plant that bears fruit. Notice the four traits of people who respond to God's Word in faith—they hear it, they retain it, they obey it, and they persist in it until they bear fruit.

How do you bear fruit? By obeying God's Word continually.

This is persistence, that we keep living in obedience until we see fruit. The fruit doesn't come before the persisting. If it did, we wouldn't grow spiritually.

Do you want to hear from God? Decide in advance, before you even open your Bible, that you will obey God's Word. Commit to doing whatever God tells you to do. God is ready to speak to you. Get yourself ready to listen.

Wise People Consider Other People's Feelings

"The wisdom that comes from heaven is first of all pure;
then peace-loving, considerate, submissive,
full of mercy and good fruit, impartial and sincere."

JAMES 3:17 (NIV)

One of the biggest mistakes we make is reacting to what people say instead of considering how they feel.

We focus too much attention on their words and not enough on the emotions behind the words. What a person is saying isn't as important as why they are saying it.

The Bible teaches us to try to understand others. We can't be peace-loving, considerate, submissive, and full of mercy without considering other people's feelings. When a person is angry or insecure, they might use words they never intended to use. Wisdom looks beyond the words to the emotion because people don't always say what they mean—but they always feel what they feel.

Wisdom in your relationships—with your kids, boss, spouse, or friends—will require you to develop the skill of looking deeper than their words. Be more mindful of the feelings of others. Pause your reactions until you've had a chance to understand their feelings.

We all have people in our lives who are difficult to love. But the people who treat us unkindly need our kindness the most! It's a fact of life that hurt people hurt people. It's difficult to show mercy and respond peacefully to others if we don't make the effort to consider the emotions that are prompting their words.

As you consider their feelings, your goal is to be impartial so you don't repeat their mistakes.

God Knows Everything

*"Nothing in all creation is hidden from God's sight.
Everything is uncovered and laid bare before the eyes of him
to whom we must give account."*

HEBREWS 4:13 (NIV)

Have you ever gotten out of bed to make a midnight refrigerator raid, even though you're on a diet? You stand there with the refrigerator door open, thinking, "Just one bite . . ."

We get into debates with ourselves like that: "Go ahead; it won't hurt this one time." "No, I'm on a diet!"

You may not be standing in front of the refrigerator, instead you are at the crossroads of another decision. You may be at work or filling out your income tax form or someplace your parents wouldn't want you to be. But you go ahead and do something questionable because you believe the lie that "no one will ever know."

But God already knows! God is never surprised. He knows everything!

The fact that God knows everything about you is good news, not bad. He's not shocked by your sin; and when you admit it to him, it will never change the way he feels about you. He loves you unconditionally.

What can you say to the God who knows everything?

Anything. Why? Because you know that no matter what you tell him, he will still love you unconditionally.

What do you need to tell him today?

Trust God to Provide

*"Since he did not spare even his own Son for us but gave him up
for us all, won't he also surely give us everything else?"*

ROMANS 8:32 (TLB)

The major cause of stress in your life is worry. You worry because you wonder if you will have what you need when you need it.

If you want a cure for stress, you need to learn to turn to God to meet your needs.

Some people find their security in their job. But when they lose their job, they lose their peace of mind. Others put their security in their marriage. But when their spouse dies or they go through a divorce, they ask, "Who am I? What is my identity?" Or maybe they put their security in their money. But when the money's gone, they lose their sense of self-worth.

Why would you put your security in anything that can be taken from you? You can lose your job, your health, your reputation, your spouse, and even your mind. But you cannot lose your relationship with Christ.

When you put your security in that promise, you can trust God to meet all your needs.

If God loved you enough to send Jesus Christ to die on the cross, don't you think he loves you enough to take care of every other need in your life? Yes, of course he does!

God is going to provide. He's going to take care of you. That's a promise. Instead of stressing out, look to him to meet all your needs.

A Heart of Devotion

*"He was successful, because everything he did . . . he did in a spirit of
complete loyalty and devotion to his God."*

2 CHRONICLES 31:21 (GNT)

God wants you to serve others with a heart full of devotion. However, over time, the compassion you once had for people can grow dull, leaving you unmotivated.

What's the antidote so you don't lose your heart? How do you maintain your spiritual passion?

Motive is everything! Never forget your motive for serving. The "why" behind it all: It's all for Jesus. You owe your life to him. The gratitude you have for what he lovingly did for you on the cross, knowing that one day you're going to stand before him and hear him say, "Well done thou good and faithful servant"—that's what motivates you. It's not about making a name for yourself or always having fun.

Maintain your prayer life, you need to keep seeking God so that you depend on him for everything. Do you pray about your ministry, or do you just jump in and do it? You ought to pray about the work God places before you. Ask God for wisdom and ask him to bless it.

Hezekiah was a king who had a lot of work to do. He slowly brought revival to Judah because he basically had to clean house after following the reign of his evil father, King Ahaz. Hezekiah was successful in everything he did because of his loyalty to God. He would pray, and God would answer. He would trust in God, and God would give victory over his enemies.

Think back to when your compassion for others was off the charts. Do you remember the thrill, the freshness, the newness of it all? You can serve with a heart like that again! Stay in step with Jesus, and never stop loving him.

You Can Trust the Bible

"For truly I tell you, until heaven and earth disappear,
not the smallest letter, not the least stroke of a pen, will by any means disappear
from the Law until everything is accomplished."

MATTHEW 5:18 (NIV)

You may have heard someone say, "I trust Jesus, but not the other guys who wrote the Bible." There's a problem with that logic.

Jesus trusted the Bible—every word of it! He taught that the Bible was more than just a unique book; it was above all other books.

Jesus said the Bible will last until the end of time. It will accomplish everything God wants to do in this world. There can be no doubt: Jesus proclaimed the truth of the Bible.

When Jesus talked about the Bible, he would often base his arguments about the truth of the Bible on a single sentence or even a single word. For Jesus, Scripture is the Word of God.

If you trust Jesus, why wouldn't you trust the Bible?

When Jesus talked about the Bible, he doesn't just talk about it as poetry and history. He saw the Bible as something that changes lives. Jesus doesn't just want us to read the Bible, he wants us to obey it.

When Jesus talked about the Bible, he talked about it as if the people and events in it were real. Jesus believed in Adam and Eve, Noah, Sodom and Gomorrah, Daniel, the prophets, and Jonah. If Jesus really believed in Jonah, then you should too. We don't know how God created a fish that could swallow a person, but he did.

You should trust in the Bible because Jesus trusted in it.

Learn Love Through Relationships

"I'm eager to encourage you in your faith,
but I also want to be encouraged by yours.
In this way, each of us will be a blessing to the other."

ROMANS 1:12 (NLT)

We can't live for ourselves if we want God to bless our lives. You need to be a part of a church family and develop relationships with other believers. The Bible calls this fellowship.

In today's verse, Paul tells the Christians in Rome, "I'll encourage you in your faith. You can encourage me in my faith. And we will bless each other in the process."

Most of the blessings God has in store for you in the coming months and years will come through other people. If you never build those relationships, you will never get the blessings.

The most important thing God wants you to learn in life isn't how to be rich or how to be successful or even how to make the world a better place.

The most important thing God wants you to learn is to love.

You learn to love by being in relationships. Whether at school, at church, in your neighborhood, or in the workplace, you need relationships to help you become who God wants you to be.

If you're not a part of a local church, you need to find one. Make it a top priority. If you're in a church but disconnected from other people, get involved in a small group (or Sunday school). Another great way to get connected in fellowship is by volunteering in a ministry.

You can't be blessed by living an independent, isolated life. We're better together because we encourage one another.

God Is Hope

"May God, the source of hope, fill you with joy and peace through your faith in him. Then you will overflow with hope by the power of the Holy Spirit."

ROMANS 15:13 (GW)

In 1927 an American submarine collided with a Coast Guard vessel off the coast of Provincetown, Massachusetts, and began to sink. The Coast Guard sent divers to assess the damage and begin a rescue operation. As the divers got close to the sub, they heard a sailor tapping on the hull in Morse Code. He asked, "Is there hope?"

That's a fundamental question of life. It's asked every day by thousands of people in thousands of different ways:

- When sitting in the doctor's office awaiting test results

- When a couple puts months and months into counseling and gets nowhere

- When dealing with a tax accountant in a bankruptcy court

- When a family hears their child is missing

You can survive forty days without food, three days without water, and eight minutes without air. But you can't last a single second without hope. It's an essential part of life. When hope is gone, life is over.

So where do you turn to find real hope? God is your true source for hope. He is the way to joy, peace, and power of the Holy Spirit.

Godly Habits

*"Practice these things. Devote your life to them
so that everyone can see your progress."*

1 TIMOTHY 4:15 (GW)

God's truth will set you free, but it may make you miserable at first. For instance, when you think about facing your weaknesses with honesty, fear can keep you in a prison of denial.

But when you allow God to shine the light of his truth on your faults and failures, you'll be set free from the old habits and patterns that have held you in bondage. You'll finally be free to replace your old way of doing things with God's way of doing things.

So how can you find this kind of freedom? It begins with understanding how much God loves you. He is already aware of all your weaknesses and mistakes, and he is actively working to help you change. It won't happen overnight. The truth is, even though you were given a brand-new nature at the moment of conversion, you still have old habits and patterns that need to be replaced. Doing that takes time.

You may wonder if it's really possible to be free from your habits, hurts, and hang-ups. That doubt might lead you to say things like, "It's just the way I am, and it's the way I'll always be." That's fear talking, loud and clear. Fear of change will slow your growth and keep you from experiencing the freedom Jesus died to give you.

Freedom requires you to practice the godly habits every day that point you to truth and make you more like Christ—habits like a daily quiet time with God and accountability to small group fellowship. The more you practice these new habits, the more the old habits will fade away.

God's Gift of Courage

"For the Holy Spirit, God's gift, does not want you to be afraid of people, but to be wise and strong, and to love them and enjoy being with them."

2 TIMOTHY 1:7 (TLB)

If you want to connect with others, you need to be willing to take the first step. This often requires courage. Why? Because fear disconnects human beings. When we're afraid of being rejected, manipulated, hurt, or used, we pull back and keep our distance.

Playing it safe keeps us isolated.

Fear makes you defensive. When people point out your weaknesses, fear makes you retaliate and defend yourself. But God wants you to understand that he loves and accepts you. Since he accepts you, what does it matter what others think or say about you?

Fear keeps you distant. If you let people get close to you they might see everything wrong about you. So in fear, you withdraw and hide your emotions. But since God loves you even when he's looking at you close-up, you don't need to be afraid of being real with others.

Fear makes you demanding. The more insecure you are, the more afraid you'll be of losing control. Fear drives you to dominate or have the last word. But God wants you to understand that he is the one in control, no matter how things appear. You can trust that he understands your circumstances.

Where do you get the courage to take the first step to connect with someone? Today's verse says it comes from the Holy Spirit. He gives you the gift of courage, so you no longer have to give in to your fears.

With God's Spirit in your life, you can replace your fear with faith.

What Does God Say to Lonely People?

"He was despised and rejected by mankind, a man of suffering, and familiar with pain. Like one from whom people hide their faces he was despised, and we held him in low esteem."

ISAIAH 53:3 (NIV)

If you woke up feeling lonely this morning, God has something to say to you: "I understand exactly how you feel." God is with you during this difficult season.

If you think Jesus didn't understand loneliness, you'd be wrong.

Jesus was despised and rejected by the people he created. He experienced loneliness throughout his entire life, especially during his final moments, when he went to the Garden of Gethsemane to pray. This was an emotional time for Jesus, for he knew the very next day he would be crucified on the cross, separated from his Father.

Since Jesus had a need for human companionship, he took his three best friends into the garden—Peter, James, and John—and said to them, "I'm very sad; stay here and watch with me awhile." And what did they do? They fell asleep! Jesus came back and said, "Can't you even wait with me one hour?"

The next day, he was nailed to a cross, where he cried out, "My God, my God, why have you abandoned me?" Since Jesus was carrying the sins of the world, the Father couldn't look at sin— *at him*. He was truly alone.

Jesus cares about you, he wants to help you and relieve your loneliness.

Maybe loneliness isn't an issue for you. However, you would be surprised by who the lonely people are. Whether a person is beautiful, wealthy, successful, or popular, loneliness affects everyone. Even married people can be lonely. Some couples never share any true intimacy, closeness, and fellowship.

Not only does Jesus understand your loneliness, but his death and resurrection also made it possible for you to truly belong as a member of God's family.

The Body of Christ Needs You

"All of you together are Christ's body,
and each of you is a part of it."

1 CORINTHIANS 12:27 (NLT)

You need to be connected to a church family to fulfill your calling to serve other believers in practical ways. Your service is essential to the body of Christ. Each of us has a role to play, and every role is important. There is no small service to God; it all matters.

No ministry in the church is insignificant. Some are visible and some are invisible, but all are valuable. Small or hidden ministries often make the biggest difference. In your home, the most important light is not the large chandelier, but the little night-light that keeps you from stubbing your toe when you get up at night.

There is no correlation between size and significance when it comes to ministry. Every ministry matters because we are all dependent on each other to function.

When one part of your body fails to function, the rest of your body suffers. Imagine if your liver decided to start living for itself: "I'm tired! I don't want to serve your body anymore! I want a year off just to be fed. I've got to do what's best for me! Let some other part take over."

What would happen? Your body would die.

Today, thousands of local churches are dying because of Christians who are unwilling to serve. They sit on the sidelines as spectators, and the body suffers.

The body of Christ needs you. How will you serve?

Trust God to Defend You

"You prepare a table before me in the presence of my enemies. You anoint my head with oil."

PSALM 23:5 (NIV)

King David knew God would defend him when he was attacked emotionally, verbally, and physically. As a young man, he was anointed by the prophet Samuel to be the next king of Israel, but he didn't become king right away. Saul, the reigning king, felt threatened by David and tried to kill him several times.

However, David never retaliated because he recognized God's goodness to him. He didn't have to use up all his energy defending himself because he trusted God to be his defender. David's cup overflowed, which meant God kept blessing him abundantly, even when others attacked him.

It takes a lot of faith and humility to rest and trust God when you're under attack, when you're misunderstood, and when rumors are spreading about you. When that happens, everything in you wants to rise up and defend yourself.

But you are most like Christ when you remain silent under attack. Jesus was constantly attacked, yet he never retaliated, even on his way to the cross. He remained silent before his accusers because he had entrusted himself to the care of the Father.

No matter what you face, you can trust God to defend you.

Let Jesus Lighten Your Load

"Come to me, all who labor and are heavy laden, and I will give you rest. Take my yoke upon you, and learn from me; for I am gentle and lowly in heart, and you will find rest for your souls. For my yoke is easy, and my burden is light."

MATTHEW 11:28-30 (RSV)

A yoke is a wooden crosspiece that connects two animals, so they can pull a load together. The yoke cuts the load in half because each animal is pulling part of the load.

When Jesus says to take his yoke upon you, he's not saying he's going to give you his problems. Jesus doesn't have any problems! Instead, he's going to share your load. He's going to take your problems on himself and bear them with you.

He uses three verbs in today's verse: come, take, and learn. Jesus says, "Come to me. In other words, team up with me. Then, take on a lighter load. Learn how I do it. This is going to reduce your stress. This is going to make it easier for you to navigate through life."

What burden are you carrying on your own? What's weighing you down? You don't have to do it alone. You can take that load to Jesus.

When you're yoked with Christ, you move together with him in the same direction and at the same speed, letting him direct you as you go.

What can you give to Jesus to lighten your load? How can you learn from him?

Your Pain Reveals God's Purpose

"God comforts us in all our troubles so that we can comfort others. When we are weighed down with troubles, it is for your comfort and salvation! For when we ourselves are comforted, we will certainly comfort you. Then you can patiently endure the same things."

2 CORINTHIANS 1:4, 6 (NLT)

God never wastes a hurt! Your pain often reveals God's purpose for you. If you've gone through a hurt, he wants you to help other people going through that same hurt. He wants you to share your story with them. God can use the problems in your life to give you a ministry to others. In fact, the very thing you're ashamed of and resent the most could become your greatest ministry in helping other people.

Who can better help somebody going through a bankruptcy than somebody who went through a bankruptcy? Who can better help somebody struggling with an addiction than somebody who's struggled with an addiction? Who can better help parents of a special needs child than parents who raised a special needs child? Who can better help somebody who's lost a child than somebody who lost a child?

The very thing that caused you pain, God wants to use for good in your life. This is called redemptive suffering. Redemptive suffering is when you go through a problem or a pain for the benefit of others.

This is what Jesus did. When Jesus died on the cross, he didn't deserve to die. He went through that pain for your benefit so that you can be saved and go to heaven. In the same way, he will use your pain to bring life and healing to others.

March

The Word of Truth

"He chose to give us birth through the word of truth."

JAMES 1:18 (NIV)

God wants to use his Word to give you a fresh start in life.

Without God's Word, you wouldn't be headed for Heaven. You wouldn't know about Jesus' death on the cross. You wouldn't know about God's purpose for your life.

God wants to give you all of these things—but it starts with his Word. Through the Bible, God recreates your life. When you feel like you're at the end of your rope, God uses the Bible to give you a fresh start, a do-over.

In Luke 8:11, the Bible is compared to a seed. Once the Bible takes root in your heart, it begins to sprout, grow, and bear fruit. As God's Word does that, God changes your life for the better.

God's Word isn't just words on a page. It is Spirit and life. It's spiritual power. His Word can transform society and transform history. It can do the impossible. It can change your life.

D. L. Moody, an influential nineteenth century evangelist, said, "The Bible was not given to increase our knowledge; the Bible was given to change our lives."

How do you need your life changed? What part of your life do you feel powerless to change?

The Word of God can change things that you cannot change on your own.

Seeking a Feeling Is Not Worship

*"I go east, but he is not there. I go west, but I cannot find him.
I do not see him in the north, for he is hidden. I look to the south,
but he is concealed. But he knows where I am going."*

JOB 23:8-10 (NLT)

God promises to never leave you, but he doesn't promise that you will always feel his presence.

When God seems distant, you may think that he is disciplining you for some sin. However, feeling disconnected from God often has nothing to do with God's discipline. Job didn't sin, and yet he still couldn't find God no matter where he looked—north, south, east, or west.

Losing the feeling of closeness to God can be frustrating and even painful; it's something that eventually happens to every Christian. However, feeling distant from God is vital for the development of your faith because

God wants to ask you this question: "Am I worth your worship even when the feelings fade?"

A common mistake many Christians make is seeking an experience rather than seeking God. They evaluate church based on how they feel after the service. "Service" has become "Serve Us." No wonder they are often dissatisfied with their church.

Job couldn't see God in the midst of his pain, but he trusted that God was watching over him as he waited faithfully for his presence.

The choice is yours: Will you base your worship on your feelings or God's faithfulness?

Don't Fear the Shadows

*"Even though I walk through the valley of the shadow of death,
I will fear no evil, for you are with me; your rod
and your staff, they comfort me."*

PSALM 23:4 (ESV)

In life's dark valleys, there is loss. When people go through loss, there are two common reactions. One is fear, and the other is grief. Grief is good. Grief is the way you get through the transitions of life. In fact, if you don't grieve, you get stuck! Grief will only hurt you if you don't let it out.

On the other hand, fear is a bad thing. Not once in the Bible does it say, "Grieve not," "Sorrow not," "Weep not," or "Cry not." What it does say is "Fear not." And it says that 365 times!

Shepherds carried a rod and a staff to guide and protect their sheep. In the same way, David knew that God had the tools to protect him, and he trusted God—even in the darkest valleys.

Perhaps you are going through the valley of the shadow right now—maybe even the valley of the shadow of death. It may be the valley of the shadow of debt. It may be the valley of the shadow of conflict. It may be the valley of the shadow of depression. It may be the valley of the shadow of discouragement.

Here's the good news: God is our Shepherd! We can say "no" to fear and be comforted by him when life is dark.

Thinking Carefully

"Be careful how you think; your life is shaped by your thoughts."

PROVERBS 4:23 (GNT)

God is far more interested in changing your mind than changing your circumstances.

We want God to take away all of our problems, pain, sorrow, and suffering. But God wants to work on you first. Transformation won't happen in your life until you renew your mind and your thoughts begin to change.

Your thoughts are powerful. They have tremendous ability to shape your life for good or for bad. For example, maybe you believed the lie someone told you about yourself when you were growing up: "You're worthless. You don't matter." If you accepted that thought, even though it wasn't true, it shaped your life.

The way to be careful with your thoughts is to examine them because some thoughts are good, others aren't. Careless thoughts lead to a careless life.

This is one reason you get mentally fatigued: there's a battle going on in your brain 24 hours a day. Satan is trying to neutralize your mind—your greatest asset. He wants you focused on negative and destructive thoughts that will distract you from God's love and goodness. The struggle can be debilitating.

Your thoughts determine your feelings, and your feelings determine your actions. To change your life, change your thoughts.

How can you be careful with your thoughts today?

Grief Doesn't Have the Last Word

"My flesh and my heart may fail, but God is the strength of my heart and my portion forever."

PSALM 73:26 (NIV)

Grief can cause a devastation that is debilitating. The hurt can be so deep that it feels like your heart is failing. Unfortunately, on this side of eternity, we will experience nearly unbearable loss.

The good news is, God can do something good in your life during these painful seasons.

For starters, God uses your grief to get your attention and to renew your focus. When grief shakes you up, you'll search for something solid— something trustworthy and unchanging to stand on. Your heavenly Father is the only one who can provide a steady foundation during times of loss and uncertainty; you were created to stand on nothing or no one else! He is your rock and your fortress.

God also uses grief to build your trust in his ability to do what only he can do: Bring good out of bad. If you've seen him turn sorrow into gladness once, you'll look for him to do it again and again. If you put your hope in God, he promises to not waste an ounce of your pain. Once you have experienced this from God, you will help others experience God in this way.

Not only does grief help you focus on God and trust in his promises, it prepares you for eternity. Grief reminds you that life on earth is a struggle, causing you to long for a place where there is no death, mourning, crying, and pain. Thankfully, your grief doesn't have the last word; God has eternity in heaven waiting for you!

Determining the Truth

*"Since only your rules can give me wisdom and understanding,
no wonder I hate every false teaching."*

PSALM 119:104 (TLB)

The U.S. Treasury Department trains its agents to spot counterfeit currency by touching and examining authentic bills. They're trained like this because there are many ways to counterfeit currency, but there's only one version of the real bills.

The way to really know what's fake is to know what's real.

Many people today fall for foolish ideas because they don't know the truth. That's why it is so important to study God's Word. By knowing biblical truth, you're able to spot false teaching.

How can you find time to study God's Word? Spend less time in front of screens.

By the time a typical American student graduates from high school, he or she will have spent more than 30,000 hours in front of a screen (including video games, tablets, laptops, and televisions).

Any guess how long it takes to read the entire Bible—all 66 books? It takes just 80 hours. With commitment and self-discipline, you could do this in a year.

So, since you do have the time, the question is: "How will you use your time?" God's Word gives you the wisdom you need to live a fulfilling and productive life. Study his Word. Examine it. It's the only way to protect yourself from the "counterfeit currency" of Satan's lies.

God Gives Advice Through Other People

*"The godly give good advice to their friends;
the wicked lead them astray."*

PROVERBS 12:26 (NLT)

God speaks to you through friends and family, particularly if they are believers. We all have blind spots. You have things in your life you're never going to see that need to be corrected, so God puts people around you to tell you the truth.

Do you have anybody like that in your life? Do you have godly friends who don't just tell you what you want to hear but love you enough to level with you and say, "You know what? You're blowing it right now. You're making a big mistake. You're full of pride. You're going the wrong direction"? If you don't have anybody in your life who loves you enough to do that, you need to find them.

You also need to be that kind of friend for someone else. Maybe you know somebody who is headed down the wrong path. They're getting involved in an affair or some kind of addiction. Or they're walking away from the Lord. You can see it, but you haven't said anything. Maybe you've thought, "It's none of my business."

It is your business if you love them. Love cares. Love says, "I love you enough to not let you do this. Don't waste your life. I care enough about you to risk this relationship." When you do that, God will speak through you.

Learn to Pray at All Times

*"Rejoice always, pray without ceasing,
give thanks in all circumstances."*

1 THESSALONIANS 5:16-18 (ESV)

The Bible tells us to pray all the time, but how can you do that? One way is to use "breath prayers" throughout the day, as many Christians have done for centuries. Choose a brief sentence or a simple phrase that can be repeated to Jesus in one breath: "You are with me." "I receive your grace." "I'm depending on you." "I want to know you." "I belong to you." "Help me trust you."

You can also use a short phrase of Scripture:
"For me, to live is Christ."
"You will never leave me."
"You are my God."

Pray it as often as possible so it will get rooted deep in your heart. Practicing the presence of God is a skill, a habit you can develop. Just as musicians are in the habit of practicing scales every day, you can learn to think about God at different times in your day. You can train your mind to remember God.

At first, you will need to create reminders to help bring your thoughts back to the awareness that God is with you. Do this by placing visual reminders around you. You might post little notes that say, "God is with me and for me right now!"

Your goal is not a feeling but a continual awareness that God is always present. If you are seeking an emotional experience rather than his presence, you've missed the point. We don't praise God to feel good— but to do good. That is the lifestyle of worship.

Count the Cost

*"People with understanding control their anger;
a hot temper shows great foolishness."*

PROVERBS 14:29 (NLT)

There's a cost to getting angry. You're going to get in trouble. You're going to sin. You're going to cause arguments. You're going to make mistakes. When you lose your temper, you always lose, whether it's respect, the love of your family, your health, or even your job.

If you count the cost first, you'll be less likely to lose your temper when somebody's pushing your buttons.

Maybe you use retaliation to motivate people to do the right thing. Don't do it! In the short run, you may get the short-term payoff. But in the long run, anger produces more anger, more apathy, and more alienation.

How many kids have become alienated from their dads or their moms because of out-of-control anger? How many people have been alienated from a boyfriend, a girlfriend, a husband, a wife, or a friend because one of them lost their cool? Anger is one of the fastest ways to destroy relationships.

So when someone starts pushing your buttons, before you retaliate, just ask yourself, "Do I really want to do this while I'm angry? Do I want to make a mistake because I'm upset right now? Do I want to sin by reacting to someone else's sin? Do I want someone else to control me by making me angry?"

There is always a price for anger. Before you retaliate, calculate the cost.

There Is No Excuse Not to Rest

*"Six days you shall labor, but on the seventh day you shall rest;
even during the plowing season and harvest you must rest."*

EXODUS 34:21 (NIV)

The Bible is filled with instructions about rest, recreation, and relaxation. In fact, it's so important that God put it in the Ten Commandments. It's right up there with "Don't commit adultery" and "Don't murder." He says that every seventh day, he wants you to take a day off.

This day off is called the Sabbath, and God commands this rest so you won't burn out.

Today, many people, even believers, no longer take a day off for rest. They might go to a church service, but afterward they go home and get right back to work, trying to finish everything they didn't accomplish during their work week. That's not a Sabbath!

Even in your busiest season, there is no excuse not to rest. You may be a tax accountant, but you still have to take a day off in April. You may work in retail, but you still have to take a day off during the Christmas season. Even a farmer must take a day off in harvest or planting season.

What are you supposed to do on your Sabbath?

Rest your body, because sometimes the most spiritual thing you can do is take a nap.

Refocus your spirit by attending a worship service at your church. Spend time alone with God to talk to him in prayer and read his Word.

Recharge your emotions by doing something that re-energizes you like a hobby or a sport.

Even though it can be a struggle to slow down and rest, it's important that you obey God and take your weekly Sabbath. He knows what's best for you.

Worship God the Right Way

"True worshipers will worship the Father in spirit and in truth. The Father is looking for those who will worship him in truth."

JOHN 4:23 (NLT)

There's a right way to worship God (and there's a wrong way).

The wrong way to honor God is with *heartless worship*. This is when your mouth is in gear but your mind and heart are not engaged. God says, "I don't want that kind of worship. It's apathetic and fake. I want you to love me with all your heart and soul and mind and strength." Worship isn't a meaningless ritual, it's the building of a relationship.

Wholehearted worship makes God smile. Why? Because he loves passionate worship, the kind that comes from the deepest places within your heart. God loves it when you acknowledge his presence with a joy that's bigger than your circumstances. God wants you to express your love to him and thankfulness for what he's done in your life. When you worship like this, Jesus says you are a true worshiper who worships in spirit and in truth.

Spirit and truth and worship can't be separated.

Worshiping in spirit is devotion that comes from the heart. To worship in truth means your life is aligned with God's Word. The truth ought to matter enough to move you to a life of worship and obedience to God

Are you genuinely devoted to God?

God is looking for you to be a true worshiper. This will draw you closer to him, make you more like Jesus, and bless your life.

The Power of a Focused Life

"Good planning and hard work lead to prosperity,
but hasty shortcuts lead to poverty."

PROVERBS 21:5 (NLT)

If you want God to use you in great ways, you need focus. The more focused you are, the more effective you'll be—and the more God will use you. Being focused is "good planning."

Diffused light doesn't have much effect on what it touches. But when you focus light—like the rays of the sun through a magnifying glass—you can start a fire.

The same is true with your life. If you lack direction, you'll just drift by without much impact. But if you focus on a few key goals, then you will make a powerful impact on the world for God.

The problem with a vague goal is that you'll never know if you've completed it. A focused life requires specific goals. For example, a vague goal is to be a better parent by spending more time with your children. But if you commit to spending an hour with them every Tuesday evening, that's a specific goal. It's measurable. You can know whether or not you've completed it. These kinds of goals focus your energy—and that can change your life.

How is God leading you to be more focused?

You Are Called to Be Free

"You, my brothers and sisters, were called to be free."

GALATIANS 5:13 (NIV)

God wants you to live in freedom. Let that sink in for a bit.

In fact, the Bible says freedom is your calling. God doesn't want you to live a buttoned-down, constrained life. He wants you to have an abundant life.

If you're not living a full and satisfying life, it's not because God doesn't want you to have it.

God wants to set you free from the pain of your past. Regret and resentment keep you from being all that God wants you to be.

Jesus also frees you from the pressures of the present. The everyday complexities of life can lead to stress and exhaustion, which distract you from hearing God and following his plan for your life.

Finally, pessimism about tomorrow is a trap from which Jesus sets you free. You no longer need to worry about the future because God is in control, and he is good.

So plug into his power. The same power that God used to raise Jesus Christ from the dead is available to you today. And that lets you live in freedom. The same power that blew the door off Jesus' tomb will blow open the prison doors that hold you back.

Trust God for the Help You Need

"Then the man said, 'Let me go, for the dawn is breaking!'
But Jacob said, 'I will not let you go unless you bless me.'"

GENESIS 32:26 (NLT)

When God allows a crisis in your life, he doesn't solve it immediately. Look at the life of Jacob. When he and God had their wrestling match in Genesis 32, God could have overpowered Jacob and ended things instantly—but instead, they wrestled until dawn. Why did God let the struggle continue?

You might be asking God the same question about your life. God lets your struggle continue because he wants to see how serious you are about seeking him. If God answered every prayer immediately, you'd begin to think he was a vending machine: Put in a prayer and pull out whatever you need.

For example, if God instantly bailed you out of a financial crisis caused by your own poor choices, then tomorrow you might overspend again. You wouldn't learn discipline or how to manage your money. God will help you get out of debt, but he wants to build your character in the process.

If you're in a crisis right now, don't give up! Don't run from it. Your problems didn't show up overnight. You may have some ingrained patterns, poor responses, and unhealthy habits that have built up over the years. God won't remove them all at once. But there is hope: God is with you and he is for you. When you ask God for help and trust him to provide, you will experience the peace of his wisdom and blessing.

Use Your Words to Build Others Up

*"Do not let any unwholesome talk come out of your mouths,
but only what is helpful for building others up
according to their needs, that it may benefit those who listen."*

EPHESIANS 4:29 (NIV)

God wants you to use your words to build others up. Your words can be like an out of control sledgehammer. You swing away without thinking, and suddenly you look around and realize that you are surrounded by a pile of relational rubble. When you thoughtlessly sling your words around and tear people down, your relationships suffer.

Your words have great power to lift a person up or tear them down. Remember this and you'll be more thoughtful with what you say. Accept responsibility for the power of your words and stop making excuses. Don't say, "I didn't really mean to say that," or "That's just how I am before my first cup of coffee." Realize that what you say impacts everyone around you.

Make a commitment to a "zero tolerance" attitude toward unwholesome talk. What's unwholesome talk? Anything that hurts. Gossip and bitterness are toxic. Jokes and sarcasm are offensive. Condescending talk and condemnation take away dignity. Make the decision to stay away from verbal landmines.

Listen more by talking less. You can't build people up according to what you think is best, you must build them up according to their needs. You need to work alongside the Holy Spirit to do them the most benefit.

Don't wait, start building others up today. Don't let excuses get in the way. Ask God for the wisdom to speak words of encouragement.

Make this your prayer today: *"May the words of my mouth and the meditation of my heart be pleasing in your sight, O Lord, my Rock and my Redeemer"* (Psalm 19:14 NIV).

Jesus' Last Prayer

"My soul is overwhelmed with sorrow to the point of death . . . Going a little farther, [Jesus] fell with his face to the ground and prayed, 'My Father, if it is possible, may this cup be taken from me. Yet not as I will, but as you will.' He went away a second time and prayed, 'My Father, if it is not possible for this cup to be taken away unless I drink it, may your will be done.'"

MATTHEW 26:38-39, 42 (NIV)

If you knew, with certainty, that you were going to die tomorrow, what would your prayers look like tonight?

On the last night of his life before the cross, Jesus knew what would happen. The Father's plan to save humanity would be fulfilled. The journey to the cross would involve betrayal, ridicule, torture, loneliness, and then a slow death by suffocation—all while taking upon the sins of the world.

We'll never understand the price Jesus paid, but he did.

And he asked God to take it all away.

Jesus prayed, *"May this cup be taken from me."* The cup represented the terror that awaited him during his final hours.

Jesus also prayed, *"Yet not as I will, but as you will."* Ultimately, Jesus was committed to obey the Father. Jesus offered a prayer of absolute surrender.

You can be honest about your feelings with God—he knows them anyway! You also need to surrender your life to him if you want his will to be done in your life.

If God calls you to care for a sick family member, you need to not only be honest about your feelings, but also be obedient to his calling. When you know doing the right thing at work may set your career back, be honest about the injustice of the situation, but also be obedient to God.

Are you ready to pray like Jesus?

Salvation Is a Gift to Be Received

"All need to be made right with God by his grace, which is a free gift. They need to be made free from sin through Jesus Christ."

ROMANS 3:24 (NCV)

If you were to ask 50 random people, "How do you get to Heaven?" you'd get close to 50 different answers. You'd hear things like, "Do more good things than bad things in life," or "Be a religious person." Many of their answers would be based on working to please God instead of resting in his grace.

Salvation is a gift from God. It's absolutely free! You can't earn it or buy it. You can only receive it in faith.

This is the fundamental difference between Christianity and every other religion. Other belief systems can be summarized by one word: "Do." You have to do certain things in order to gain bliss, heaven, or God's approval.

On the other hand, if you summarized Christianity with one word, it would be "done."

Many people ask, "What can I do to be saved?" The answer is, "You're too late! You're about two-thousand years too late! What needed to be done for your salvation has already been done."

Jesus paid for your salvation on the cross, and now he offers his grace as a free gift to you. That's why Jesus Christ, when he was hanging on the cross, stretched out his arms and said, "It is finished." What's the "it"? It's the payment for your salvation—the plan to provide grace for every person who needs it.

You don't get to heaven based on what you do. You get to heaven based on what has already been done for you by Jesus Christ. Praise God for his gracious gift!

Maintain Your Integrity

*"Whoever walks in integrity walks securely,
but whoever takes crooked paths will be found out."*

PROVERBS 10:9 (NIV)

The test of integrity is that your private life and your public life match; your heart and your actions are headed in the right direction. Ask yourself, "Would I want everyone to know about this decision I'm making?" The truth is that when it comes to integrity, even if you have everyone else fooled, you can't fool yourself. And you can't fool God.

Sometimes you're tempted to do the wrong thing, and this thought comes to your mind: "I know it's wrong, but I'm going to do it anyway because I know God is a forgiving God."

Do you think you can do something that God says is wrong and not face consequences? That's the very reason he doesn't want you to make that decision. It's because he loves you, not because he wants to keep you from having fun. God knows there are consequences to every decision. He knows bad decisions leave scars in your life. He wants better for you.

Does this mean that God does not forgive you for the wrong things you do? Of course he forgives you. He's a forgiving and gracious God. But forgiveness does not free you from the consequences that come from poor decisions. You can be forgiven and still have regrets. You can be forgiven and still face pain. You can be forgiven and still have a broken relationship.

Whose Voice Are You Listening To?

"Noah did everything just as God commanded him."

GENESIS 6:22 (NIV)

Have you noticed that the moment you establish a goal in your life, you start hearing people say, "Who do you think you are?" or "It can't be done," or "Forget about it"?

The antidote to the voices of doubt is to listen to the voice of God instead. Imagine all the critics in Noah's life who said, "That guy Noah thinks God speaks to him, but he's just messing up all of our property values by building that ark in his front yard."

The Bible tells us Noah listened to God. And what did he hear? He heard God's warning that the world was going to be destroyed. Noah believed—and acted on—what he had not yet seen. That's what faith is—being certain of something we don't see.

Noah didn't turn his back on the vision God had given him. Instead, in faith and obedience, he built the ark.

God is going to give you a goal for your life, and some people may think it's pretty crazy. But you have to stay focused on what you know God has said to you through prayer and through his Word. Then, go "build your ark"—tackle the assignment God has given you.

God's goal for your life can only be accomplished with God's help. If it doesn't require faith, it isn't big enough. But if you, like Noah, do *"everything just as God commanded,"* God will reward your faith and show his power to those who doubted your goal.

Sow Generously to Reap Generously

"Whoever sows sparingly will also reap sparingly, and whoever sows generously will also reap generously . . . And God is able to bless you abundantly, so that in all things at all times, having all that you need, you will abound in every good work."

2 CORINTHIANS 9:6, 8 (NIV)

You reap what you sow, good or bad. That's true about money; it's also true about everything else. If you sow affirmation, people will affirm you. If you sow criticism, they will criticize you.

You always get back more than you put in. If you plant a kernel of corn in the ground, you won't get just one kernel back. You'll get an entire stalk with several ears and hundreds of kernels.

When you plant a seed in the ground, do you get an ear of corn the next day? Of course not. You plant in one season, and you harvest in another.

The same is true in giving. You give to other people. You give to God. You give your life away, but do you reap the results the next day? No. There is a season of waiting before God gives you the harvest. Why? He's testing your faith to see if you'll trust him during the delay.

While you're waiting, you can trust God to bless you abundantly.

Living Your Best Life

"Be very careful, then, how you live—not as unwise but as wise, making the most of every opportunity, because the days are evil. Therefore do not be foolish, but understand what the Lord's will is."

EPHESIANS 5:15-17 (NIV)

We all have the same amount of time every week: 168 hours. It's what you do with it that counts! You've only been given a certain number of days in this world, and if you waste them, you can't get them back.

If you waste your time, you're wasting your life.

You have to develop a practice of stopping and asking, "Is this the best use of my time? Is this the best use of my life?" You don't have time for everything. The good news is that God doesn't expect you to do everything. So don't feel guilty about not being able to do everything. The truth is, there are only a few things worth doing.

Effective people know how to live their best life because they figure out the difference between what's essential and what's trivial. They spend more time doing the essential things and less time doing the trivial. You can't eliminate all the minutiae in your life, but you can reduce it.

Sounds easy, right? But do you find yourself wasting too much of your time?

Wisdom chooses what's best for your life over what's convenient. Don't settle for second best. Don't go through life just existing. You were not created to just coast along. God made you for a mission and a purpose. Commit your life to understanding God's will so that you can live in obedience to him.

Gratitude Lowers Stress

*"Whatever happens, give thanks, because it is
God's will in Christ Jesus that you do this."*

1 THESSALONIANS 5:18 (GW)

Gratitude isn't just great worship, it's also a great stress reducer.

Being thankful is the world's healthiest human emotion. Ungrateful people are never satisfied. They're always stressed and never have enough. When they're renting a house, they want to own—and if they already own a house, they want a bigger one . . . or even two houses! When it's warm and sunny out, they want it to be ski season; but when it's time to hit the slopes, they'd rather surf. Even when they go out to dinner, they get upset when they order the "wrong" dish at a restaurant.

You don't want to get to the end of your life and declare: "Nothing ever worked out for me; I never got what I wanted." That would certainly be a tragic ending!

Paul gives us a better way to approach life: *"Whatever happens, give thanks."*

There's always a reason to be thankful. If you look hard enough, you can find reasons to be satisfied. First and foremost, we have the presence of God—both in this life and forever in heaven. That truth alone should wipe out stress completely!

Gratitude can change everything. Try doing this: If you're feeling depressed, make a list of 50 things you are grateful for. That may sound like a lot, but start with the little things you are thankful for and don't stop until you get to 50.

Your gratefulness will shift your focus away from your stress toward everything good God has done and is doing in your life. It's easy to take things for granted. Choose to worship God with gratitude and watch your stress level go down.

Friends Who Build You up

"Do not be misled: 'Bad company corrupts good character.'"

1 CORINTHIANS 15:33 (NIV)

God wants you to have friends who are non-believers. If you don't have any non-Christian friends, you won't be around anyone who needs to hear the Good News. But your best friends should be Christians. They should be strong believers.

One reason is that it's easier for people to pull you down than to pull you up. That's why you must make sure the people you spend the most time with are moving you in the right direction in your walk with Christ. If you want that kind of friend, you have to be that kind of friend. It's a mutual relationship.

What kind of person do you want to be in ten years? The people you spend your time with is one of the key factors that determine your future. You become like the people who are closest to you.

Your friends are too important to pick by chance. You must be intentional. That's why you need a church home. Do whatever it takes to build relationships there. Join or start a small group. It's easy. Just gather some friends to study the Bible and pray together.

Look at your key friendships in life. Who are you investing in, and who is investing in you? Are they building you up spiritually or tearing you down?

Find friends who build you up and be a friend who does the same.

Worship with Others

"Let us not neglect our meeting together, as some people do, but encourage one another, especially now that the day of his return is drawing near."

HEBREWS 10:25 (NLT)

These days you don't have to go to church to see a worship service. You can just stay home in your pajamas and watch it online.

But the Bible makes it clear: you need a church family. This is why you need to gather with a group of believers and do life together as you follow Jesus.

Without a church family, you'll drift when it gets tough to trust Christ. You will lose your sense of belonging. You will collapse under the weight of the burdens of life. The Bible says we are to *"share each other's burdens, and in this way obey the law of Christ"* (Galatians 6:2 NLT).

What is the law of Christ? It is to love one another. And how do we obey that law? By sharing each other's burdens. It is impossible to love others in isolation. It is impossible to *"share each other's burdens"* if there is no one to share your burdens with.

A church is like a campfire with red-hot coals. If you remove one single coal and set it aside, it will cool in a matter of minutes. But if you take a coal that has lost its heat and put it back into the fire, it gets hot again. That's the power of fellowship. If your faith is losing its fire, be sure you are connected in fellowship with other fired-up followers of Christ.

Where are you connected to the body of Christ, the church? Who's encouraging you spiritually?

Life Doesn't End with Death

"The Spirit of God, who raised Jesus from the dead, lives in you. And just as God raised Christ Jesus from the dead, he will give life to your mortal bodies by this same Spirit living within you."

ROMANS 8:11 (NLT)

One day your heart will stop beating, and that will be the end of your body.

But your life doesn't end with death.

You were made in God's image, which means you were designed to last forever. Death is not the end; it's just a transition into eternal life with God or eternal life without God. For Christians, death is not leaving home, it's a homecoming.

This world is not all there is, and that's a good thing because sometimes things get pretty bad. As a believer, one of the reasons we have hope is because no matter how bad it seems on earth, it's only temporary. After death, you'll spend eternity with God. In heaven, there will be no more sorrow, no more sadness, no more sickness, and no more suffering.

We have this hope because of our faith in Christ. God is the God of hope, and it is a hope that will not disappoint. We believe in the hope of the resurrection because the same power that resurrected Jesus will resurrect you.

In Jesus, the Holy Spirit lives in you. You get to live a guilt-free life, a life with no condemnation. You are forgiven, no matter what you do. Your life is no longer controlled by sin because you are set free. Eternal life with Jesus begins the moment you say "yes" to Jesus, and it continues for eternity after death.

More Than Listening

"Everyone who hears these words of mine and puts them into practice is like a wise man who built his house on the rock."

MATTHEW 7:24 (NIV)

Satan doesn't mind you going to Bible studies as long as you don't do anything with what you learn. We fool ourselves when we assume that just because we've heard or read or studied a biblical truth, we've also internalized it, making it a part of how we live our lives.

We can be so busy going to the next class or seminar or Bible conference, that we take little time to implement what we've learned from God's Word. We may even forget it on the way to the next study. Unless you apply what you've learned from the Bible—allowing it to change the way you live and letting it mature you as a believer—all your studies are worthless. That's why Satan doesn't mind you being in a Bible study as long as the Bible doesn't end up in

you! He doesn't care what you know as long as you don't do anything with it.

Jesus told a parable about two builders. One built his house on rock, the other built on sand. When the storm hit both houses, only one stood: the house built on rock.

The way you build your life on the rock is to hear Jesus' words and put them into practice.

Jesus said God's blessing comes from obeying the truth, not just knowing it.

Bible *study* must always lead to Bible *application*. You are missing the point if you don't ask, "How am I going to put this truth into practice?"

Following Jesus is more than just listening to him.

Only God's Opinion Counts

"It is no shame to suffer for being a Christian.
Praise God for the privilege of being called by his name!"

1 PETER 4:16 (NLT)

Here's a truth that will liberate your life: You don't need people's approval to be happy.

You may have been trying to win the approval of a certain person for many years. I hate to tell you, but if you don't have it by now, you're not going to get it. The good news is, you don't need it! You don't need anybody's approval in order to be happy.

Consider the answer to these questions: Is an insult going to kill you? No. Is a putdown going to ruin your life? No. Is being called names for making a stand for Christ going to hurt you? No.

No matter what you do in life, somebody's not going to like it. You can't avoid disapproval. So, if you're going to have people's disapproval either way, you may as well have it for doing the right thing rather than the wrong thing.

This is important to remember as you face opposition. If someone else's opinion matters more to you than God's opinion, then you're going to crumble when people attack you because of your faith in Jesus. But if you focus on God, then you can make a firm stand: *"Stand firm against [Satan], and be strong in your faith. Remember that your family of believers all over the world is going through the same kind of suffering you are"* (1 Peter 5:9 NLT).

Suffering Makes You More like Jesus

"Those who suffer according to God's will should commit themselves to their faithful Creator and continue to do good."

1 PETER 4:19 (NIV)

Some people think that following Christ is like having a golden ticket, which guarantees millionaire status and a life with zero problems.

The truth is, we live in a broken world, and suffering is a reality.

Some suffering is shared by everyone. It doesn't matter if you're Baptist or Buddhist or Muslim or atheist. When a hurricane hits, it doesn't just pick on Christians. It affects everybody. Sickness and tragedy are common to all humans.

Suffering can also be the result of poor decisions. If you gossip, your friends will stop confiding in you. If you steal from your company, you'll lose your job. If you become addicted to something unhealthy, your relationships will suffer. When you choose to sin and go against God's will, there are real consequences. Your choices are up to you—not God or anyone else.

However, some suffering is God's will. God allows it to happen to make you more like Jesus. Suffering helps you discover what matters most, moving you to greater dependence on God. Suffering deepens your faith and is rewarded in heaven.

In all seasons of suffering, renew your commitment to God. He is faithful. No matter what life throws at you, God is with you. He is worthy of your trust. When everything is falling around you, build your life on him.

Your commitment to God is also a commitment to do good to others. It's hard to do the right thing in the middle of suffering, but helping others often makes our own problems more bearable.

Sharing Helps You Heal

"When I kept things to myself, I felt weak deep inside me.
I moaned all day long."

PSALM 32:3 (NCV)

The worst possible response to hidden wounds in your life is to clam up. It's like shaking a can of soda. One day, you'll just explode!

Bottling up your hidden wounds will wear you out.

You'll never get over your hidden wounds until you face your feelings head on by admitting them to yourself, God, and one other person.

Many people try to move past their pain by admitting it to God and themselves, but then they skip the third part of the equation. Admitting your pain to others is absolutely essential to your healing. Getting better depends on it: *"Confess your sins to each other and pray for each other so that you may be healed"* (James 5:16 NIV).

You don't have to confess to a pastor, a priest, or a therapist to obey this Scripture, (although you can). You just need a friend you can trust.

If you use all your emotional energy trying to cover up the past, you'll have little left for today. Ask God to help you be honest with yourself. Open up about your hidden pain to someone.

Dealing with the past isn't easy, but it's necessary. Why? Because sharing helps you heal.

Eliminate Negative Self-Talk

*"You will keep in perfect peace all who trust in you,
all whose thoughts are fixed on you!"*

ISAIAH 26:3 (NLT)

Long before psychologists came up with theories for human behavior, God said your thoughts determine your feelings and your feelings determine your actions.

Even though research indicates that most people speak at a rate of 150 to 200 words per minute, our thoughts can race through our brains at about 1,300 words per minute. Often it's an internal dialogue (self-talk) that echoes Job: *"Everything I say seems to condemn me"* (Job 9:20 GNT).

Chances are, you are your own worst critic. You're always putting yourself down. You could walk into a room smiling, but inside you're thinking, "I'm not smart enough. I'm not good-looking enough." Most of this dialogue is unconscious, we're not aware it's even happening.

God wants you to stop putting yourself down. When you put yourself down, who are you really putting down? You're actually pointing to the Creator who made you. When you say, "I'm worthless; I'm no good; I can't do anything," you're actually saying, "God, when you made me, you made a mistake."

How do you eliminate negative self-talk? Praise God for the good things he has done for you. Here's the truth: you were made wonderfully and God loves you unconditionally. God doesn't make junk, and he didn't send his Son to die for junk.

Praise him for what he has done and start believing what God says about you.

God Wants to Bless Your Career

"Seek the Kingdom of God above all else, and live righteously, and he will give you everything you need."

MATTHEW 6:33 (NLT)

If you want your life to turn from emptiness to overflowing, give Jesus complete control of your life, including your career.

Peter, James, and John were fishermen before they became disciples. One night, they worked nonstop and caught nothing. Then Jesus stepped into their boat and told them to cast their nets again. Luke 5:6 says, *"When the fishermen did as Jesus told them, they caught so many fish that the nets began to break"* (NCV). It was the same lake, the same boat, the same nets, and the same fishermen. In other words, it was the same business. The only difference between nothing and fullness was Jesus in their boat.

Here's the point: You have to get Jesus in your boat. What's your boat? It's how you make a living. It's how you earn your daily bread. What does it mean to have Jesus in your boat? It means you dedicate your career to God; you give him control of your livelihood.

When Simon Peter gave his job to Jesus, he was blessed with incredible results. But don't miss the sequence. We sometimes think, "God, if you'll make me really successful in business, then I'll serve you with the success." Wrong! It's the exact opposite. We first give Jesus control, then comes the success. That's the correct order.

April

Fortify Your Faith

"Strengthen yourselves so that you will live here on earth doing what God wants, not evil things people want."

1 PETER 4:2 (NCV)

Spiritual growth isn't automatic. God is working to draw you closer to him, but you must also take steps to strengthen your faith.

Your faith will grow when you make daily appointments with God. Use this time to talk to him and read his Word. The Bible will fully equip you for everything God wants you to do and prayer is a simple conversation with God. He wants to hear anything you have to say, but make it a habit to ask for his forgiveness for your sins, help with your problems, and direction for your decisions.

Do yourself a favor and learn all you can by reading Christian books. Keep feeding your soul with what other believers have to say. If all you do is study the Bible for yourself and don't listen to what other Bible-believing Christians have to say about it, you're not gaining from their wisdom and experience.

Keep your testimony fresh. Ask yourself, "What is God doing in my life?" Take some time to write out your testimony. When God gives you an opportunity to share about him with others, you will be prepared because you took the time to write it out. When you share your testimony with others, not only does it encourage them, but it also fortifies your faith.

Be faithful to a small group of believers. You need a place to share your burdens and celebrate your victories. You need a committed group of people who are praying for you. You also need to do these same things for others. We are better together because we help one another strengthen our faith.

Come As You Are

*"God showed his great love for us by sending
Christ to die for us while we were still sinners."*

ROMANS 5:8 (NLT)

It's a myth that you must clean up your act before you can come to God.

To think you have to make things right first is like having a broken bone, but waiting until it is healed before going to the doctor. That doesn't make sense! You go to the doctor because you have something that needs to be fixed and you can't get well on your own. The same is true with God.

The Bible doesn't day, "God helps those who help themselves." Nothing could be further from the truth!

God helps the helpless.

God says, "You don't have to clean up your act. In fact, you can't. Just bring it all to me—the good, the bad, and the ugly. Come as you are, and I'll clean it up for you."

God's love for us is unlike any other love we will experience from the world.

God has *great* love for us. Do you know how he demonstrated that love to us?

Jesus died for you long before you knew you needed him.

He did for you what you could never do for yourself. He made the way for you to come to God when there was no hope of getting there on your own. If you don't act on this news, then the death of Jesus Christ and his resurrection are wasted for you personally. You may recognize the gift, but if you do not receive it, then it makes no difference in your life.

God is not asking you to make a promise you cannot keep: "I can get better on my own."

God is asking you to receive a promise that only he can keep: "I will accept your great love for me."

You Can Rely on God's Power

*"We stopped relying on ourselves and learned
to rely only on God, who raises the dead."*

2 CORINTHIANS 1:9 (NLT)

God's strength will carry you through every storm. Sometimes we experience storms that push us to the limit. The apostle Paul would agree. He was once so depressed by his circumstances, he felt like he was out of options. Paul had come to the end of his strength. On his own, he could no longer endure.

How did Paul get through that difficult time? He plugged into God's power—the same power that raised Jesus from the dead.

How about you? Have you come to the end of your own strength? Are you out of options and wondering where you'll find the power to take another step forward?

There is just one condition for receiving God's power in your life: humility.

God doesn't give his power to arrogant people. Humility is simply admitting to God, "You are God, and I am not. I am powerless to change this situation, so I am giving it to you." The moment you do, God brings his resurrection power into your situation.

What's dead in your life? If God can raise a dead man, he can certainly raise a dead marriage, a dead career, or a dead dream. God specializes in turning crucifixions into resurrections.

Where do you need God's resurrection power in your life? When you learn to rely on him instead of yourself, you will begin to see just how much God can do.

The Door of Salvation

"I am the door; if anyone enters through Me, he will be saved."

JOHN 10:9 (NASB)

You will encounter many doors in your life: doors to happiness, doors to sadness, doors to success, and doors to failure. Some doors are traps, and others are opportunities.

Your success in life largely depends on which doors you decide to walk through. But there is one door you just can't afford to miss: the door to salvation.

Your salvation is important to God. That's why he sent Jesus. God doesn't want you enslaved to guilt, resentment, grief, fear, or anything else. He wants you to live free in Christ.

The biggest prisons in life aren't physical. They're the prisons in your mind. Maybe you feel trapped in an immoral relationship. Maybe it's debt you can't escape. Perhaps it's a habit you can't seem to shake. It could be a fear that holds you captive or a painful memory you can't forget.

Jesus saves you for eternity, and from your problems. You can't enter the doors of opportunity God has planned for you until you walk out of the prison that holds you back.

Where do you need God's help today?

Rejoice in God's Goodness to Others

"Rejoice with those who rejoice, weep with those who weep."

ROMANS 12:15 (ESV)

When you see God providing for others, you can respond with joy or resentment. In some ways, the second half of today's verse is much easier to do than the first half. It's easy to weep with those who weep.

On the other hand, it's much more difficult to rejoice when someone has a success. You might feel threatened by it, or even resentful. Maybe you think it's not very fair—she got the promotion and the dream house; they have well-behaved kids and a new car. You figure all of God's blessings have already been doled out. There's nothing left for you.

That kind of thinking limits God. He doesn't run out of blessings. He doesn't run out of grace. There's more than enough to go around for everybody. Just because God blesses somebody else doesn't mean there aren't enough blessings for you. He wants to bless you, but it may be in different ways.

We can rejoice with others when we remember that God is good. He blesses people because he loves us, and he is constantly working to draw us closer to him. You can be happy for the success of others when you remember that God has a perfect plan for each of us.

That plan includes blessings and success—just not the same kind of blessings for everyone. In the parable of the vineyard workers (Matthew 20), the owner hired some workers at the start of the day and others later in the day. At the end of the day, he paid them all the same. The first workers thought they'd been cheated—although they were paid what they agreed to work for. Instead of enjoying the extra blessings God gave to others, they resented the owner.

If you choose to rejoice in God's goodness to others, you can be joyful all the time—because something good is always happening to somebody.

God Will Build Your Faith

"Lord, I believe. Help my unbelief!"

MARK 9:24 (NKJV)

Your faith will be tested in one of four different ways.

If you're in the "Where? Test," you are asking God where you should live, go to school, work, plug into church, or meet new friends. God is telling you, "Get moving. Do what you already know is right and I will show you the rest along the way."

The "When? Test" stretches your patience because you are waiting on God. You've been praying, "God, I need your help! When are you going to answer?" God says, "Trust me, for my timing is perfect."

You are experiencing the "How? Test" when facing an impossible situation. You are wondering how to get out of debt, parent a difficult child, or reach your sales goals. God says, "trust me because I am bigger than your circumstances."

The "Why? Test" is the ultimate trial for your faith. In these situations, things don't make sense and you are looking for answers. You may be grieving over a pointless tragedy, and your heart is broken, but in these moments, God is saying, "I'm right here beside you. Trust me."

The Bible tells us about a Roman soldier who faced the "How? Test." His son needed healing, so he brought him to Jesus and said, "Lord, help my son—if you can." Jesus said, "If you believe, anything is possible." The man replied, "I believe; help my unbelief!" What a great prayer! The man believed in Jesus, but he knew he needed God to help his faith grow.

Tests are uncomfortable, but they reveal our progress. When God is testing you, he's working to draw you closer to him. Today, are you being tested? Make this your prayer, "Lord, I believe, help my unbelief."

How to Deal with What You Feel

"To be controlled by human nature results in death;
to be controlled by the Spirit results in life and peace . . .
Those who obey their human nature cannot please God."

ROMANS 8:6, 8 (GNT)

When you give your heart to Jesus, that commitment includes your emotions, not just what you think and do. God's Word gives four reasons we need to manage our emotions.

Your emotions can be unreliable. Not everything you feel is true or authentic.

Your emotions can be manipulated. If you're always guided by your feelings, other people will take advantage of you. Worst of all, negative emotions are Satan's favorite tool. He will use fear, resentment, and worry to wreak havoc in your life (1 Peter 5:8).

Your emotions can lead to bad decisions. When emotions rule your life, God doesn't. If you make decisions based on how you feel, then God isn't God in your life.

Your emotions can undermine your success. How many people do you know who ruined their reputation because of something they said in anger? Or who missed an opportunity because of a lack of self-control? (Proverbs 5:23).

So, when you give your heart to Jesus, also give him your emotions so he can help you manage them.

Truth Is Eternal

"Heaven and earth will pass away,
but my words will never pass away."

MATTHEW 24:35 (NIV)

The Bible is the most despised, derided, denied, disputed, dissected, and debated book in all of history. Yet the Bible has flourished in spite of unrelenting attacks during the past two-thousand years. It is still the most read, most published, and most translated book in the world. It's still changing lives all over the world.

Voltaire, the brilliant eighteenth century French philosopher, was an atheist. He authored a number of tracts deriding the Bible. Voltaire defiantly proclaimed, "One hundred years from today the Bible will be a forgotten book."

Today, that quote has been forgotten—but not the Bible. After Voltaire died, the French Bible Society used his property for nearly one hundred years and sold Bibles out of his house! God's Word is eternal. It will always be true and it will always be relevant.

We live in a world with information overload. We are constantly flooded with much more than we can handle. Companies spend billions of dollars to filter content, and we still end up overwhelmed. What you need to know has already been "filtered" by God, and it can be found in his eternal Word.

God's eternal truth will change your life.

Disciples Stay in God's Word

"If you continue in My word, then you are truly disciples of Mine."

JOHN 8:31 (NASB)

Following Jesus means connecting consistently with his Word.

You start with a decision. You need to choose to make this a priority in your life. Here's the reality about your schedule: you have time for everything that is important to you.

You need to set a realistic goal. If you aren't in the habit of reading the Bible daily, start out small—maybe 10 minutes a day—and let it grow.

If you are in a small group, tell them about your new commitment to read the Bible. Ask them to hold you accountable because if you keep your commitment a secret, it will be easier to give up. Pick one person to be a spiritual partner to come alongside you for support and encouragement. Share with them what you are learning and how you are challenged to live differently.

Be prepared for distractions and dry spells! Don't allow anything to knock you off your commitment. Be absolutely determined to make this a permanent habit in your life, particularly in the early months. If you skip a day, don't beat yourself up, but keep in mind: the more you skip, the harder it will be for you to stay committed. To form a new habit, you need to do it every day for six weeks, so be determined!

Discipleship isn't easy, it takes self-discipline. There will always be a reason to skip your time with God. With his help, you can develop this habit in your life.

Release Your Grief

"Pour out your heart to him, for God is our refuge."

PSALM 62:8 (NLT)

When we lose someone or something important, the result is grief. Grief always produces strong emotions—anger, fear, depression, worry, and sometimes guilt. These feelings can be confusing and difficult to manage, and you don't always know what to do with them.

Some people never directly deal with grief in their life. They stuff it down and pretend it's not there. That's why they're still struggling with emotional pain from a loss that occurred 10, 20, or even 30 years earlier.

There's a myth that says God wants you to walk around with a smile on your face all the time, saying, "Praise the Lord!" In reality, you can't pretend away all of your pain. This is not a way to live, if you want to live with integrity. You won't always have a smile on your face because life can be hard. Even Jesus grieved the loss of his friend Lazarus.

What should you do with your feelings? Don't repress them, release them! Let God be your refuge. You need to cry out, "God, I'm hurt! I'm grieving! This is a tough one to take." The book of Psalms is a good example of this, where many times David spills his guts and says, "God, I'm in a difficult time. I am really, really hurting."

If you are going through a loss right now, understand that if you don't release your grief, it will pour out eventually. The feelings that are pushed down fester, and eventually they erupt!

Release your grief so that God can begin to heal your heart.

Change Yourself

"Let us examine our ways and turn back to the Lord."

LAMENTATIONS 3:40 (GNT)

The most important change is up to you. When your life feels like it's falling apart, knowing what you can change—and what you can't change—will make all the difference.

You can't change your past. You can't change your parents. You can't change the gifts and talents God has or hasn't given you. You can't bring a dead loved one back to life or force somebody to love you.

But there's something important you *can* change: you.

When Jeremiah's world was falling apart, he knew he needed to make a change and return to God.

Is something going on in your life that doesn't line up with what God wants? Sometimes God will put you in a crisis to get you to change.

He wants your life to align with his will, and he knows that requires a gut-level, fearless self-evaluation. This means taking an inventory of every area of your life. Look at your relationship with God, your spouse, your kids, and your co-workers. Look at hurts, habits, and hang-ups that you may still carry around with you. Nothing is off-limits. In fact, if you think something is off-limits, that's the first thing you need to hand over to God.

This won't be easy. It will get messy. It's always tough to turn from sin.

But you won't find lasting change without repentance. You can't change everything—but you can change you by letting God have control of every part of your life.

God Calls You to a Higher Road

"A fool expresses all his emotions, but a wise person controls them."

PROVERBS 29:11 (GW)

The high road is always the right road. You cannot control what other people do to you, but you can control how you choose to react. You can get angry and stressed out, or sink into depression . . . or you can respond graciously. The choice is yours: Will you be foolish or wise?

Why is it foolish to express all of your emotions? Without a filter, they are too destructive. Your feelings need to be examined. You can't act on all of your feelings, and you shouldn't share all of them either. You don't have to say everything you are thinking!

Your mouth is controlled by your mind. You need to shift gears in your mind if you want to have self-control with your words. Wise words come from wise thoughts.

When others cause pain in your life, you might be tempted to feel entitled to express everything you are feeling. This is a choice; you don't have to erupt verbally just because you've been hurt.

When you are mistreated, the proper reaction isn't to blow up or clam up. Strike the right balance by sharing enough to restore the relationship. This is wisdom: Saying the right thing, at the right time, in the right way.

Getting "even" may feel like the right thing in the moment, but resist that urge. Sinking to the other person's level isn't satisfying and it won't improve the relationship. Take the high road and be wise by demonstrating your self-control.

Open Your Eyes

"Open my eyes, that I may behold wondrous things out of your law."

PSALM 119:18 (ESV)

God has so much he wants to show you, but you must be willing to look into his Word with open eyes.

When you study the Bible, seek answers from the text by asking questions. There's no limit to how many questions you can ask about the Bible because there's no limit to its wisdom and insight. Asking questions will challenge your assumptions and help you dig into the Bible. The deeper you dig, the more gold you'll find. Asking questions will help you look at the Bible through a new set of eyes. Suddenly, every time you pick up God's Word, you'll discover new truths that will help you as you mature in Christ.

Never study the Bible without pen and paper or an electronic device in hand so you can make notes. When you ask questions, write down the answers. You can read the Bible without writing something down, but to really study it, write down the things God is telling you through his Word. The act of writing will open up new thoughts.

Write down the application. Always ask, "What does this mean for my life, and what will I do about it?" Consider the details of your life under the light of what you have just read. How does the passage challenge you to think and act differently? How does it apply to your relationships and your responsibilities? Will you see anyone soon who needs to hear about what you've read? Studying God's Word will change your life if you put what you learn into practice. But it all starts with your willingness to *study* his Word.

Don't Fool Yourself

*"But don't just listen to God's word. You must do what it says.
Otherwise, you are only fooling yourselves."*

JAMES 1:22 (NLT)

What role does God's Word play in your life?

According to James, you must listen to the Word and do what it says. Without listening and doing, you are fooling yourself.

Listening without doing does not make you spiritually mature.

You must learn what God wants, and then put it into practice. Maybe you already know that Jesus said to forgive a person 77 times. But if you don't actually forgive others as many times as they need it, you are fooling yourself if you think you are mature in Christ.

As you read the Bible, one great habit to develop is to write a one-sentence application about what you've just read. Putting the application in writing will clarify your thoughts and help you put biblical truth into practice. Start by asking, "God, what do you want me to do?"

A good application is personal. It should address your current situation. You can't write an application for somebody else. It's not about what the world needs to do, or what your spouse needs to do, or what your kids need to do. It's about what you need to do!

Your application should be practical; it needs to be a specific statement that you can do. "Always forgive everyone" is too generic. Broad generalities won't help you take action. Additionally, put a timeline on it so you can check your progress.

Unrealistic application sentences will leave you feeling defeated. For example, let's say your application is, "Pray five hours every day, three times." That's probably not a rational goal!

Don't fool yourself: Do what you've learned from God.

Do You Want to Hear from God?

*"I will climb up to my watchtower and stand at my guardpost.
There I will wait to see what the LORD says and how he will answer."*

HABAKKUK 2:1 (NLT)

You will hear God when you *want* to hear God. It's just that simple. He wants you to desire communication with him. He wants you to come to him with a willingness to obey before he even says a word.

That's why Habakkuk begins by saying: *"I will."* He made a choice to listen to God.

Once you decide you want to hear from God, withdraw to a quiet place. That's what Habakkuk did after he said, *"I will climb up to my watchtower."* This is a Hebrew expression that means to get alone.

You cannot hear God's voice if you're surrounded by noise. That's why you must find a quiet place.

Jesus gives us some very specific advice in Matthew 6:6: *"Find a quiet, secluded place so you won't be tempted to role-play before God. Just be there as simply and honestly as you can manage. The focus will shift from you to God, and you will begin to sense his grace"* (The Message).

How can you stay motivated to get alone with the Lord each day? The secret is found in two words: God cares. God cares about what you're going through. If God didn't care, then why would he want you to get alone with him? He cares about the details of your life. He cares about your circumstances. And he wants to spend time with you today.

Let God's Love Save You from Fear

"Save me from the insults I fear ... I want to obey your commands ...
Show me how much you love me, Lord, and save me according to your promise.
Then I can answer those who insult me."

PSALM 119:39-42 (GNT)

You are loved fully by your heavenly Father, and his perfect love casts out all fear.

The fear of rejection comes from all directions: your marriage, family, friends, school, and work. This fear is fed by words of condemnation, disappointment, and criticism. It doesn't even take words! Just a non-verbal facial expression of disappointment can be devastating.

The fear of rejection prevents you from connecting with others because it hinders your ability to both give and receive love. How does the fear of rejection work?

You were created to be loved by others, this is God's intentional design. When you don't experience healthy love, you are vulnerable to being hurt by others. Many of us experience conditional love which says, "I love you when you . . ." To be loved, we are trained to meet the conditions of others.

Your vulnerability increases when you believe other people should meet all of your needs. This is an unrealistic expectation because people can't meet all of your needs. Expecting people to meet your needs leads to frustration and eventually, the fear of rejection.

God's love for you is perfect. He's the only one who can meet all of your needs. He's the only one who can love you unconditionally—just as you are! When the fear of rejection rears its ugly head in your life, trust God to meet your needs and remember that his love comes with no strings attached.

Spiritual Food for Spiritual Strength

*"I am the bread of life. I am the living bread
that came down from heaven."*

JOHN 6:48, 51 (GNT)

Just like you need physical food for physical strength, you need spiritual food for spiritual strength. The Bible describes itself as the water, milk, bread, honey, and meat of our spiritual lives. It is everything we need for spiritual sustenance.

A general wouldn't send a soldier into battle who hadn't eaten in a month. A football coach wouldn't send a player onto the field who had not eaten in two weeks. Why? Because they know the soldier or the player wouldn't have the physical stamina to defeat the opposition. In the same way, you won't have much success in the spiritual battles you face if you're starving yourself. That's why you need to feed on the Word of God every day.

God has not only given us his written Word, but he also gave us his Word through Jesus. The apostle John tells us that Jesus is God's Word wrapped up in human flesh. When you spend time with Jesus, you are feeding yourself spiritually.

When you feast upon God's Word, your life is filled with his wisdom, his strength, and his love. The more you taste and see how good God is, the more you will hunger for the living bread only God can provide.

Choose Forgiveness, Not Gossip

"Fire goes out without wood, and quarrels disappear when gossip stops."

PROVERBS 26:20 (NLT)

Let's just admit it: Some people get on your nerves. When you have a person in your life like that, and he's just done that "thing" *again*, it's almost impossible to not call somebody and say, "You won't believe what he just did!" You want someone to agree with you that this person belongs in the "people who irritate you" hall of fame.

When a person constantly frustrates you, it's difficult to let it go. It may make you feel better to tell others about it, but that's not love. That's gossip.

The fire goes out of our frustrations when we stop spreading the latest gossip and choose to forgive.

Gossip is incredibly destructive. It damages churches, families, friendships, and businesses. It is destructive to your life, and it tears you up on the inside.

The worst thing about gossip is that the person you're gossiping about wins! He becomes the one who controls your conversations and your emotions. Don't let that person win by making the choice to gossip.

Instead, respond to the situation with love. Don't retaliate with gossip; instead choose God's way and offer them the blessing of forgiveness.

Don't Pretend Anymore

*"It is dangerous to be concerned with what others think of you,
but if you trust the LORD, you are safe."*

PROVERBS 29:25 (GNT)

Children love to play make-believe. So do many adults. They pretend they're somebody they're not to win the approval of others.

Maybe that's you. Perhaps you've been pretending for so long that you don't know who the real you is anymore. You're wearing a mask, and it's wearing you out. Everyone else thinks you've got plenty of money, plenty of joy, and plenty of time. But you know the truth, and you're exhausted.

You pretend for one of two reasons.

You fall into the people-pleasing trap. Meeting the expectations of others becomes your purpose in life.

You fall into the perfectionism trap. You think you must be perfect to be loved.

Freedom comes when you look to God for approval and not anyone else. Only God knows you completely, loves you unconditionally, and knows exactly what you were created to do.

You don't need to earn his love. You don't need to be perfect to please him. You can't buy his approval or fake your way to earn it. He knows everything you've ever done, and he still loves you completely.

Living for God, rather than the approval of others, simplifies your life. You're living for an audience of one. You'll enjoy the freedom that comes when you stop pretending and really start living as the person God created you to be.

To the Ends of the Earth

"Life is worth nothing unless I use it for doing the work assigned me by the Lord Jesus—the work of telling others the Good News about God's mighty kindness and love."

ACTS 20:24 (TLB)

Today, there are still parts of the world that have no Bibles, no believers, and no churches.

These parts represent the "final frontier" for the church. The Bible tells us that one day, people from every tribe and nation will worship Jesus. Will we be the generation that finishes the task of taking the Gospel to the ends of the earth, or will we punt it to the next generation?

How can you be a part of reaching the final frontier?

Start with consistent prayer. Ask God to send people into the mission field and for God to bless their ministry. Pray for the response to the message, that people would say "yes" to Jesus. Everyone in the world needs to hear the Gospel. If God moves you to pray for a specific country or region, learn more about what is happening there so you can pray specifically.

Consider offering financial support, as this enables others to share the Gospel. When you give your money, you are participating in their work to take the Good News to all nations.

Like Paul, God may be calling you to step out in faith and go yourself. For some people, this is a scary idea! If God is telling you to go, do you want to ignore him? God won't force you; the choice is yours. Remember that God knows what you need, and maybe your next step spiritually is to serve in another country.

What's your role in taking the Gospel to the final frontier? What is the work that Jesus has assigned to you?

Choose Faith over Fear

"That Sunday evening the disciples were meeting behind locked doors because they were afraid of the Jewish leaders. Suddenly, Jesus was standing there among them! 'Peace be with you,' he said."

JOHN 20:19 (NLT)

You can experience God's best for you if you learn to live without fear.

Think about the first Easter evening two thousand years ago. The disciples hadn't seen Jesus, but they heard he had risen from the dead. They didn't know if they could believe the news. They were scared: If Jesus was put to death, would they be next?

The Bible says they locked the doors because they were afraid. That's what fear does. It locks God out, and you miss the miracle.

Maybe your heart has been broken, and you're afraid to let anyone get close to you again. Maybe you took a risk on a new job that didn't work out. Now you're afraid to try a new career path again. Maybe you've been hurt by people in a church, and you've locked God out of your life because of it.

You can't protect yourself from pain. It's foolish to even try because the pain of isolation simply replaces the pain of failure.

But you can choose to respond with faith instead of fear by acknowledging God's presence, watching for signs of his work in your life, standing on his promises in the Bible, and believing in the goodness of his plans.

You can be confident that God is with you and that he is working through every circumstance and situation in your life: *"Do not be afraid or discouraged, for the LORD will personally go ahead of you. He will be with you; he will neither fail you nor abandon you"* (Deuteronomy 31:8 NLT).

Jesus appeared to the disciples and replaced their fear and confusion with peace. His offer still stands, will you choose faith over fear?

Your Commitments Shape Your Life

*"Since everything around us is going to melt away,
what holy, godly lives we should be living!"*

2 PETER 3:11 (TLB)

You are defined by your commitments.

You might be committed to worldly goals such as wealth, fame, or power. You'll put most of your time and energy into these goals. You may even achieve these things, but ultimately you will remain unsatisfied. Why? Because none of it will last; one day, it will all *"melt away."*

One thing that will last for eternity is you!

The commitments you make today will determine your tomorrow, so don't you want to be committed to what matters most?

Your commitment choices have real consequences.

Since this life is a preparation for the next life, your choices have eternal consequences. When you commit to the wrong things, you miss out on God's purpose for your life. Don't settle for less than God's best for your life!

The most important commitment you can make with your life is to follow Jesus. This leads to a life that is holy and godly. By making this commitment, you commit to becoming more like Jesus and following his best for your life.

Take an inventory of the biggest commitments in your life. If you are having a difficult time identifying them, look to where you spend most of your time, energy, and money. Write your commitments down so you can examine them to determine if they are worth keeping or not.

Are your commitments keeping you from a life of holiness and godliness?

No Condemnation

"There is no condemnation for those who belong to Christ Jesus."

ROMANS 8:1 (NLT)

Conviction comes from God, and condemnation comes from the devil. The purpose of conviction is to correct something that's wrong in your life. The purpose of condemnation is to put you down, to make you feel guilty and ashamed.

God's motivation for convicting you is that he loves you and wants to help you mature. Satan's motivation for condemning you is that he hates you and wants to make you miserable.

When God speaks to you about an area in your life that needs changing, the conviction is very specific. He will tell you what is wrong, and then he'll give you the solution. When you confess the issue to God, the sense of conviction goes away instantly.

When Satan condemns you, it comes as a general sense of disapproval and guilt about nothing in particular. It can leave you with a sense of hopelessness—that there's nothing you can do to get out from under the endless condemnation.

Many Christians live under condemnation and guilt, thinking it's the voice of God. But it's not. It's the devil speaking!

If you hear a voice telling you, "You're hopeless! You're worthless! You're unlovable!" it's not the voice of God.

When you're feeling guilty, ask yourself, "Is this convicting or is it condemning?" If it's from God, he'll tell you what needs to change and how you need to change it.

What's Your Foundation?

"By the grace God has given me, I laid a foundation as a wise builder, and someone else is building on it. But each one should build with care. For no one can lay any foundation other than the one already laid, which is Jesus Christ. If anyone builds on this foundation using gold, silver, costly stones, wood, hay or straw, their work will be shown for what it is."

1 CORINTHIANS 3:10-13 (NIV)

A building is only as good as the foundation it's built on. The same is true of your life: What's your foundation?

Are you building your life on what everybody else is doing? Popular culture doesn't provide a firm foundation because the world's values are constantly shifting. God's values never change.

Some people build their life on reason or logic. This isn't consistent either. If you were to ask ten really smart people a controversial question, you won't get a unified response—far from it! With enough mental gymnastics, you can rationalize just about anything.

Sometimes we let our feelings lead the way. This foundation says, "If it feels right, you do it." The problem with this is that one day you'll feel one way, and the next you'll feel the opposite.

If you're building your life on "the way it's always been done," you're building your life on a tradition. This can get your life stuck in a rut. While the past can hold a lot of good lessons, the truth always trumps tradition.

What should you build your life on? The only foundation is Jesus. Be wise and build your life with care, don't settle for a weak foundation. Jesus is the only firm foundation because he is always the same and his love for you never wavers.

Learn to Recognize the Truth

"Now the Berean Jews were of more noble character than those in Thessalonica, for they received the message with great eagerness and examined the Scriptures every day to see if what Paul said was true."

ACTS 17:11 (NIV)

We live in the age of information.

Countless ideas bombard us constantly from every angle, whether it be from friends, TV, the internet, radio, social media, and the list goes on and on.

How can you filter through the noise to separate opinion from wisdom and lie from truth?

The Berean Jews teach us how to have better discernment. When Paul came to teach, they eagerly accepted the message about Jesus but with reservation. They examined the Bible to see if what Paul said was in alignment with what God had already said.

When you hear something new, turn to the Bible.

God is consistent and he will never contradict what he's already said in his Word. God will never tell you to do something that violates a principle that's in the Bible. God's Word is true, it has always been true, and it will always be true.

Some people say, "God said it, I believe it, and that settles it." But the truth is, if God said it, that settles it—whether or not you believe it!

Trends change, popular opinions change, but the truth of God's Word never changes. That should encourage you. You never have to wonder what God thinks about something because he has clearly stated what he thinks in his Word.

If you want to be sure an idea is from God, see if it agrees with the Bible.

Refining Fire

"I have refined you, but not as silver is refined.
Rather, I have refined you in the furnace of suffering."

ISAIAH 48:10 (NLT)

Trials turn up the heat in our lives and make us uncomfortable. When you are experiencing financial hardship, poor health, conflict at home, or a stressful work deadline, you may wonder, "What is God doing?"

God uses heat in your life to burn off things that are tying you down and holding you back. It could be a bad attitude toward your circumstances. Maybe you are holding a grudge or wallowing in self-pity. Here's the point: You have "impurities" in your life that are limiting you from being all God meant for you to be.

When a silversmith works with metal ore, he uses intense heat to separate out the impurities. This leaves behind the pure metal. The silversmith watches his work closely, knowing when the heat has done its refining work. The silver has been refined when he can see his reflection in the metal.

God refines your life because he wants to see his own reflection in you.

Yes, the refining process hurts. It's hard, and suffering is painful. But you need to trust God while you are being refined. God can use your trials to eliminate what's holding you back. This process will make you more like Jesus.

We have a lot of impurities in our lives. Therefore, God will use the refining process several times as you follow Jesus. You can trust that God has great plans for you and is working through the tough times to draw you closer to him.

Next time you experience a trial, ask God how he is refining you and making you more like Jesus.

Set Free

"Suddenly there was such a violent earthquake that the foundations of the prison were shaken. At once all the prison doors flew open, and everyone's chains came loose."

ACTS 16:26 (NIV)

Sometimes we need God to shake up our lives so we can experience freedom.

This is particularly true when we find ourselves locked up in prisons of our own making. We may be trapped by a habit we can't escape, a fear we can't overcome, or a dead-end relationship. These prisons keep us from fulfilling God's purpose for our lives.

God did this for the apostle Paul. In Acts 16, Paul was in a real, physical prison. He needed a miracle to get out of it—so that's what God gave him. The chains came loose, the doors flew open, and Paul walked out of prison.

Sometimes God must also shake your foundations to set you free. You may lose your job, face a health crisis, or experience the end of a treasured relationship.

In the earthquake, you might be tempted to think that God has forgotten you or that he is angry with you. Neither is true because God's love for you is perfect. There is a unique opportunity when your foundations are being challenged: It's in the shake-up that you start re-examining what you believe about God, yourself, and others.

The earthquake opens you up to learning something new and changing the way you think.

Don't let an earthquake in your life create distance between you and God. Instead, use it to draw closer to him. How can you do this? Ask God what prison he is trying to free you from.

Then watch the chains come loose and the doors fly open.

How Your Courage Grows

"Never be ashamed to tell others about our Lord . . .
With the strength God gives you, be ready to suffer
with me for the sake of the Good News."

2 TIMOTHY 1:8 (NLT)

When you lift weights, you strain, stretch, and stress your muscles. That's how they grow.

Courage is like a muscle, and the only way to build your courage muscle is to put it to the test.

Courage isn't the absence of fear; it's moving forward with what God wants, regardless of your fear. Standing up for God when you're afraid builds your courage, and it builds your character.

Giving in to fear—instead of standing up to it—keeps your courage from developing. When you let fear win, you lose the courage to follow God's will for your life. But when you stand strong for what God wants, your courage grows.

What are you willing to do to be true to your faith? Are you willing to be teased? Are you willing to have people gossip about you? Are you willing to be shunned?

Historically, Christians have suffered in ways we can't begin to imagine. They've been fed to lions and crucified for their faith in Christ. Even today, people are being martyred for their faith. It's much more common than you may realize. Would you have the courage to die for your faith?

Stand up for God today. When you overcome your fears, your courage grows, your character grows, and your faith does too.

Wisdom Keeps the Peace

"Fools start fights everywhere while wise men try to keep peace."

PROVERBS 29:8 (TLB)

Do you want more wisdom in your relationships?

The Bible tells us it's foolish to start arguments, but it's wise to keep the peace. It's important to understand the misconceptions about peace in order to become a practical peacemaker.

You can't achieve peace by avoiding a problem. Peace is not running away from the issue or pretending that it doesn't exist. Often people will avoid issues rather than face them, saying, "Let's not talk about it," or "Don't make waves." Making the peace doesn't mean avoiding the problem! Unresolved conflict is like having termites in your relationship. If you don't deal with the issue, eventually it will destroy the relationship.

Avoiding conflict doesn't keep the peace; it gives fear the steering wheel.

Peacemaking is also not achieved by appeasing the other person. In other words, if you always give in to the other person's ways, you're allowing yourself to be manipulated. God certainly doesn't expect you to be a doormat! When you study the ministry of Jesus, you learn that he never backed off from controversial issues, and he didn't settle them by compromising. Here's the truth: Appeasement always results in resentment.

Resentment swallows your feelings and your stomach keeps score.

Next time you need to keep the peace, spend time talking about it to God—he cares about your problems! He will give you the wisdom, courage, and strength to keep the peace. Jesus is right there with you!

Personalize God's Word

"And I am certain that God, who began the good work within you, will continue his work until it is finally finished on the day when Christ Jesus returns."

PHILIPPIANS 1:6 (NLT)

God's Word changes your life when you learn to take it personally. That's what application is all about. The Bible won't become dynamic until it becomes specific.

How do you make God's Word personal? Try the personalize-it method of Bible meditation. It's easy to do, and you don't need any special tools or advanced theological training.

Simply put your name in the place of pronouns or nouns in Scripture. For example, you can personalize John 3:16 like this: *"For God so loved (your name), that he gave his one and only Son so that (your name) would not perish but have* *everlasting life."* Put your name in the text, and you'll strengthen your faith and encourage yourself.

You can also rewrite the verse as if God is talking directly to you. For example, Philippians 1:6 would say, *"[I], who began a good work in you, (your name), will carry it on to completion."*

Practice this type of Bible meditation, and many passages of Scripture will literally bring tears to your eyes. You'll start reading the Bible as God's love letter to you. Reading your Bible isn't just about getting to know the content of the Word; it's about getting to know the author of the Word—personally.

May

Quiet Time with God

*"The plans of the diligent lead surely to abundance,
but everyone who is hasty comes only to poverty."*

PROVERBS 21:5 (ESV)

The abundant life starts with a plan. A plan will keep you diligent in many things, including your daily quiet time.

Following a plan similar to the one below can get you started on a rewarding time with God.

Start by simply sitting down and staying quiet before the Lord. This helps you focus on God and what he has to tell you.

Start with a short opening prayer. Ask God to cleanse your mind and open your heart.

Read a portion of Scripture slowly. This is where your conversation with God begins as he starts speaking to you through his Word. Don't try to read too quickly or too much.

Practice meditating on the verse. Think about what God is saying and repeat it over in your mind. You can even say it out loud.

Keep a journal and write down what you learn. When God speaks to you through his Word, write it down. Writing helps you remember what God says to you, and you can look back at it when you need encouragement and clarity.

Pray and have a conversation with God. Talk to him about what he's said to you, and tell him what you're thinking about. Prayer is an intimate conversation with God. You can talk to him about anything that's on your mind. He wants to talk with you, and he will always listen.

Praying with Confidence

"I remain confident of this: I will see the goodness of the Lord in the land of the living. Wait for the Lord; be strong and take heart and wait for the Lord."

PSALM 27:13–14 (NIV)

Knowing who God is influences the way you pray. So what is God really like?

He is all-knowing (omniscient), he is all-powerful (omnipotent), he can be everywhere at the same time (omnipresent). The Bible tells us God is holy, just, kind, loving, and faithful.

There are many characteristics of God that we could study, but let's look specifically at the goodness of God. God's goodness is the basis for all prayer. If God is not a good God, then we have no motivation to pray and no hope of being heard.

The only reason there is any good in the world is because God, our Creator, is a good God. If there is no God, then there is no right and wrong, no good and bad.

People often ask, "Why is there evil in the world?" The answer is simple: Evil exists because God gave us free choice. God doesn't force us to do good, so we sometimes choose the opposite.

Evil is easy to explain. The hard thing to explain is why there is any good in the world. In a "dog eat dog," tough luck world, the only reason there is good is because God is a good God.

Because God is always good, you can pray with confidence. The more you understand how good God really is, the more you're going to enjoy prayer. Prayer won't be a duty anymore; it will be a delight!

Perfectionism Paralyzes Potential

*"If you wait for perfect conditions,
you will never get anything done."*

ECCLESIASTES 11:4 (TLB)

Fear is at the root of all indecision—fear that you'll make a mistake, that you'll embarrass yourself, that you'll make a commitment you can't keep, or that somebody will reject you.

We don't like to admit that we're afraid, so we make excuses when God tells us to do something. We see this throughout the Bible. Moses said, "I can't talk." Gideon said, "I'm too young." Abraham said, "I'm too old."

What's your excuse?

You might be saying, "I don't have the time or the money. I don't have the experience or the education. If only I were older or younger, in another country, in another year." It's fear that's keeping you from making the decision you know God wants you to make. You're afraid that you won't do it perfectly.

Perfectionism paralyzes potential. But God has always used imperfect people in imperfect situations to accomplish his will. If you're waiting for circumstances to be just right before you fully commit to doing what God is telling you to do, you'll never get started. Decisions and commitments must be made when God calls, not when everything is perfect.

What's the antidote to fear? Hand your fears over to God and step out in faith. God isn't looking for perfection, he's just waiting for you to take a step in the right direction.

Turning Back to God

*"You don't love me or each other as you did at first! Look how far
you have fallen! Turn back to me and do the works you did at first."*

REVELATION 2:4-5 (NLT)

You will experience dry seasons in your spiritual life.

Next thing you know, serving God becomes more of a duty than a delight. You continue to pray because it's the right thing to do, but there's no joy, power, or excitement in your conversations with God. You'll show up to small group, but you don't experience connection and encouragement.

What do you do when you are in a spiritual slump?

The first thing you need to do is to admit to God that you're not as close to him as you used to be. You're no longer as close as you want to be. You need to pray, "God, my heart has grown cold. Things don't move me like they used to. I need you to light the fire again in my heart. I need the passion back."

Then you need to depend on God to restore your passion—and fully expect him to do it. This is the faith step. You must believe that God can and will and wants to bring you back into a close relationship with him. It's something you can start right now, for God has the grace, the power, and the energy to restore you.

God will help you get out of your spiritual slump, but you also have a responsibility. Think back on a time in your life when you were closest to God, living with joy and in obedience to him. During those days, what were you doing to maintain your faith?

Work alongside the Holy Spirit by returning to those habits to restore your connection with God.

Every Decision Has a Price Tag

*"It is a trap to dedicate something rashly
and only later to consider one's vows."*

PROVERBS 20:25 (NIV)

Every time you give a minute of your life to anything, you're giving a piece of your life away. You'll never get that minute back, so use every minute wisely.

Every decision has a price tag. Every decision will cost you time, money, energy, reputation, talents, or resources. You're always making some sort of investment whenever you make a decision. It doesn't matter if the decision is good or bad, all decisions have a cost.

It is a trap to decide without deliberating, to make a promise without pondering, to make a commitment without first considering the cost.

When people pressure you to make a decision, it's okay to just say, "I'll get back to you." Making the right decision is more important than making a quick decision.

One of the rules of life is that it's always easier to get into something than to get out of it. It's easier to get into trouble than to get out of it. It's easier to get into a relationship than to get out. It's easier to get into debt than to get out. It's easier to fill your schedule than to fulfill your schedule.

That's why it's important to count the cost before you make a decision. Don't choose too quickly. Slow down to gain perspective. It can save you a lot of heartache in the long run.

Seek God's Wisdom in Everything

"A man is a fool to trust himself!
But those who use God's wisdom are safe."

PROVERBS 28:26 (TLB)

The Bible gives a simple, workable plan to make wise decisions. Whether it's about career, marriage, finances, health, children, or the future, follow these three principles for decision-making from God's Word.

Dedicate time to pray for guidance. Before you do anything else, get God's perspective on the issue. Have you ever made a foolish decision that you thought was the best thing to do at the time? You need to make decisions based on something greater than simple intuition or a gut feeling. You need to base your decisions on absolute truth. You do that by getting God's guidance.

Get all the facts before you make a decision. We make mistakes when we base decisions on uneducated enthusiasm. The Bible says in Proverbs 18:13, *"What a shame—yes, how stupid!— to decide before knowing the facts!"* (TLB).

It's important to ask for advice. Talk to people who have made a similar decision. Talk to friends who know your weaknesses. Learn to ask for advice!

It is wise to learn from experience, but it is wiser to learn from the experiences of others. You don't have time to learn everything from personal experience. You don't have time to make all the mistakes in life. Life is too short to learn everything by trial and error. But you can learn from God's Word, by knowing the facts, and by listening to people with experience.

God Is Always at Work in Your Life

"We know that God causes everything to work together for the good of those who love God and are called according to his purpose for them."

ROMANS 8:28 (NLT)

Where is your hope when your life is upside down?

God doesn't promise that every event in your life will be good. He doesn't guarantee that everything will work out like you want it to, or that every story will have a fairytale ending. Not every business decision will make you a million dollars. Not every married couple will live happily ever after. Not every doctor's report will be positive.

God is not your genie because your wish is not his command.

Because you love him, God does promise to work everything—the good and the bad—for your good. It's like putting a puzzle together. On its own, each piece doesn't look like much. When all the pieces are connected together, a beautiful picture appears.

God can take all the pieces of your life and make something wonderful.

God created the universe! He can work good from anything that's bad. God will use confusion to teach wisdom, frustration to develop patience, pain to show comfort, disappointment to refine where we put our hope, and anger to remind us that some things in our world simply aren't right. In every season of your life, God is moving you closer to him.

God is bigger than all the bad stuff that happens in your life.

On this side of eternity, you won't have all of the answers, but you can have something better: God's presence and his promise. Truth is, the answers don't bring peace. You can be confident that God is working in your life, and he is working everything together to be good for you.

Today, how is God working in your life?

Bless Those Who Oppose You

"Love your enemies! Do good to those who hate you.
Bless those who curse you. Pray for those who hurt you.
If someone slaps you on one cheek, offer the other cheek also.
If someone demands your coat, offer your shirt also."

LUKE 6:27-29 (NLT)

When you're persecuted, harassed, and faced with opposition, respond with a blessing.

It's what sets Christians apart from others because it's not a natural, popular, or easy response. It takes a lot of courage to be kind in the face of opposition.

Anyone can fight back and retaliate. But God wants you to love your enemies, do good to those who hate you, bless those who curse you, pray for those who hurt you, and turn the other cheek. Are those things easy to do? No, but you can do them when you are filled with God's love.

Stephen, the first Christian martyr, is a courageous example of turning the other cheek. He was falsely accused of blasphemy and was stoned to death by his enemies. Even then, Stephen refused to retaliate; instead, as he was dying, he shouted, *"Lord, don't charge them with this sin!"* (Acts 7:60 NLT).

God doesn't want you to retaliate, no matter what gets thrown at you. Instead, respond in love, trusting that God will give you the courage you need.

What Kind of Goal Does God Bless?

"When you eat or drink or do anything else, always do it to honor God."

1 CORINTHIANS 10:31 (CEV)

God wants to bless your goals. But not every goal you set is a goal that God will bless.

How do you know which goals are best? You can figure that out by following these guidelines.

It's important to determine if your goal will honor God. Goals that bring glory to God are those that cause you to trust him more. If your goal doesn't require faith, then you don't need God to bless it. You just need to get to work. If you want God's blessing, you need a faith-based goal because the Bible says, *"Without faith it is impossible to please God"* (Hebrews 11:6 NIV).

Determining the motivation of your goal is a big step in the process because God won't bless a goal motivated by

greed, envy, guilt, fear, or pride. But he does honor a goal motivated by a desire to demonstrate love to him and to others. If you want God's blessing, you need a love-based goal.

Why is it important to have goals that are based on love? Because if you set loveless goals, you're going to treat people like projects. You're going to run all over them to get to your goal. God says, "No. You've got it all wrong. Life is not about accomplishments. It's about relationships. Life is about learning how to love."

The number one goal in your life should be to learn how to love—your family, your neighbors, and even your enemies. That makes you more like God—because God is love.

Talk to the God Who Is Good

"For the Lord is always good. He is always loving and kind, and his faithfulness goes on and on to each succeeding generation."

PSALM 100:5 (TLB)

Have you ever noticed how you act more formally when talking to someone you don't know very well?

What you know about somebody influences how you communicate with that person.

The same is true with God. Your understanding of what God is like shapes everything else in your life, including your prayer life.

A lot of people have misconceptions about God. Some think he's cranky and upset all the time. Some people picture a god who is ready to pounce when they make a wrong move. Others think he's moody, always changing his mind.

Have you ever heard somebody say, "I like to think of God as . . . ," and then they cobble together a description based on guess work and hearsay? It doesn't really matter what they *think* God is like. What matters is what the Bible says God is like.

It's important that you know the real God. If you have a misconception about him, then prayer is going to be a duty rather than a conversation between friends. God wants you to talk to him because you love him, and you will love him more as you get to know him better through his Word.

The more you understand God's goodness, the more natural and relaxed your conversations will be with him. You can tell God anything! Tell him everything you care about, if it's on your mind, God wants to hear it.

Knowledge Requires Action

"Remember, it is sin to know what you ought to do and then not do it."

JAMES 4:17 (NLT)

God wants you to apply the Bible to your life, not just read it. The Bible is about transformation, not just information. And when you study the Bible without doing what it says, you literally limit your spiritual growth.

It's important to apply God's Word to your life because knowledge without application produces pride. The Bible says, *"Knowledge puffs up while love builds up"* (1 Corinthians 8:1 NIV). If you never apply God's Word, it doesn't matter how much of the Bible you know. You can still become mean-spirited, cranky, critical, or judgmental.

But when you allow God's Word to speak into your life, it will transform you.

Acquiring knowledge requires action. You need to take what you learn from the Bible and do something with it. It doesn't get any plainer than that. It's God's plan for your life.

Knowledge of the Bible increases your responsibility. As you learn more about God's Word, he calls you to a greater responsibility to do the things he wants you to do. The more you put God's Word into practice, the more you become like Christ.

Let Go Of Your Hurt

"Make allowance for each other's faults, and forgive anyone who offends you. Remember, the Lord forgave you, so you must forgive others."

COLOSSIANS 3:13 (NLT)

If you've ever been hurt by another person, you might think, "I know the Christian thing to do is to forgive, so I will forgive him as soon as he apologizes."

There is a big problem with this way of thinking. He may never apologize. He may not even realize what he's done. So you will end up stewing over something the other person forgot long ago. You'll hold on to the hurt, and your resentment will eat you up inside!

Resentment is like drinking poison and hoping it kills someone else. You have to decide to forgive the person who wronged you, even if they never ask for forgiveness.

When Jesus was being crucified, he forgave the people who put him on the cross. Jesus didn't wait for an apology. He just forgave.

We are called to make allowance for each other's faults. In the Greek language, the phrase for "make allowance" can also be translated "to bear with, to endure, to be tolerant." It means to cut people some slack. After all, everyone does things that require forgiveness, including you.

When you struggle with forgiving, remember the great gift of God's forgiveness in your life.

God Is Never in a Hurry

*"Don't try to get out of anything prematurely.
Let it do its work so you become mature and well-developed."*

JAMES 1:4 (THE MESSAGE)

One of life's frustrations is that God's timetable is rarely the same as yours. You are often in a hurry when God isn't, and you get frustrated with the seemingly slow progress you're making. But remember, God uses your entire lifetime to prepare you for your role in eternity.

The Bible is filled with examples of God taking his time when developing someone's character, especially in leaders. He took eighty years to prepare Moses, including forty in the wilderness. For 14,600 days Moses kept waiting and wondering, "Is it time yet?" But God kept saying, "Not yet."

The key is not to get discouraged. When the prophet Habakkuk got depressed because he didn't think God was acting quickly enough, God asked him to be patient and reminded him it will take time for the vision to be fulfilled.

Great souls are grown through struggles, storms, and seasons of suffering. Be patient with the process. Allow the source of your frustration to do its work in your life.

Remember how far you've come, not just how far you have to go. You may not be where you want to be, but you're also not where you used to be. God isn't finished with you, so keep moving forward.

Fix the Problem, Not the Blame

*"If you want to enjoy life and see many happy days,
keep your tongue from speaking evil and your lips from telling lies."*

1 PETER 3:10 (NLT)

When you're trying to resolve conflict in a conversation, you can either fix the blame or you can fix the problem. You need to decide which is more important—to blame the other person or to resolve the conflict.

To help resolve the conflict, you need to establish ground rules for fighting fairly, including identifying words you both agree not to use. There are some things you should never say in a marriage, in a family, or in a friendship because certain words can become relational weapons of mass destruction.

During the Cold War, the Soviet Union and the United States both had weapons of mass destruction aimed at each other. This created a tense situation called MAD, which is short for mutually assured destruction. If the weapons were used, both sides would be destroyed, so both sides agreed not to use them.

In a way, certain words are like personal weapons of mass destruction. For instance, in a marriage, you should both agree to never threaten divorce, say you'll walk out, or speak negatively about one another's parents. No matter how upset you are with each other, some words are off limits because they will destroy the relationship by tearing down trust.

Focus on fixing the problem and not the blame. Blaming is a form of judging, and only God has the right to judge. You can't figure out anybody else's motivation. In fact, you may not even know your own motivation! Only God knows. Let him be the judge as you focus your attention on working toward creating peace with each other.

Stand Up to Fear

"Lord, take notice of the threats they have made, and allow us, your servants, to speak your message with all boldness."

ACTS 4:29 (GNT)

We all have fears. Too often, though, we let them rule over our lives and stop us from taking a stand for what God wants us to do.

If you want to overcome a fear that's dragging you down, start doing the things God desires. Only then will you have victory over the fear in your life.

Fear grows every time you refuse to do what God wants you to do. Eventually, you feel cornered. When fear grows, your life shrinks.

On the other hand, faith grows every time you take a step of obedience and do what God wants you to do. Eventually, you find freedom. When faith grows, your fear shrinks.

What can you do?

Follow the lead of Peter and John. In Acts 4, they came up against fierce opposition. After they prayed, the Bible says they were filled with the Holy Spirit and spoke the Word of God boldly.

The answer to your fear isn't to give in to it. It's to move forward boldly in spite of your fear by trusting God.

When you take a step of faith, regardless of your fears, you'll find God actively working in your circumstances. Fear will diminish when you step out boldly for God.

Only God Can Unlock Your Potential

"Whatever I am now, it is all because God poured out his special favor on me—and not without results. For I have worked harder than any of the other apostles; yet it was not I but God who was working through me by his grace."

1 CORINTHIANS 15:10 (NLT)

You are far more capable than you ever imagined. You can't even fathom your full potential. But God, your Creator, knows all you are capable of becoming. Your parents, your spouse, your friends, your boss—they only get a glimpse of your potential.

That's why you risk falling short of your potential when you live for the approval of others. They may tell you that you're not capable of doing something when, in truth, it's the very thing God created you to do. They may point you in the opposite direction of your life mission.

God knows your capabilities, and he can unlock your potential. As God pours out his special favor on you through his Word and his grace, you will be able to do things you never thought possible on your own.

Paul had firsthand experience with God unlocking his potential. He had immeasurable impact on the Kingdom. Paul planted churches, invested in others, and his letters make up more than half of the New Testament. Paul worked hard, but the true power was God's grace.

Perfect and Flawless

*"As for God, his way is perfect: The LORD's word is flawless;
he shields all who take refuge in him."*

PSALM 18:30 (NIV)

If you are ready to take refuge in God, he is ready to protect you.

Taking refuge in God means you are ready for God to answer your prayers whenever and however he thinks is best. When you look to God for help, you need to believe that his *"way is perfect"* and that his *"word is flawless."*

What would have happened in the story of Zechariah and Elizabeth if God had answered their request for a baby immediately? They would have gotten a sweet little baby they would have loved and cherished—but God had a plan. He delayed the request for a number of years before he gave them John the Baptist. When John grew up, his ministry prepared the people of Israel for Jesus. God's timing was perfect.

Do you ask too little of God and want it too soon?

If God answered your prayers exactly how you wanted and according to your timeline, you'd end up shortchanged. His answers are much greater than your requests. In fact, be thankful God hasn't answered every single one of your prayers the way you had hoped. Accept that God will answer your prayers in his time and in his way.

If you want God's help, you need to ask for it, and you need to spend time reading the Bible. To know God's will for your life, you need to look at God's Word. Building your life on the truth will protect you from the harm that comes from the lies of the world.

Your power and perspective is limited, that's why you need to trust God's ways and his Word. They are perfect and flawless.

Pray for Your Purpose

"'I know what I am planning for you,' says the Lord. 'I have good plans for you, not plans to hurt you. I will give you a hope and a good future. Then you will call my name. You will come to me and pray to me, and I will listen to you.'"

JEREMIAH 29:11-12 (NCV)

You are not an accident.

There are accidental parents, but there are no accidental children. Your parents may not have planned you, but God did, and he wanted you alive and he has a purpose for your life.

Did you know that God can't do everything?

God can't be evil. God doesn't just do good things, God is good. Everything that is good in this world comes from him. God is good, all the time, and this means that his plans for your life are good. You don't have to wonder or worry about your future because God has that covered. Your hope for tomorrow is secure!

Once you are convinced that God has good plans for you, ask him what they are.

God wants you to believe in his goodness, to believe in it enough to go call on his name, to go to him in prayer. God's open invitation to a great future must be accepted—he's not going to force you to follow his purpose for your life.

A watch on your wrist is useless if you never look at it. If you want to know what time it is, you'll look at your watch because you trust that it's accurate. If you want to know your purpose in life, look to God in prayer.

Do you know God's purpose for your life? If not, make a commitment today to begin seeking him.

God Grows Us One Step at a Time

"So get rid of your old self, which made you live as you used to —the old self that was being destroyed by its deceitful desires. Your hearts and minds must be made completely new, and you must put on the new self, which is created in God's likeness and reveals itself in the true life that is upright and holy."

EPHESIANS 4:22-24 (GNT)

God could instantly transform us; instead he matures us slowly.

Most of us are slow learners. We often have to relearn a lesson several times to get it. The history of Israel illustrates how quickly we forget the lessons God teaches us and how soon we revert to our old patterns of behavior. The good news is, God is patient and committed to helping us mature.

In order to learn something new, we often have to take the time to unlearn something that's holding us back. Growth requires the hard work of removal and replacement. The Bible calls it "taking off the old self" and "putting on the new self." God understands this process; he's made it part of his plan for us.

The bottom line is, we all fear change. Growth can be painful and scary. Sometimes we hang on to our old ways because, like a worn-out pair of shoes, they are at least comfortable and familiar. But God loves you so much that he is more interested in your growth than your comfort. He wants you to become more like Jesus.

What's your next step? Where is God calling you to put off your old self?

Surrender What Jesus Uncovers

"If anyone would come after me, he must deny himself and take up his cross daily and follow me. For whoever wants to save his life will lose it, but whoever loses his life for me will save it."

LUKE 9:23-24 (NIV84)

Jesus wants you to surrender your whole life to him. He doesn't want just a part of your life, he wants all of it.

You may think you've surrendered enough to him, but Jesus wants it all. C.S. Lewis, the Christian apologist and author of the Narnia series, says Jesus is like a dentist. When you go to the dentist, you want him to fix your toothache. You want him to stop the pain. But the dentist isn't willing to stop there. If he's a good dentist, he's going to poke and prod around your teeth to find out what is causing the toothache. He doesn't just want to stop you from hurting, he wants to heal what is causing the pain.

This is what Jesus wants to do in your life. He wants to uncover all the sin and hurt and heartache that is keeping you from being the person he created you to be. As he uncovers these things, he corrects, comforts, and heals you.

He simply wants you to give control of your life to him. If you keep holding onto parts of your life, even as you follow Jesus, you will not experience the fullness of your new life in Christ.

But when you surrender everything to Jesus, there will never be a doubt about the outcome. When you "lose" your life for Jesus—surrendering it to him— you will gain real life.

Your Choices Control Your Calendar

"We are each responsible for our own conduct."

GALATIANS 6:5 (NLT)

Your choices are far more powerful than your circumstances. You may not like how complicated your life has become. But with few exceptions, no one is forcing you to keep your life complicated.

You have the power to simplify your life. In fact, God expects you to assume responsibility for your life and carefully choose how you spend your time.

You've been given just enough time to do God's will while you're here on earth. You've been given just enough time to fulfill your purpose. When you try to do more than God planned for you, you'll find yourself constantly out of time or stressed over your schedule.

When you do only the things God created you to do, you will find relief from stress and a new sense of satisfaction. When you trust God with your time, committing every plan and circumstance to him, you are taking godly responsibility for your conduct.

Where do you believe God wants you to focus your time and energy? Make a list of activities and responsibilities that cause you stress. Ask God to help you determine which things he doesn't intend for you to do. Then begin to focus on his plans.

When You Are Tired, Trust in the Lord

"Those who trust in the LORD will find new strength. They will soar high on wings like eagles. They will run and not grow weary. They will walk and not faint."

ISAIAH 40:31 (NLT)

When you are tired, your endurance is being tested.

If you're discouraged, don't give up without a fight. Nothing worthwhile ever happens without endurance and energy. Where can you get the energy to keep moving forward? It comes from trusting in the Lord. He is the one who gives you the ability to rise above your temporary discouragement and to keep pressing on toward success.

Why does trusting God work? For starters, your decision to ask God for help opens the door for the Holy Spirit to work in your life. Also, trusting in God works because he's the only one who won't let you down.

When an artist creates a sculpture, he doesn't hit the chisel with the hammer once, and suddenly, all the excess stone falls away. He keeps hitting it and hitting it, slowly revealing a beautiful masterpiece.

That's true of life, too. Nothing worthwhile ever comes easy. But if you keep chiseling away at it, little by little your life becomes a masterpiece of God's grace.

Let God Guide You

"He guides me along the right paths
for his name's sake."

PSALM 23:3 (NIV)

Are you ever paralyzed with fear that you'll make the wrong decision?

Maybe it's about a major issue: "Should I hold on, or should I let go?" "Should I get in, or should I get out?" "Should I get married?" "Should I find a new job?" "Should I move?"

When you're afraid to make up your mind, you may stagger through life. In fact, the Bible says, *"A double-minded man is unstable in all his ways"* (James 1:8 KJV). In the Greek, the word for "unstable"gives a picture of someone "staggering like a drunk." When you're unstable, you're no longer in control of where you're going; your direction is haphazard instead of intentional.

God gives you a solution for overcoming fear and indecision. It's not too complicated. Here's the solution: Let God guide you. He wants you to know his will more than you want to know it. How can you know if he's guiding you? His guidance will always align with Scripture, point you toward clarity, and lead you to peace.

So, here's a decision for you to make right now. Will you take a step of faith and say "yes" to God? You can trust him to guide you *along the right paths for his name's sake."*

Find Freedom in God's Word

"You will know the truth, and the truth will set you free."

JOHN 8:32 (NIV)

Do you ever wonder why you do things that you know are bad for you? Even after you become a follower of Christ, there's a tension inside of you. You have your new nature that God gave you, but your old nature still pulls at you. But Jesus promises a way out!

The secret to personal change is not willpower. It's not a New Year's resolution or a self-help program. It's not something you do or say. The secret to personal change is something you know—God's truth. When you know the truth, it changes the way you think. When you change the way you think, it changes the way you feel. When you change the way you feel, it changes the way you act.

Behind every self-defeating act is a lie you believe. It might be a lie about yourself, about others, or even about God. You're convinced there will be a positive payout for negative behavior. So, you rationalize your decision to do the wrong thing. But when you rationalize, you're just telling yourself "rational lies." You expose those lies by discovering and embracing the truth of God's Word.

This is why you need a daily quiet time with God. When you read God's word and spend time talking to him, you will encounter the truth and it will set you free.

Justified Through Faith

"Since we have been justified through faith, we have peace with God through our Lord Jesus Christ."

ROMANS 5:1 (NIV)

To have peace with God, you need to be justified.

To be justified means to be made right with God—it's "just-as-if-I'd-never-sinned." No one is perfect—not by your own standards, let alone God's standards—and the result is guilt. When you carry your guilt, you lose your sense of peace with God.

Wouldn't you love to have a heart as clean as freshly fallen snow?

No matter how deep the stain of your sin, God can take it out—all of it. You need to ask to be justified. The Bible says, *"Let us come boldly to the throne of our gracious God. There we will receive his mercy, and we will find grace to help us when we need it most"* (Hebrews 4:16 NLT).

You don't have to be fearful or shy about coming to God for forgiveness.

When you come to God and confess your sins, you will not be scolded, punished, or rejected. Instead, you will receive God's mercy and grace. To have a relationship with God, you need his forgiveness.

You don't need to beg for God's forgiveness. God wants to forgive you more than you want to be forgiven. Don't try to bribe him: "God, I promise I'll never do it again! I'll even tithe 20 percent!" God sees right through those kinds of empty promises.

Instead, believe God's promise in Hebrews 4:16. Come to God in faith and confess. You won't be telling God anything he doesn't already know. Just admit that you've blown it, and receive his mercy and grace. When you do, you too will be able to say, "It's just-as-if-I'd-never-sinned."

Who Needs Your Hospitality?

"[Cornelius] was a devout, God-fearing man, as was everyone in his household. He gave generously to the poor and prayed regularly to God."

ACTS 10:2 (NLT)

People who have the gift of hospitality are warm and welcoming to others. They're not strangers to the stranger because hospitable people are gracious and generous. Hospitality accepts others and helps them feel like they belong.

Did someone model hospitality to you as a child? When parents teach their children that they are not the center of the universe—that they have a God-given ability to connect with and care for others—it pleases God.

Showing hospitality doesn't require a big house, a ton of friends, or a pool in the backyard. You don't even need a house! You only need a "How may I serve you?" attitude as you interact with others throughout the day—and a willingness to welcome the lonely, the hurting, the hopeless, the shy, and the weary into your life.

Hospitality is a matter of the heart.

A good example of this is Cornelius' family in the book of Acts. His entire family demonstrated hospitality to those in need. What a great legacy! Wouldn't you like people to say that about you and your family someday?

The best example of hospitality is found in the life of Jesus. He's the One who first initiated hospitality. Although not many people welcomed Jesus, his generosity to others was unparalleled—especially when he went to the cross, the greatest act of generosity ever shown.

Today, what opportunities will you have to show hospitality to others?

Change Requires New Thinking

"Let the Spirit renew your thoughts and attitudes."

EPHESIANS 4:23 (NLT)

The battle to change your life begins in your mind. If you want to change your behavior, you must start with your thoughts and attitudes.

The renewal of your mind is related to the word "repentance." Repentance is a negative word for some people. They think of a guy on a street corner, holding a sign—"Repent! The world's about to end."

Repentance is a good thing. It does not begin with your actions. It begins with learning to think differently. "Repent" simply means to make a mental U-turn. It's something that starts with your mind, not with your behavior. Changing the way you think will change the way you act.

This means turning from guilt to forgiveness, from purposelessness to purpose, from no hope to new hope, from frustration to freedom, from darkness to light, from hell to heaven, from hatred to love.

Repentance also changes the way you think about God. He's not mad at you; he's mad about you! It changes the way you think about yourself, your spouse, your kids, your loved ones, and how you think about your past, present, and future.

Renewal is powered by the Holy Spirit. In other words, God is actively working to help you change the way you think, so that you will become more like Jesus.

Trusting God Completely

"Trust in the LORD with all your heart
and lean not on your own understanding."

PROVERBS 3:5 (NIV)

Many people make the mistake of worrying about God's will. They get anxious and uptight: "Am I in the will of God? Have I missed it?" Such people think God's will is like a tightrope, where each careful move is up to them. If they make one misjudgment or one false move, they're doomed!

Knowing God's will for your life is not your ultimate responsibility—it's God's, so trust him to speak to you. It's your responsibility to respond in faith with obedience. Even though it's human nature to want to figure it all out and come up with rational explanations for everything, God wants you to trust him.

The fact is, you don't need to know the reason for everything. You're called to obey.

You can't see the grand scope of things, but God does. You are a finite being and you have very limited understanding. That is why God says to *"not lean on your understanding"* and to trust his understanding, which is infinite and perfect and good.

Trusting God with all your heart means you are fully abandoned to doing what God wants you to do. This isn't easy because we live in a world that says, "You deserve to have it your way." God wants you to trust him, even more than you trust yourself.

What if it's time to make an important decision and God has yet to show you what to do? If you've prayed about it, and it aligns with what God has already revealed to you in his Word, you are free to make the decision— without guilt, stress, and worry.

Call on God in Times of Trouble

"Call on me in times of trouble. I will rescue you, and you will honor me."

PSALM 50:15 (GW)

God wants you to ask for help when you are in trouble.

Psalm 50:15 is a "microwave" prayer because it is quick and to the point. For instance, when temptation strikes and you don't have time for a long conversation with God, simply cry out! David, Daniel, Peter, Paul, and countless others have prayed this kind of instant prayer in times of trouble.

God is telling you to call on him when you need help, so you can be sure that he will hear you. Your God is the one who saves you and rescues you when you need it.

If God is waiting to help us, why don't we turn to him more often?

Honestly, sometimes we don't want to be helped. We are convinced that we know what's best, as if we are more qualified than God.

At other times, we are too embarrassed to ask God for help. We feel like we're not good enough to deserve help, so we let our guilt keep us from God.

Neither of these reasons are valid. We aren't more qualified than God, and his love for us is unconditional. God's help is the best help, and he offers it to you no matter what you've done!

When we call on God for help and he rescues us, the natural response is to honor God. If you want to honor God more with your life, ask for more of his help! When you make it a habit to ask God for help, you will honor him more and more.

Where do you need God's help? Who do you know who also needs God's help, and how can you be praying for them?

You Were Made by God and for God

"Some of these people have missed the most important thing in life —they don't know God."

1 TIMOTHY 6:21 (TLB)

There are about 18 inches between your head and your heart. Sadly, some people will miss heaven by those 18 inches. They know about God in their heads, but they don't know him in their hearts. They intellectually believe the Gospel, but they've never let it change their hearts.

You're going to forget much of what you've learned in the past, but don't ever forget this: You were made by God, and you were made for God. Until you understand that, life will never make sense. You were not made for your own sake.

You might know quantum physics. You might understand chaos theory.

You may even know how to build a rocketship. But if you don't know God, you've missed the purpose of life.

At the end of your life, God will give you a final test. He won't ask you if you got straight A's in school. He won't care how well you did in your career. He won't ask to see your bank account balance.

Instead, he'll ask you this: "Did you get to know me? Did you build a relationship with my Son whom I sent to earth to die on the cross for you?"

The most important thing in life is that you would know God—not knowing about him, but knowing him personally.

Pride Is Destructive

"Love is . . . never boastful or proud."

1 CORINTHIANS 13:4 (TLB)

Pride ruins relationships.

Pride produces misunderstandings because it says, "I know it all, I don't need to listen." When your ears are closed, your mind jumps to conclusions. Pride causes you to presume and take liberties you shouldn't. It leads to assumptions that simply aren't true. These misunderstandings hurt deeply and damage the relationship. Have you ever heard anybody say love is blind? Love isn't blind. Pride is blind. It blinds us to our own faults.

Pride provokes arguments because it says, "Look at how good I am." Bragging doesn't impress anyone, it just creates conflict. The person who has the right to boast doesn't need to. Greatness is its own advertising. Bragging always gets you into trouble.

Pride prevents intimacy. The fear of rejection hides behind pride. Inside, you're thinking, "If you knew the real me, you would not like me!" Ego moves us to build walls in order to hide our faults, fears, and feelings. It pushes people away, keeping them at arm's distance while projecting a false sense of "I've got this!"

Pride postpones reconciliation when there's conflict. Have you ever done something wrong to someone you love, and you knew it was thoughtless, but you couldn't bring yourself to admit it? You can't say "I'm sorry. I was wrong" when you are filled with pride. When your ego is in charge, you can't restore a relationship.

Is pride ruining any of your relationships? How can you be more loving with humility?

June

OPEN DOORS

Your Money Management Matters to God

"Whoever can be trusted with very little can also be trusted with much, and whoever is dishonest with very little will also be dishonest with much. So if you have not been trustworthy in handling worldly wealth, who will trust you with true riches?"

LUKE 16:10-11 (NIV)

God uses money to test you. He doesn't automatically give his blessings to just anybody; he tests you first to see if you're responsible. If he can trust you with material possessions, then he can trust you with spiritual power. If you're not managing your money well, why would he give you the stuff that really matters?

What does your relationship with money reveal about you?

Money shows what you love most. If you really want to know what's important to you, look at your calendar and your credit card statement. The way you spend your time and money reveals what you love the most.

Money shows what you trust most. Do you trust in your money for security, happiness, and identity? Or do you trust in God? Generosity reveals a heart that trusts God.

Money shows whether or not God can trust you. Today's verse is a reminder that money doesn't only reveal how much you trust God; it also shows how much God can trust you.

Our world creates a culture of coveting versus contentment. When you find yourself wanting more, pause to consider how you could be more responsible with what you have. When you are trustworthy with very little, God will trust you with more.

God's Spirit Is Working in You

*"God is working in you, giving you the desire
and the power to do what pleases him."*

PHILIPPIANS 2:13 (NLT)

You cannot reproduce the character of Jesus in your life by your own strength. New Year's resolutions, willpower, and best intentions are not enough. Only the Holy Spirit has the power to make the changes God wants to make in your life.

Christlikeness is not produced by imitation but by inhabitation. You allow Christ to live through you.

The Bible says, *"The Lord—who is the Spirit—makes us more and more like him as we are changed into his glorious image"* (2 Corinthians 3:18 NLT). This process of changing you into a living, breathing image of Jesus is called sanctification.

Mention the "power of the Holy Spirit," and many people think of miraculous demonstrations and intense emotions. But most of the time the Holy Spirit transforms you in quiet ways that you aren't even aware of. He often nudges you gently.

How does he do it? Primarily by enabling you to understand the Word of God. The Holy Spirit is your advocate and will guide your thoughts toward truth that pleases God.

As the Holy Spirit transforms you, your faith matures. He gives you immediate and constant access to God's power, love, faith, and wisdom. These are available just for the asking because God's Spirit lives inside you. Through the Holy Spirit, God enables you to live a bold, powerful, joy-filled life full of purpose.

Grief Can Lead to Good

"There is a time for everything, and a season for every activity under the heavens . . . a time to weep and a time to laugh, a time to mourn and a time to dance."

ECCLESIASTES 3:1, 4 (NIV)

Would you agree that life is tough and full of losses? The world is broken and imperfect. Your body, the weather, the economy, and even your relationships don't work perfectly.

If you never grieve, it means one of three things: You're out of touch with reality, you're not listening to your emotions, or you don't love others. You need to understand a couple of truths that will give you a better perspective as you face the inevitable losses in your life—and rise above them.

God doesn't expect you to be happy all the time.

Sometimes the only appropriate, logical response to life is grief. The Bible says you are to grieve over your losses, including your disappointments, your sin, the suffering in the world, and your friends who are spiritually lost.

Grief is painful, but it's also healthy. Grief is God's gift because it helps you get through the tough seasons of life. Grief allows difficult transitions to transform you. If you don't grieve, you get stuck emotionally.

When you experience a painful loss, you need to grieve over it. If you were hurt many years ago but didn't grieve, you need to go back and mourn your loss. Don't keep the pain to yourself! Share it with God and share it with a close friend.

When you take the time to grieve, it opens your heart to receive comfort from God.

Learn to Say No

---

*"We must get rid of everything that slows us down,
especially sin that distracts us. We must run the race
that lies ahead of us and never give up."*

HEBREWS 12:1 (GW)

Sometimes, the most important word to remember to grow spiritually will simply be *"no."*

Your faith journey is a long, and you can't run a marathon with a couple of barbells in your hands. Too many people start off well but quit early because everything they're carrying drains their energy. You need to declutter because God wants you to go the distance.

Do you find yourself always feeling drained? That's what happens when you say yes to everything. Why? Because you end up trying to do too much. You need to learn to say "no"— even to some of the good things— because they slow you down and keep you from running the race God has set before you.

This may surprise you: Busyness is not a virtue. God has given you just the right amount of things to do with the time you have. He never gives you too little or too much. If you're experiencing burnout—or are quickly headed there—you need to remove the extra weight in your life. Don't take a shortcut and only remove some of it. You've got to remove all of it.

Weights aren't necessarily bad or sinful. They are unnecessary distractions that slow you down from doing what God wants you to do with your life. A weight could be a relationship, a hobby, or a habit like watching TV.

The dead weight isn't worth it. Learn to say "no" so you can grow.

Engage the Truth

"You must continue to believe this truth and stand firmly in it. Don't drift away from the assurance you received when you heard the Good News."

COLOSSIANS 1:23 (NLT)

God doesn't just tell the truth, he is truth. God is the ultimate standard of truth. What does it mean to believe and stand firm in the truth?

Make it your regular habit to take action on what you know to be true. If you don't believe an idea to be true enough to act on it, you don't really believe it. If you believe God is all-powerful, you'll trust him when life is uncertain.

Meditate on the truth. This simply means focused thinking. If you know how to worry, you know how to meditate. The more you think about the truth, the better you will understand it and the more it will change your life.

Share the truth with a friend. When God teaches you something new, he may provide an opportunity for you to pass that along to others. God wants to work both in and through your life!

When challenged, stand up for the truth. This can be very uncomfortable, but it will radically grow your faith. For example, if someone says, "Jesus was just a moral teacher, he wasn't God," stand up for what you know is true. Standing up for the truth doesn't mean you get to be rude. Defend the truth with gentleness and respect.

When you have questions (or are asked a question you can't answer), don't ignore them, look for answers. Putting your questions before God is a great way to open the door to let him work in your life.

There will be times when the truth is confusing or uncomfortable—that's normal. Continue to honor God by doing what you know to be true, and he will draw you closer to him.

Love Others the Way God Loves You

"Love never stops being patient, never stops believing, never stops hoping, never gives up."

1 CORINTHIANS 13:7 (GW)

The same love God gives to you, he wants you to offer to everyone around you. It's not an option or a suggestion. It's a command from Jesus: *"Now I am giving you a new commandment: Love each other. Just as I have loved you, you should love each other"* (John 13:34 NLT).

If you are a follower of Christ, you must love everybody—whether you like them or not—in the same way Christ loves you. That means you are to accept them completely, love them unconditionally, forgive them totally, and consider them extremely valuable.

Today's verse tells us that God never stops loving you. God will always be patient with you, believing in you, and hoping for the best in your life. God never gives up on you. And that's what God wants you to do with everybody else!

Loving others in this way will transform your relationships.

Start by asking God to help you love others the way he loves you:

"Father, help me to accept others, just as you've accepted me. Help me to love others unconditionally, just as you have loved me. Help me to forgive others totally, just as you've forgiven me. Help me to value others as much as you value me. Help me to extend grace to others, just as you've extended grace to me. And help me to expect the best in others and endure the worst when it happens. I ask this in Jesus' name. Amen."

Surrender Every Day to God

"Surrender your heart to God, turn to him in prayer, and give up your sins—even those you do in secret. Then you won't be ashamed; you will be confident and fearless. Your troubles will go away like water beneath a bridge, and your darkest night will be brighter than noon. You will rest safe and secure, filled with hope and emptied of worry."

JOB 11:13-18 (CEV)

How can you learn to live in God's love so that you can live free of fear? You have to surrender your heart to God every day. 1 John 4:18 says, *"Where God's love is, there is no fear, because God's perfect love drives out fear"* (NCV).

Each morning, before your feet hit the floor, pray, *"God, before I even start this day, I surrender my emotions to you. I want you to be Lord of my feelings. I want you to control my mind. I surrender my heart to you. I want you to fill me with your love."*

There are three commands and eight promises in today's Scripture. God says, if you do this, then he'll do that. When you follow his commands, God will follow through on his promises.

God gives three commands to follow: Surrender your heart to God. Talk to him in prayer. Confess all of your sins to God.

Then, God follows through on eight promises: You won't be ashamed. You'll be confident. You'll be fearless. Your troubles will be like water under the bridge. Your dark night will be brighter than noon. You'll sleep well because you are safe and secure. You will be filled with hope. You'll be emptied of worry.

Who wouldn't want to benefit from these promises? Surrender every day to God and follow his commands, and you'll live a life free of fear.

Compromise Keeps You from Your Purpose

"But Daniel resolved not to defile himself."

DANIEL 1:8 (NIV)

Once you say "yes" to Jesus, your faith will be challenged every day. And you'll have to choose to honor God or not.

Daniel faced the same choice. Either he could take the king's food, compromise on obeying God's Word, and follow the ways of the Babylonian Empire. Or, Daniel could refuse to defile his body and stay true to the biblical values he believed in and lived by.

Daniel stayed strong. He didn't compromise. He never forgot who he was. He said, "You can change my address. You can change my clothing. You can change my name. But you're not going to change my heart. I will not compromise my beliefs. I won't become someone God never meant for me to be."

Too many of us choose differently. Instead of sticking to our values, we live like everyone else. We let the culture shape us into its image instead of letting God transform us into the image of Jesus.

Most people can't figure out what God wants them to do with their lives. It's because they live by the world's standards instead of God's standards. They seem more interested in being like everyone else than in being the unique person God made them to be. As long as you're focused on adapting to the culture around you, you'll be distracted from God's plan to transform you, and you won't be able to discover God's will for your life.

But if you refuse to compromise and instead choose God's best for your life, you'll begin to see how he transforms you into a reflection of Jesus, the light of the world.

God's Solution for Our Failures

*"[God] canceled the debt, which listed all the rules we failed to follow.
He took away that record with its rules and nailed it to the cross."*

COLOSSIANS 2:14 (NCV)

You are going to fail in life. That's a given. Thankfully, you can live free from guilt and learn to move beyond your mistakes.

The Bible is painfully honest about the failures of its heroes. God saved the world from the flood through a man named Noah—yet his story ended in shame. Moses led the children of Israel through the Red Sea and into freedom—yet his anger kept him out of the Promised Land. King David was a man after God's heart—but had an affair and murdered the woman's husband so he wouldn't be discovered.

God realizes your frailty—and he has a solution for it: grace. If he only used perfect people, the Bible would be a short book. Jesus canceled our debt; he paid for our brokenness when he went to the cross.

God transforms failure into triumph, and he transforms broken lives into trophies of his grace. This is what the world needs, this is what it must be shown.

Just like those heroes of the Bible, you are an example of God's grace. Your primary witness to the world around you isn't all the great things you do for God—it's how you handle the mistakes you've made. Do you wallow in guilt, or do you revel in the grace of God?

You are a trophy of God's grace! You are forgiven in Christ and given the power to start over.

Pray Before You Commit

"Be very careful, then, how you live—not as unwise but as wise, making the most of every opportunity."

EPHESIANS 5:15-16 (NIV)

When you pray before making a decision, you slow your life down enough to make a wise choice.

Consider your commitments very carefully, and pray before taking action. God wants you to *ponder* before *promising. Deliberate* before *deciding. Muse* before you *choose. Reflect* before you *select.* When you do those things, you will discover what God wants you to do.

The Bible says, *"It is a trap to dedicate something rashly and only later to consider one's vows"* (Proverbs 20:25 NIV). Are you careful, or are you rash?

Do you ever keep adding things to your schedule without eliminating others? Every time you add a new activity, you need to take something off. One mark

of wisdom is knowing what to stop and what to cut out.

If you have a hard time deciding which activities to cut from your schedule—and which ones to add—ask yourself these three questions:

Is it worth it? It may not be worth your time, energy, effort, reputation, or money.

What am I going to give up? Consider the cost.

Can I just say no? Chances are, the answer is "Yes, you can."

You will reduce stress when you count the cost of committing to something new. Take time to pause and pray before saying "yes."

A Journey of Lifelong Learning

"Commit yourself to instruction; listen carefully to words of knowledge."

PROVERBS 23:12 (NLT)

Your journey of lifelong learning starts with a choice that only you can make. It's an incredibly important decision that will impact your entire life.

Your education doesn't stop when you graduate. I've heard people say, "I'm glad my education is over so that I can start my career." Tell that to God, and he'll laugh. God has so much more he wants to teach you! Your education will never end.

Learning isn't a stage of life; it is your life! God wants you to learn something new every day. Don't ever stop. Commit to becoming a lifelong learner. You can start by learning a new skill this year. God wants you to keep growing.

Lifelong learning will make you a better leader, a better parent, a better spouse, and a better friend. It will make you more effective in your job. It will bring both success and profit.

The Bible says, *"If the ax is dull and its edge unsharpened, more strength is needed, but skill will bring success"* (Ecclesiastes 10:10 NIV).

In other words, the sharper the ax, the less effort it takes to do the work. In the same way, the more you sharpen your skills, the more you will be able to accomplish.

The Bible is saying to work smarter, not harder. You're never wasting time when you learn new things—it's like sharpening your ax.

Never stop learning.

God Doesn't Want You to Worry

"Never worry about anything."

PHILIPPIANS 4:6 (ISV)

The number one source of stress in your life is not work—it's worry. Work doesn't keep you up at night; worry does.

God makes clear in the Bible what he thinks about worry. When you worry about something, you are telling God that you don't think he can handle it. Worry is an offense to God. Why do you need to let go of your worry?

Worry is unreasonable. It exaggerates the problem. When somebody says something bad about you, the more you worry about it, the bigger it gets.

Worry is unproductive. It's like sitting in a rocking chair: "Should I or shouldn't I, should I or shouldn't I? Will he or won't he; can she or can't she; what if it happens, but what if it doesn't?" You'll be wasting a lot of energy, and it won't get you anywhere.

Worry is unhealthy. Your body wasn't designed to handle worry. When people say, "I'm worried sick," they're telling the truth. Doctors say many people could leave the hospital today if they knew how to get rid of guilt, resentment, and worry.

Worry is unhelpful. Worry has never solved a problem. Worry cannot change the past, and it cannot control the future. All it does is mess up today. The only thing worry changes is you. It makes you miserable!

You know all those things you're stressing, anxious, and worried about? Let them go. Give them to God.

It's Always Too Soon to Quit

"That is why we never give up. Though our bodies are dying, our spirits are being renewed every day. For our present troubles are small and won't last very long. Yet they produce for us a glory that vastly outweighs them and will last forever!"

2 CORINTHIANS 4:16-17 (NLT)

Faithful people remain hopeful even when things seem hopeless. In fact, God uses difficult circumstances to test your faith. He wants you to stay determined, persistent, and obedient, regardless of how confusing things may seem.

Consider the testimony of Noah: God warned him about things that were to come, and in obedience, Noah built the ark even though he had never seen rain. Building the ark wasn't just a quick weekend project; it took more than 50 years to complete! The ark was as tall as a four-story building, as long as one-and-a-half football fields, and as wide as a tennis court is long.

In faith, Noah never gave up. Imagine how Noah's neighbors must have mocked and ridiculed him. He didn't give up because he trusted God. Experiencing the first rain, the flood, and 40 days on the ark would have also required faith. After the flood, Noah and his family had to start all over again with nothing but dependence on God and what he provided for them. That's resilient faith!

No matter how bad things may seem right now, don't give up. It's always too soon to quit! God is testing your faithfulness.

There's No Contest

"The one who is in you is greater than the one who is in the world."

1 JOHN 4:4 (NIV)

You were born into a war that began a long time ago. You didn't start it, and you can't escape it. It's the war between God and Satan, good and evil.

It's important to know that God and Satan are not equal enemies—not by a long shot! Although popular culture likes to paint a picture of God struggling with Satan, it simply isn't true. God is the Creator, and Satan was created. Only God is all-knowing, all-loving, and all-powerful. Only God can be everywhere at one time. He is far superior in every way.

One day God will completely wipe Satan out. But until then, he allows you to choose whose side you're on. When you choose God's side through Jesus Christ, he comes to live in you by his Holy Spirit—and that's when you become a real threat to Satan. Why? Because God will use you to take back "ground" from Satan. The more you live your life in obedience to Jesus, the more of a threat you are to Satan.

Satan cannot hurt God, so he tries to hurt God's children. He can't take us out of God's family, but he uses temptation to take us "out of the game." Satan is constantly working to make us ineffective.

But here's the good news: You were born to win because God is greater than Satan, there's no contest. Satan isn't afraid of you, but he is afraid of who is in you—the Spirit of God. You don't have to be afraid of Satan. You can face him with confidence because you're on the winning side.

Are You Teachable or Unreachable?

"Conceited people do not like to be corrected;
they never ask for advice from those who are wiser."

PROVERBS 15:12 (NCV)

Have you noticed how small children are eager to learn? They're not wise in their own eyes or resistant to learning new things. They're not defensive. In fact, they're exactly how God wants you to be—willing to listen, learn, and be open to suggestions and corrections from others.

Teachable people understand that it's impossible for anyone to know everything about every subject. You can't learn all there is to learn in life from personal experience. It's wiser to learn from the experiences of others.

The Bible says in Proverbs 15:12, pride, at its root, is insecurity. Prideful people act like they know it all. Does that sound familiar? When you're afraid to admit you don't know how to do something or how to answer a question, it may be a signal that you're not teachable. When someone corrects you and you get defensive, that may also be a sign you're not teachable.

You have a choice: Will you be humble and open to learning, or will you live in prideful denial? Will you be teachable or unreachable? God is for you, and he'll support you as you learn new things. In fact, like a child growing to maturity, God wants you to keep learning.

Learn Your Purpose Through Relationships

"We are like the various parts of a human body. Each part gets its meaning from the body as a whole, not the other way around . . .
Each of us finds our meaning and function as a part of his body.
But as a chopped-off finger or cut-off toe we wouldn't
amount to much, would we?"

ROMANS 12:4-5 (THE MESSAGE)

You'll never learn who you really are by yourself. You only learn it in relationships. That means being connected with others in fellowship.

Think about it this way: If you lived your entire life with no human contact, you wouldn't have the slightest idea who or what you were. You wouldn't even know you were a human being. You only know that because of your relationships with other human beings.

The Bible says you need to be connected to God's family, the Body of Christ. And here's why: Your ear only

functions and fulfills its purpose by being connected to your body. If your ear was cut off, then it would have no value because it would not be able to fulfill its purpose. It's the same for your nose and eyes. If they're disconnected from your body, then they have no way to fulfill their purpose.

In the same way, if you are not connected to the Church, then you won't know the purpose of your life. Your value, your meaning, and your identity become apparent in relationship to the Body of Christ— the Church.

God Brings New Life out of the Fire

*"Praise be to the God of Shadrach, Meshach and Abednego,
who has sent his angel and rescued his servants! They trusted in him
and defied the king's command and were willing to give up their lives rather than
serve or worship any god except their own God."*

DANIEL 3:28 (NIV)

How you handle pain reveals the maturity of your faith and is a great witness to the world.

Remember the story of Daniel's friends being tossed into the fire? They trusted God, and God rescued them in a miraculous manner.

King Nebuchadnezzar recognized they would rather defy his order and risk death than defy their God. Their actions impressed the king and moved him to trust God.

God will refine you through the furnace of suffering many times in your life. The psalmist saw the greater purpose for the suffering Israel experienced, *"For you, God, tested us; you refined us like silver"* (Psalm 66:10 NIV).

The refining process is meant to make you look more like Jesus. God knows you're purified when he sees his own reflection in you. God is more interested in your character than your comfort, and he is working to make you more like Christ. God is also working in your suffering to draw others closer to himself.

It's the furnace of suffering that does both.

When you trust God in spite of suffering, you'll become more like Jesus and point unbelievers to him.

Ready for Every Good Work

"If you keep yourself pure, you will be a special utensil for honorable use. Your life will be clean, and you will be ready for the Master to use you for every good work."

2 TIMOTHY 2:21 (NLT)

God uses all kinds of people.

He uses people from all different races, ages, stages of life, backgrounds, and personality types. God will use vessels that are plain or fancy, big or small. But there is one kind of vessel that God will not use: He won't use a dirty one. You don't have to be perfect to be used by God, but he wants you to be clean on the inside.

How do you become clean for God? The answer is confession.

Confession means to admit your sin to God. It's not about bargaining ("I'll never do it again"). It's not about bribing ("I promise to read my Bible every day if you'll forgive me"). Confession puts down pride,

picks up humility, and says, "God, I was wrong."

That may seem too simple to you. Grace is simple!

Take time this week to sit down with a pen and a pad of paper, and write, "God, what's wrong in my life? Show me." Then, when God gives you an idea, write it down.

The first time you do this, it may feel like you are writing a book! But make a list, and then write "1 John 1:9" over it and say, "God, I admit these to you. These are wrong. I don't want them in my life." Ask God to cleanse your life. He will forgive you!

Stop hanging on to your guilt. Instead, give it to God.

Sometimes God Speaks by Saying Nothing

"If God is silent, what's that to you? If he turns his face away, what can you do about it? But whether silent or hidden, he's there, ruling."

JOB 34:29 (THE MESSAGE)

When Saul, the first king of Israel, was preparing for battle, he went to God and asked for his instructions. But God didn't give Saul an answer. Saul got impatient and turned to a witch for advice—something he himself had outlawed. He knew it was wrong but did it anyway, and he lost everything. He lost the battle, his reputation, and his life. Saul didn't wait to hear from God, and he suffered great consequences.

Even when God is silent, he is still in control over everything—he still has a plan. God's silence doesn't lessen his power! When you don't put your confidence in God, you'll grow insecure.

Waiting for God—following his lead—is always difficult, more so when you are impatient! Frustration can make you act like Saul, who failed to wait for God and took matters into his own hands. Sometimes God is silent when developing your patience. Waiting for God shows that he is first in your heart. Running ahead of God will only lead to problems.

If God seems silent right now, remember that he is in control, deserving of our trust, and worth the wait.

God Will Bless Your Obedience

"When [Jesus] had finished speaking, he said to Simon,
'Put out into deep water, and let down the nets for a catch.' Simon answered,
'Master, we've worked hard all night and haven't caught anything.
But because you say so, I will let down the nets.'"

LUKE 5:4-5 (NIV)

Jesus expects you to obey whatever he tells you to do—even if it seems foolish, confusing, or scary.

After teaching the crowds from Peter's boat, Jesus gave Peter instructions on how to fish. Notice Peter's reaction. He didn't argue with Jesus. He didn't say, "Excuse me, Lord. You're a carpenter. I'm a fisherman. And the fish aren't biting! Who are you to tell me how to do my job?"

Peter didn't look for a second opinion either. When Jesus told him to launch the boat, Peter didn't say, "Why don't we think about this for a minute? Let's form a committee, create a survey, and then vote on it."

Peter didn't delay. He didn't say, "We've been out here a long time—literally all night. We're dirty and tired. Jesus, how about we try again tomorrow afternoon?"

What did Peter say? "Because you say so." Peter responded to Jesus with unquestioned obedience and he netted the biggest catch of his fishing career.

Disobedience always hurts us because we miss God's blessing. If you become a "because-you-say-so" follower of Jesus, God will bless your life.

His instructions will not always make sense to you. But you can trust God because he always has your best interest in mind, even if you can't see it right away.

When God says, "do it," just do it. Obedience is faith in action.

Run the Race Together

> *"Let us consider how we may spur one another on toward love and good deeds. Let us not give up meeting together, as some are in the habit of doing, but let us encourage one another—as you see the Day approaching."*

HEBREWS 10:24-25 (NIV84)

Spiritual growth isn't a sprint. It's a marathon.

If you want to go the distance in your relationship with Jesus, don't run the marathon alone. No one can run the race for you, but other people can—and should—run the race with you.

An old African proverb says, "To run fast, run by yourself. But to run far, run with other people."

You don't need 100 people with you. You don't even need ten. You just need three or four people running with you, supporting you in all God wants to do through your life.

That's why you need to be in a small group. You need three or four people who can spur you on in your spiritual

life. You need to be able to spur others on as well.

Do you know why so many people give up on their spiritual lives? Usually, it's fear. They're afraid of failing. They're afraid they won't measure up. They're so afraid they can't keep their commitment that they just give up. As a result, they miss God's best for their life.

But when you're in a small group, where you're loved and accepted by others, they'll give you the courage to keep going in your spiritual journey. They'll give you the courage to finish your race strong.

Do whatever it takes to find a group of people who give you that kind of courage. It could mean the difference between giving up or giving it your all.

When You Need to Delay

*"Daniel went at once to see the king and requested more time
to tell the king what the dream meant."*

DANIEL 2:16 (NLT)

When you're asked to do something that feels impossible, ask for more time. The biggest temptation in the midst of a crisis is to be impulsive. Pain makes us act quickly, but our reflex in moments of emotional pain might not lead to wise reactions. During an impossible situation, you're typically not thinking rationally; instead you are controlled by your emotions.

You want to make a quick decision to ease the tension you feel inside. You may want a fast decision, but that doesn't mean it's the best decision. In fact, there's a good chance it'll be the wrong decision. To make the wisest decision, you may have to ask for more time. When everything feels out of control, reconnect to the One who is always in control. Step back from the situation, take a deep breath, calm down, and talk to God.

This is what Daniel did when the king asked him to interpret a dream.

The stakes were high! The king was impatient! But David asked for more time and the king granted his request. David asked his friends to pray for him as he sought God's wisdom. Daniel didn't make a fast decision; he made the right one. Eventually he solved the king's problem, not on his own power or skill, but through God's power.

Important decisions have effects that are long lasting and far reaching. Life is hard enough without adding the negative consequences that come from poor decisions. When you are overwhelmed or in pain, and facing an important decision, you need God's help to make the right choice. The first step is to hit the pause button. Then, ask a few people to begin praying for you as you seek God on your own.

When you face odds that you can't fathom solving on your own, start praying. God won't leave you to your own talent, logic, and education—they won't solve your problem. And he will give you more time when he knows it's needed to make a wise decision.

How Do You Handle Your Fear?

*"Do not fear, for I have redeemed you; I have called you by name; you are Mine!
When you pass through the waters, I will be with you."*

ISAIAH 43:1-2 (NASB)

When you are afraid, the problem isn't your fear. It's what you do with the fear that really matters. Fear is actually an opportunity to grow closer to God, because your fears reveal where you ought to be trusting him.

God has a plan for you to handle your fear.

When fear becomes overwhelming, remember to practice the presence of God. When you are in trouble, God is with you, even if you can only see the fear. Say throughout the day, "God is with me." Practice talking to him all the time, no matter what you are doing—when you're walking down the street, driving in your car, or sitting in a meeting. Talking to God keeps you focused on him and on his presence.

God is always with you; it's your job to acknowledge him.

To face your fear, walk straight through whatever is causing it. Don't avoid it! You can't go around, over, or under it. You cannot let your fear keep you from moving forward.

Fear is always worse than reality. The fear of failure is worse than failure itself. The fear of rejection is worse than rejection. The fear of embarrassment is worse than the actual embarrassment. Today, make a list of your fears. Then, give them to God, one by one.

Keep your eyes on Jesus, keep moving forward, and he'll take care of you and replace your fears with his peace.

How Do You Forgive?

---

*"God has done it all! He sent Christ to make peace
between himself and us, and he has given us the work
of making peace between himself and others."*

---

2 CORINTHIANS 5:18 (CEV)

In 1956, five American missionaries traveled to the rainforest in Ecuador to tell the Huaorani tribe about Jesus. Upon their arrival, they were speared to death by members of the tribe. The brutal murders of the missionaries, including Nate Saint and Jim Elliot, made news around the world.

A couple years later, Jim's wife Elisabeth, daughter Valerie, and Nate's sister, Rachel, moved into the Huaorani village to show love and forgiveness to the very people who had killed their family. Eventually, all the men responsible for the murders became Christians.

How could Elisabeth, Valerie, and Rachel extend so much forgiveness to those men? They did what God commands all of us to do: the work of making peace with others. Here are two things you can do to model their forgiveness:

Relinquish your right to get even. Leave it up to God. He'll handle things much better than you ever could.

Respond to evil with good. How can you tell when you've completely forgiven someone? When you can actually pray for God to bless the person who hurt you.

When you forgive, God will use you in amazing ways to bless others and draw them closer to him.

Shine Bright in the Darkness

"If you feed those who are hungry and take care of the needs of those who are troubled, then your light will shine in the darkness . . . The Lord will always lead you. He will satisfy your needs in dry lands."

ISAIAH 58:10-11 (NCV)

There is always a cost to compassion—a sacrifice of time, money, energy, reputation, or privacy. Jesus sacrificed for you, and you become more like Jesus when you sacrifice for others.

Jesus told a parable about a Samaritan who found a man beaten and abandoned on the side of the road.

The Samaritan served a total stranger. First, he administered first aid at the scene of the crime. Then, he put the man on his donkey—which means the Samaritan walked. He checked the man into a motel, cared for him through the night, paid the bill in the morning, and pledged to cover any additional costs. What did the Samaritan gain from serving? Nothing. He didn't even know the guy! No one gave him any awards. He stepped in to help without any concern for the sacrifice it might require. His focus was on the injured man's needs.

Would you agree that the world is a dark place? There are needs everywhere—people are hurt, struggling, and looking for hope. When you step up to serve others, you shine brightly in the darkness of this broken world.

The Giants You'll Face

"Everyone assembled here will know that the Lord rescues his people, but not with sword and spear. This is the Lord's battle, and he will give you to us!"

1 SAMUEL 17:47 (NLT)

Before David fought Goliath, he actually fought three other giants. They weren't physical giants, but they were just as big and intimidating—and you'll fight them too. You will need to overcome these giants to fulfill God's plan for your life.

David's first giant was delay. The prophet Samuel anointed David as king, but then his father sent him back to tend sheep. Can you imagine how he must have felt? That's like telling someone they are going to be the President and CEO of a large company and then sending them to the mailroom. Our timing doesn't always line up with God's timing. This results in a waiting period in which we need to learn patience. You can defeat the giant of delay by trusting in God's timing, for he is never early or late.

Discouragement was David's second giant. Goliath created a climate of fear in Israel. King Saul and the entire army had given up hope. No one had the courage to face Goliath. David showed up to bring some food to his brothers. When he heard what was happening, he refused to give in to the fear that had plagued the army for 40 days. Fear looks at the size of your problem rather than the size of your God. You can defeat this giant by knowing that God is on your side. You have nothing to fear.

The third giant David faced was disapproval. His oldest brother, Eliab, made a brutal verbal attack against David. He challenged David's motives and integrity. In his anger he wouldn't even let David talk. David didn't let his brother's disapproval keep him from fulfilling God's purpose. You can defeat the giant of disapproval by listening to who God says you are, not others.

Jesus Came to Help Hurting People

"The Spirit of the Lord is on me, because he has anointed me to proclaim good news to the poor. He has sent me to proclaim freedom for the prisoners and recovery of sight for the blind, to set the oppressed free, to proclaim the year of the Lord's favor."

LUKE 4:18-19 (NIV)

Throughout the Gospels we see how much Jesus cared for hurting people.

Just look at how he preached. He always started with a hurt— poverty, blindness, brokenness, or imprisonment. Why? Because he came to share the Good News with people who needed hope.

When hurting people approached Jesus, he did not blow them off. He never told them they should only be concerned about correct doctrine. He met their needs with compassion.

Notice the last line of today's Scripture: *"proclaim the year of the Lord's favor."* This refers to the "Year of Jubilee," which God established when he created the nation of Israel. It was a year when every debt would be canceled, every prisoner would be released, every slave would be set free, and all land that had been sold to

pay off debt in the previous fifty years would revert back to its original owner.

So, as Jesus read Isaiah's words in the synagogue of his hometown, he was boldly proclaiming: "I am the Day of Jubilee when everyone's sin and debts are wiped out."

There are still broken people in the world today. And Jesus wants you to serve them, following his example— preaching the Good News of freedom in Christ.

Revealing Your Feeling
Is the Beginning of Healing

*"Admit your faults to one another
and pray for each other so that you may be healed."*

JAMES 5:16 (TLB)

There are two kinds of people in the world: Those who are broken and know it, and those who are broken and in denial.

Even when we are forgiven by God, there are times we still feel the pain of our guilt. This is a natural consequence of our sin because the root of all of our problems is relational. It's impossible to sin in a vacuum; the consequence is always felt in our community.

This is why you need to admit your faults to another person. When followed by a habit of prayer, true healing happens. God wired humans to need each other. You need at least one friend who will love you unconditionally and won't think less of you when you share your guilt—who you can offer the same unconditional friendship right back.

What's keeping you from admitting your faults to others? The fear of rejection can be a powerful force in your life Satan knows this, and he'll play on your fears to keep you isolated from others and from the healing you need.

When you find the courage to share your sins with others, you will encourage them to do the same. What was once in the dark is now brought into the light. Accountability is only as effective as it is honest.

The best place to develop friendships like this is in a small group. If you aren't in a group, you need to take care of that today. Call your church and let them know you want to join a small group. If you don't have a church home, check out a few in your area.

Some types of healing are best experienced in community. We are better together because we help heal one another.

Your Teacher, the Holy Spirit

*"The Holy Spirit. . . will be your teacher and
will bring to your minds all that I have said to you."*

JOHN 14:26 (PHILLIPS)

The Holy Spirit is real, and he is the third member of the Trinity. He is God, and he is different from the Father and the Son. The Holy Spirit isn't a myth or an impersonal force. He is God and he has a mission to draw you closer to him.

Jesus taught us that the Holy Spirit is a teacher, and he is working to tell us what we need to know. The Holy Spirit will never tell you something that contradicts the Bible because God doesn't contradict himself. If you "hear" something that goes against the Bible, it's not coming from the Holy Spirit.

The Holy Spirit will speak to you in many different ways, but he often speaks directly to your mind. He doesn't speak with an audible voice. Why would he need to? He doesn't need to go through your ears when he can go directly through your mind.

The Holy Spirit will give you thoughts, suggestions, and impressions. Most often, he brings Scripture to mind, at just the right time.

But the Holy Spirit cannot bring Scripture to your mind if you haven't already hidden it in your heart. That's why you need to get into the Bible; you need to read it, study it, and think about it. Store up the truth in your mind and the Holy Spirit will remind you when you need it most.

The next time you feel prompted to say or do something good, do it! If the Holy Spirit reminds you of a verse, he wants you to act on that teaching in some way. Develop and deepen your ability to hear the Holy Spirit—you will be amazed at what God does through your life!

Time to Tell Yourself the Truth

"The LORD gave us mind and conscience;
we cannot hide from ourselves."

PROVERBS 20:27 (GNT)

The best way to get off a guilt trip is to deal with it. Don't bury it, deny it, or ignore it. You need to own it, and that isn't easy.

Running from your guilt may feel like the better option. But it will always catch up to you. No matter how far or fast you run, you can't escape your guilt because you bring it with you—it's in your mind. When you finally slow down, the feelings of shame and regret come crashing back in again.

God doesn't want you to live with guilt.

Guilt ought to drive you closer to God, not further away. The distance grows when you live in denial. The person you lie to the most is yourself. We often say, "It's not bad!" (but it's really, really bad). Or, "Things are getting better!" (but they are actually getting worse).

To stop defeating yourself, you have to stop deceiving yourself.

What does this look like? Start by paying attention to your conscience. Your mind is like the dashboard of a car, and your conscience is like the "check engine" light, warning you of upcoming danger. When you ignore the warning, things only get worse.

Your next step is to make a confession to God. David wrote, *"Finally, I confessed all my sins to you and stopped trying to hide my guilt. I said to myself, 'I will confess my rebellion to the LORD.' And you forgave me! All my guilt is gone"* (Psalm 32:5 NLT).

Tell yourself the truth, and give your guilt to God.

July

OPEN DOORS

Tell God How You Feel

*"I was born with nothing, and I will die with nothing.
The LORD gave, and now he has taken away. May his name be praised!"*

JOB 1:21 (GNT)

When you hit a setback, it's okay to tell God you're mad, sad, or depressed. It's okay to express all your emotions to God, just don't get bitter.

Bitterness is saying you don't trust God when troubles hit. It's like a poison that will tear your life apart if you let it.

Job endured all kinds of problems. He lost his family, his fortune, and his health. But instead of becoming bitter, he kept his focus on God's goodness.

Job understood that God was still in control even though everything else seemed to be falling apart.

When setbacks come your way—and they most certainly will—you must focus on the fact that God has the big picture in mind. Many things will change in your life. Your faith will be tested and tried. No one has been promised a perfect life.

No matter what setbacks you face, remember that God will never stop loving you. He has a plan for you that is good, and he cares about every detail of your life. God is always in control, and he is never surprised. No matter how much pain you experience, God is protecting you.

When everything falls apart, instead of getting bitter, find reasons to praise God. It isn't easy, but he is worthy.

It's a Choice to Rejoice

*"Though the fig tree does not bud and there are no grapes
on the vines, though the olive crop fails and the fields produce no food,
though there are no sheep in the pen and no cattle in the stalls,
yet I will rejoice in the LORD, I will be joyful in God my Savior."*

HABAKKUK 3:17-18 (NIV)

How do people worship God in the middle of adversity? It starts with a choice to put their pain where it rightfully belongs: under the care of their heavenly Father.

Habakkuk knew this all too well, for he chose to worship God while his country, Israel, was attacked by a brutal enemy intent on wiping them out.

Despite his obvious fear and doubt, Habakkuk made a choice to direct his thoughts toward God—he didn't hold back either. He told God exactly how he was feeling. "God! Why aren't you listening? Violence is all around me! Why are you allowing this to happen?" Yet through it all, Habakkuk had an ongoing conversation with God. He mixed together his praises with complaints and admiration with honest, gut-wrenching questions. In all of this, he was joyful.

Was Habakkuk happy? No. Since happiness depends on circumstances, he had nothing to be happy about because Israel was devastated. But he had plenty to be joyful about. Habakkuk knew God was in complete control—in spite of appearances—he was able to experience joy at its best with conditions at their worst.

When your circumstances start to unravel, what is your go-to response? Do you call a friend? Do you think of ways to fix the problem yourself? Do you give God the silent treatment? Instead, make a choice to rejoice, for joy is only found in relationship with your heavenly Father.

Who Is Responsible for Your Time?

"Teach us to number our days, that we may gain a heart of wisdom."

PSALM 90:12 (NIV)

God wants to do amazing things in and through your life.

However, most people miss out on God's blessings because they don't make time for God in their schedule. They are simply too busy with their own agenda.

If you want to be used by God, you must manage your time wisely.

Time management must be learned. People are not naturally good at it because their tendency is to waste it. To make the most of your time, the first step is to assume responsibility. You have to ask God for help, and this requires a humility that says, "God, I'm not enough, but you are."

Taking responsibility means you need to stop complaining. When we spend our time foolishly, it's easy to accuse others and excuse ourselves. We need to stop saying things like, "I have too much work to do," or "There's so much I'm not getting done."

Your choices control your calendar a lot more than your circumstances do. You may not like what you're doing, but you're choosing to be busy. You can't change your circumstances until you start changing your choices.

On this side of eternity, your days are numbered. Take responsibility for your time—stop complaining and blaming.

Ultimately, this is an issue of faith: Do you believe God knows what he's doing? If so, submit to him and ask for help to make the most of your time. You will focus on what matters most and glorify God in everything you do.

You Need a New Soundtrack

"We demolish arguments and every pretension that sets
itself up against the knowledge of God, and we take captive
every thought to make it obedient to Christ."

2 CORINTHIANS 10:5 (NIV)

The good news is, your brain stores everything. The bad news is, your brain stores everything. Your brain can't distinguish between what's imaginary and what's real. It takes in both truth and lies.

You have stored all kinds of garbage in your brain. Often it's that garbage that you're basing your decisions upon.

When you were a child, adults said things you believed without question because they were authority figures. For example, maybe they said you weren't good enough, or you wouldn't amount to anything in life. That was a lie then, and it's a lie now. But you believed them anyway!

You need to change the soundtrack that's playing in your mind. Instead of playing songs based on lies, you need to play the truth of God's Word. This is what it means to take every thought captive to make it obedient to Christ.

Ask God to heal your memories. Tell God, "I need you to heal these memories of rejection, sin, resentment, guilt, and abuse. They hurt. Please heal me."

Fill your mind with God's Word. The more truth you put in your mind, the more lies you push out. Instead of spending all your time watching television and surfing the web, fill your mind with God's Word. God says you are lovable, capable, valuable, forgivable, and usable.

Let God's Word become the soundtrack of your life, and God will transform your mind.

To Move Forward, Stop Looking Back

*"Put your heart right, Job. Reach out to God. Then face the world
again, firm and courageous. Then all your troubles will fade
from your memory, like floods that are past and remembered no more."*

JOB 11:13, 15-16 (GNT)

You'll get in an accident if you spend too much time looking in the rear-view mirror. You can't heal your deepest wounds in your life by focusing on your past. You need to look ahead to the future because remembering your troubles from the past will only keep you stuck.

Job had a painful past, and while his friends weren't always right, they did have great wisdom.

You need to put your heart right before God. If hurt by another person, forgive them so you can move forward. Planning their downfall will only delay your healing.

Confession and repentance are necessary actions to get your heart right.

In humility, admit what you have done wrong, ask for grace, and commit your life to living according to God's will.

Reach out to God by asking for his help. Where are you hurting the most? Give that to God. Where do you need direction? Ask him for wisdom.

It is hard to stand firm and find courage when we are wounded. When everything in our lives is turned upside down, we are shaken to the core. If you are hiding, you need to stop. Do not withdraw from others just to avoid pain. That's not how God wants you to live.

Your past is not your future. Get right with God and build your confidence through him.

Peace Thieves

*"I am leaving you with a gift—peace of mind and heart. And the peace
I give is a gift the world cannot give. So don't be troubled or afraid."*

JOHN 14:27 (NLT)

In Christ, we have a peace that the world cannot match— it can't even come close! You need to be aware of the threats against your peace.

We can lose our peace when circumstances are uncontrollable. Much of life is beyond your control. You sit in gridlock traffic for hours and miss an important event. A couple keeps trying desperately—but unsuccessfully—to have a baby. When these things happen—big or small— we get frustrated and lose our peace of mind.

We can lose our peace when people are unchangeable. The quickest way to lose your cool is to try to change somebody else. Most people are just not going to change the way you want them to.

We can lose our peace when problems are unexplainable. We know life isn't fair and things don't always turn out right. When we don't know why, we get anxious, nervous, and stressed.

But God has promised to give you peace of mind. In fact, one of God's names is Jehovah Shalom, which means "I am the God of peace."

Accepting God's peace doesn't mean your life will be problem-free. It means that even when your world seems to be falling apart, you will be able to think clearly and sleep peacefully. How do you get God's peace in your life? God's peace is not something you work for or beg for. It's a gift you receive by faith. Turn to God in prayer and tell him what's on your mind. Focus on his goodness, and his perfect peace will fill your heart and mind.

God Won't Answer Every Question

*"For I have learned how to be content with whatever I have.
I know how to live on almost nothing or with everything.
I have learned the secret of living in every situation, whether it is
with a full stomach or empty, with plenty or little. For I can do
everything through Christ, who gives me strength."*

PHILIPPIANS 4:11-13 (NLT)

Paul knew how to focus on God in every situation.

When Paul wrote the book of Philippians, he was imprisoned in Rome, awaiting execution. As he was reflecting on his life, he could have lashed out at God and questioned what was happening to him.

Instead, he trusted God for the things he could not change.

When we are living in a dry season with "almost nothing," it's natural to ask God, "Why me? Why now?" God wants to hear your questions, because he cares about every detail of your life, but you won't always get an explanation.

God doesn't owe you an explanation. He's God and you aren't. He is always good and just, even if it doesn't seem like it.

If you had the answer for every question you asked, you wouldn't understand it all. Some answers just won't add up because we don't have a calculator big enough to figure out God. His knowledge is perfect and his power is absolute—he makes decisions we'll never understand.

Ultimately, having the answers won't guarantee peace. The explanations never satisfy. In fact, most of the time when we ask God for an explanation, we aren't really looking for an answer, we're looking for an argument.

The secret of living isn't more explanations, it's learning to be content. Our strength comes only through Jesus.

Stand up for God

"Never be ashamed to tell others about our Lord . . . With the strength God gives you, be ready to suffer with me for the sake of the Good News."

2 TIMOTHY 1:8 (NLT)

Standing up for God when you're afraid isn't just the right thing to do, it also builds your character. Reputation is what you want people to think about you. Character is what you really are. Character is who you are when no one is watching.

Character is like a muscle. Your muscle doesn't grow unless it's strained, stretched, and stressed. You lift weights to push it to its limit, so that it will grow stronger.

The same is true with your "courage muscle."

You're not developing any spiritual, emotional, or relational muscle when you give in to fear. Paul told Timothy he didn't need to be ashamed to tell others about Jesus. This isn't easy! When we have the opportunity to share our faith, our courage is being stretched and stressed.

When you stand strong for what God wants, your courage grows. Courage isn't the absence of fear; it's moving forward with what God wants in spite of how you feel.

What are you willing to do in order to be true to your faith? Are you willing to be teased? Are you willing to have someone look at you funny? Are you willing to have people gossip about you?

God gives you the strength to have courage, even when you are suffering.

In the past, Christians have gone before lions and been crucified for their faith in Christ. Persecution continues into the present and people are still being martyred for their faith. It's much more common than you may realize.

Stand up for God. When you overcome your fears, your character grows to become more like Jesus.

Choose Worship over Worry

"Now, who will want to harm you if you are eager to do good? But even if you suffer for doing what is right, God will reward you for it. So don't worry or be afraid of their threats. Instead, you must worship Christ as Lord of your life."

1 PETER 3:13-15 (NLT)

Christianity is not for weaklings, wimps, or the faint of heart. It takes courageous men and women to follow Jesus.

People all over the world are suffering in a way the United States will never experience. What is it costing you to follow Christ? It's unlikely you'll ever face violent oppression. But you will deal with silent repression every single day as our culture becomes more and more secularized and anti-Christian.

There are two choices for when you suffer for doing what is right: You can worry, or you can worship. You will either panic, or you will pray. Either you focus on the problem, the pressure, and the persecution, or you focus on promises of God.

Peter reminds us that God will reward us in eternity for the suffering we endure here. When people want to harm you for doing good, remember that your hardship won't last. It's easier to run the race when you are focused on the finish line.

When we worship Jesus as Lord of our lives, we need to remember that he is the Lord over all creation. His control is constant and absolute. He's never out of control and he doesn't answer to anyone. This is the Lord you are worshiping, and you have no reason to worry.

Next time you face opposition, will you be ready to choose worship over worry?

God Loves You Anyway

"[God] knows what we are made of;
he remembers that we are dust."

PSALM 103:14 (GNT)

Your failures don't surprise God. He expects them. He knows what we're made of—because he created us. God won't stop loving us when we mess up.

The central message of the Bible is this: God doesn't love you because of who you are or what you've done but because of who he is and what he has done.

God made you. He loves you. It's settled! You can't make God love you more. You can't make him love you less. He loves you just as much on your bad days as he does on your good days. His love is not performance based.

The Bible has a word for this. It's called grace—and it's absolutely amazing. When you understand his grace, you can relax about your failures and have the confidence to take more risks. You may have come to God multiple times for forgiveness on

the same issue. Maybe you're not sure you deserve his love and grace. And you're sure that God has grown tired of your constant efforts at change.

But you can relax. God never tires of a conversation with you and he's never too busy. No matter how many times you come to him for forgiveness, he'll be waiting with open arms.

You may have grown up in a home where conditional love was the norm. Your parents' affections may have been based on your academic, athletic, or social successes. When you failed in one of those areas, you felt the loss of your family's love. That's not how God deals with you.

The Christian life isn't a mistake-free life, but it can be a guilt-free life. God understands your failures, and he loves you anyway. That's amazing grace!

God Will Help You Succeed

*"We plan the way we want to live,
but only GOD makes us able to live it."*

PROVERBS 16:9 (THE MESSAGE)

God gives you the freedom to make plans, but it is only through God's power and grace that you succeed. God equips you to succeed in everything he calls you to do.

God's Spirit empowers you to make changes you cannot make on your own. Lasting change is not based on willpower; it's based on God's power. It's not based on trying harder; it's based on trusting him.

God's Word guides you because the Bible is the owner's manual for life. The more you read it, study it, memorize it, and meditate on it, the more successful and fulfilled you will be.

When Joshua was given the great dream of taking over the Promised Land, God had these words for him:

"Meditate on [this book of the law] day and night, so that you may be careful to do according to all that is written in it . . . and then you will have success" (Joshua 1:8 NASB).

God's people will help you succeed. You will not be able to reach your goals on your own. It takes a team to fulfill a dream! A crowd can't support you, but a small group can. The people in your small group know when you're sick, when you're having a tough time, or when you need a break. You can share your goals and successes and failures, and they will rejoice with you and encourage you to keep going. You're going to need that when you make the right kind of goals and pursue them wholeheartedly.

Failure Can Be Good for You

"A man who refuses to admit his mistakes can never be successful."

PROVERBS 28:13 (TLB)

In America, failure is almost the unpardonable sin and we idolize success. That kind of pressure creates major stress on people. It can cause you to be indecisive, a workaholic, and a perfectionist who clings to safety. When we are afraid to fail, we shun all kinds of risks. For many of us, the fear of failure has an iron grip on our hearts. Even some of the best and brightest people in the world are impacted by the fear of failure.

Failure can be good for you.

Failure doesn't have to be fatal. Wise people know how to take advantage of failure. They accept it as one of God's primary tools in making them who he wants them to be.

God uses failure to educate you, so take the opportunity to learn as much as you can. Mistakes are simply learning experiences, and some lessons can only be learned through failure. If you're not making any mistakes, you're not learning. If you're not taking any risks, you're not growing. When you're free from the fear of failure, you're free to grow.

God uses failure to motivate you to change. People don't change when they see the light; they change when they feel the heat. When you fail, maybe God's trying to get your attention to move you in a new direction.

God uses failure to build your character. Failure has a way of softening your heart. It helps you grow up and become mature and makes you sensitive to others. It makes you less judgmental and more sympathetic to people around you who are hurting.

Failure doesn't automatically grow your character. It only builds character when you respond to it correctly and learn from it.

New Life in Christ

*"Therefore, if anyone is in Christ, the new creation has come:
The old has gone, the new is here!"*

2 CORINTHIANS 5:17 (NIV)

Can a butterfly go back into a cocoon after it's come out? Of course not! Once the caterpillar becomes a butterfly, it is what it is—a butterfly.

When you become a believer, you're like that butterfly—you've come out of your cocoon. The moment you believe in Christ, there's a spiritual metamorphosis—everything changes! This is a matter of faith and not sight. It may take you some time to fly spiritually, but once you become a new creation in Christ, you are a new creation.

The greatest step of faith we can take in our lives is to believe in Jesus. He is the Son of God who lived a perfect life, died for our sins, and was resurrected from death. He paid the price we could never pay. Salvation is a free gift of grace, available to all, that can be accepted by faith.

The next step is to believe what God says about who you are. In Christ, you are free from the power of sin. The Bible says in Romans 6:14, *"Sin is no longer your master, for you no longer live under the requirements of the law. Instead, you live under the freedom of God's grace"* (NLT).

Your best life is only found in Jesus.

Do you believe what God says about Jesus? Do you believe what God says about you? Trust in him for salvation and watch everything become new.

To help you understand how to begin a relationship with Jesus Christ and join God's family, go to: PastorRick.com/know-god

God's Answer for Your Fear

*"We know the love that God has for us, and we trust that love . . .
because God's perfect love drives out fear."*

1 JOHN 4:16, 18 (NCV)

People who are afraid to give their lives fully to God generally give one of three reasons: They are afraid they will lose their freedom, lose their fun, or become some sort of religious fanatic.

If any of that were true, their fear would be justified. But none of those reasons are true.

What is God's answer for our fear of trusting him? It's simple: God loves you. Over and over in the Bible, God makes it clear that he created you to love you and to let you love him.

The greatest expression of God's love is Jesus. God came to earth in the form of a human being to show us how much he loves us, to the point of dying on the cross. God's only Son dying on the cross shows us once and for all that we can fully trust the love of God.

God's love will drive the fear out of your life. It will help you see that God isn't a cosmic killjoy. He won't take away your freedom, or your fun; he won't turn you into a fanatic. Jesus didn't die to take away from your life; his sacrifice means we can have eternal life.

No, Slow, Grow, and Go

"You fathers—if your children ask for a fish, do you give them a snake instead? Or if they ask for an egg, do you give them a scorpion? Of course not! So if you sinful people know how to give good gifts to your children, how much more will your heavenly Father give the Holy Spirit to those who ask him."

LUKE 11:11-13 (NLT)

God answers every one of your prayers. But there are times he doesn't always answer in the way you want.

When the request is not right, God says, "No." Just like parents say "no" to their kids for a hundred good reasons, God doesn't owe you an explanation every time he says "no" to your request.

When the timing is not right, God says, "Slow." There's a big difference between a delay and a denial. "No" and "not yet" are not the same thing, and learning and accepting the difference shows spiritual maturity.

When you're not right, God says, "Grow." He wants to do something in your life before he answers your prayer. It may be you're not yet ready to handle the answer.

When the request is right, the timing is right, and you're right, then God says, "Go." God often gives us the green light to our prayers—and it's a reason to celebrate!

God is never going to give you anything that is hurtful or bad for you. After all, if imperfect parents know how to give good gifts to their kids, won't God, who is good and perfect, do even more for you? He is ready to answer your prayer—in his perfect time and way.

The Power of Persistent Prayer

*"Stay alert and be persistent
in your prayers."*

EPHESIANS 6:18 (NLT)

Why should you be persistent in your prayers, even when you don't get an answer?

Persistent prayers focus your attention. When you pray over and over, it's not to remind God. It's to remind you that God is the source of your answer. If every time you prayed you instantly got results, you'd only think about the blessing. God wants you to focus on the Blesser.

Persistent prayers clarify your request. A delayed answer gives you time to clarify what you want and to refine your prayers. When you pray persistently to your heavenly Father, it separates deep longings out from mere whims. God wants to answer your prayers, but he wants you to be certain it's what you really want. This process helps you develop more wisdom.

Persistent prayers test your faith. When God delays your answer, you are at a crossroad. Will you wait for God to act, or will you take it upon yourself to come up with a solution? God is always working in our hearts to be more dependent on him.

Persistent prayer prepares your heart for the answer. Sometimes God denies your prayer requests because you're thinking too small and asking too little. He wants to give you something better. But first, he has to prepare you for it.

If you've given up on praying persistently, today is the day to renew your commitment to pray specifically.

Have you been praying for something persistently? What is God doing in your heart through that process?

Setbacks Can't Derail God's Purpose

*"Don't be afraid, Paul, for you will surely stand trial
before Caesar! What's more, God in his goodness has granted
safety to everyone sailing with you."*

ACTS 27:24 (NLT)

Sometimes a setback is rooted in your own actions. You made a mistake or hurt another person. Maybe you disobeyed God, and even though nothing you do can remove you from his love, you're now facing a storm because of your choices.

However, sometimes the storms you face in life are caused by other people's poor decisions—or even their sins.

Acts 27 gives us a dramatic example of suffering a setback caused by the foolish choices of others. Paul had been put on trial unfairly for crimes he didn't commit. He was a Roman citizen, and he had the opportunity to appeal to Caesar, which meant going to Rome.

On the way to Rome, the prison ship carrying Paul hit a storm. That storm didn't sidetrack God's purpose for Paul. The angel had told Paul he'd one day stand before Caesar and share his testimony. God's purpose wouldn't be prevented by the poor choices of others. The storm in your life doesn't have to sidetrack God's purpose for you. God's purpose is greater than any setback you'll ever go through. God is always in control; he doesn't answer to anyone.

God doesn't need a "Plan B" for your life. Hitting a setback—whether it's your fault or someone else's—doesn't mean God's purpose for you is ruined. God saw the disaster coming, and he is more than able to fit it into his plans.

When another person's decision turns your life upside down, God uses it for his glory. When someone else's mistake puts you in a difficult situation, God works through it anyway. When you feel like you've lost everything, God does the incredible so you can do the impossible.

Love Is a Choice

*"Now choose life . . . that you may love the Lord
your God, listen to his voice, and hold fast to him."*

DEUTERONOMY 30:19-20 (NIV)

God's love for you is great, but he doesn't force you to love him back.

It's a choice: You either love God or thumb your nose at him and go a completely different way. When you love God, you find real life. When you don't, it will inevitably lead to destruction. God wants everyone to love him back, and he's constantly working to draw us closer to him, but he gives us the choice.

Many people buy into the myth that love is uncontrollable. They'll say, "I fell in love," as if it were some kind of unavoidable ditch. This kind of thinking makes for popular movies, but it's terrible for life.

Love isn't something that happens to you. Love is an active commitment that is repeated over and over. When you decide to love God, it's a commitment to love him for the rest of your life.

Loving other people is also an active commitment and this has significant implications for your relationships. You choose who you love. It's not automatic, as if you were a robot. Healthy relationships are built on a lasting commitment of love, even when times are tough.

Love doesn't make everything perfect, far from it! Often, the more you love someone, the more your love is tested because you know everything about that person, the good and the bad.

You also can't force someone to love you, which is a painful truth. No matter how much you love someone, day in and day out, you can't make them love you back. Love is a choice for you, and it's a choice for them too.

The choice is yours. Will you choose to love God? How will you love others?

Keep Joy in Your Life

"It is for freedom that Christ has set us free. Stand firm ... You were running a good race. Who cut in on you to keep you from obeying the truth?"

GALATIANS 5:1, 7 (NIV)

Do you remember how you felt when you first became a Christian? You felt a deep sense of joy and freedom that comes from being totally forgiven. You had a new purpose and no longer felt guilty.

Gradually, you lose your joy because of one of these three common traps.

The trap of perfectionism is when you try maintaining a perfect performance in order to stay saved. The perfectionist says, "God accepts me because of my near-perfect living." This trap steals your joy and freedom. Your relationship with God becomes a duty instead of a delight, and you end up frustrated rather than fulfilled.

The trap of legalism is when you measure your maturity by how many rules you keep. The legalist says, "If I go to church on Sunday mornings,

do weekly Bible studies, and witness to others, I'm a good Christian." So, do you stop doing these things? No. Just change your motive from "I have to" to "I want to."

The trap of conformity is being controlled by the expectations of other Christians. It takes your eyes off the Lord and puts them on everyone else. New believers don't care what others think; they just love the Lord and talk to him without using fancy words. But conformity says, "Oh, that's how I'm supposed to be a Christian. I guess I'll do it their way."

How do you keep joy in your life? Accept God's grace. It's how you began your life in Christ; it's how you continue. *"So then, just as you received Christ Jesus as Lord, continue to live your lives in him"* (Colossians 2:6 NIV).

How Do You Know You're Saved?

"It is by grace you have been saved, through faith—and this is not from yourselves, it is the gift of God—not by works, so that no one can boast."

EPHESIANS 2:8-9 (NIV)

Your deepest need is salvation from sin because sin is what separates you from God and eternal life.

When Jesus hung from the cross, two criminals were also being crucified. One turned to Jesus and said, *"Remember me when you come into your kingdom"* (Luke 23:42 NIV).

Jesus was famous for doing miracles, but the criminal didn't ask Jesus to stop his pain or save him from death. Instead, he asked Jesus to help him with his biggest problem—separation from God. Jesus comforted the new believer, and told him that he will be with him in paradise.

How can you be sure that you're saved? How do you know you're going to heaven when you die?

Your salvation is secure because it's not based on what you've done. Jesus did all the work. Salvation is a gift; it's not something you can earn because you aren't perfect.

Your salvation is secure because it's not based on how you feel. Feelings come and go; they do not determine your citizenship in God's Kingdom.

Your salvation is secure because it's based on Jesus. We receive this gift through faith. If you believe, you belong! You don't have to wonder if you are saved, you can know with absolute certainty.

A Prideful Heart Opposes God

"'God opposes everyone who is proud, but he is kind to everyone who is humble.' Surrender to God!"

JAMES 4:6-7 (CEV)

Does this sound familiar? You make plans without consulting God. You think you can do a better job without involving the Creator of the universe. You forget his promise to show you the right path. Then, when your plans don't come together, you get angry.

The Bible calls this pride, and God opposes pride.

You really don't want to be opposed by God; there's no way you'll win that battle. In fact, when you're filled with pride, you're operating as an enemy of God. That's how serious it is.

The best thing you can do is surrender. Tell God you give up control. Stop trying to get God to submit to your plan, and tell him you are surrendering to his plan.

Romans 6:13 says, *"Give yourselves to God, as those who have been brought from death to life, and surrender your whole being to him to be used for righteous purposes"* (GNT).

A person surrendered to God prays, *"God, I'm going with your plans for my life, not my own. I've been making my own plans, chasing dreams that have nothing to do with you. I'm making decisions based on ambition, pleasure, or convenience. That's all going to stop. From now on, I will intentionally choose your plan for my life. I will seek and pursue the purpose for which you created me. I will rely upon your Word to guide me, and I will be sensitive to the Holy Spirit's direction. Amen."*

Let God Take the Driver's Seat

*"Anyone who intends to come with me has to let me lead.
You're not in the driver's seat; I am."*

MATTHEW 16:24 (THE MESSAGE)

You need to put Jesus in the "driver's seat" of your life and let him lead your every decision.

Here's what many of us do: we let him into the driver's seat, only to become backseat drivers! We're constantly giving Jesus advice—"No, turn this way, stop, wait, faster! I want to go that way." We treat Jesus as if he is our own private chauffeur who follows our instructions.

We get stuck on calling all the shots.

When you are in charge, you miss out on God's best for your life. When you refuse to let Jesus lead your life, the result is more confusion, conflict, and stress.

Putting Jesus in the driver's seat isn't a matter of understanding; the issue is surrender. The problem with most of your decisions is not confusion, you know the right thing to do. The problem is that you want to have it your way, so you argue and disagree with God. In your mind, you fight with the Creator: "I know you are telling me to do this, but I want to do something else."

Surrender is easy to understand but difficult to do.

When you put your faith in Jesus, he expects you to let him lead. Make this your prayer several times throughout the day, "Not my will, Jesus, but your will." Every night, ask God to show you where you followed your own way rather than his.

Life on this side of eternity will never be perfect, but your best life is when you hand over the keys and let Jesus lead. Today, who is going to be in charge of your life?

Encourage Others

"Encourage one another and build each other up."

---

1 THESSALONIANS 5:11 (NIV)

Encouragers are a rare commodity because we live in a negative culture. It's easy to be critical or spread gossip in order to tear someone down.

Yet God calls us to do the exact opposite. He wants you to build others up—even the people you don't like! He didn't just create the people you struggle with, he also died for them.

When you encourage others, you are sending a message that says, "You matter to God, and you matter to me."

Here are three practical ways to be an encourager:

Listen to others. The Bible says, *"Share each other's burdens, and in this way obey the law of Christ"* (Galatians 6:2 NLT). When you listen attentively to someone, you are helping them carry their burden. Everyone needs a

safe place to share their struggles. Be an encourager by listening without judgment or adding to the negativity.

Use positive words. When your goal is to build others up, it's easy to pick the right words. Before you open your mouth, ask yourself, "Will this help or hurt them? Encourage or discourage? Build up or tear down?" Choose good words!

Pray for them. Make a list of the people you see every week. Put it in your Bible and pray regularly for them. Ask God for wisdom on how to best encourage and build them up according to their needs. When the timing is right, tell them you're praying for them and ask how you can be praying for them in the future. Even unbelievers appreciate that!

Who will you encourage today?

Discovering Contentment

"It is better to be satisfied with what you have
than to be always wanting something else."

ECCLESIASTES 6:9 (GNT)

The first step in becoming a content person is to stop comparing your life to everyone else's.

You also must learn to admire without needing to acquire. You need to learn to rejoice in other people's prosperity without getting jealous and envious, feeling like you must have what they have.

This is one of the great biblical principles that many people don't understand. The truth is, you don't have to own it to enjoy it! Maybe you like to vacation in the mountains. Why buy a mountain cabin when you can just rent one every year?

The word "covet" in Greek means "to grab or to grasp so tightly that your hands are tight; you can't even let it

go." If God ever gives you something and tells you to give it away, but you can't, you don't own it—it owns you.

God is not saying you should never desire things. After all, nothing can be accomplished unless you desire to do it. You can't become more like Christ without desiring to become more like Christ. But when you desire to be like someone else, to have what they have, you will always want more. Why? Because God didn't make you to be like someone else, he wants you to be you.

To have a content life, stop comparing your looks, your house, your job, your kids, and your education to that of others. Find ways to be thankful for what God has already given you.

God Gives You Wisdom

"Trust in the LORD with all your heart; do not depend on your own understanding. Seek his will in all you do, and he will show you which path to take. Don't be impressed with your own wisdom. Instead, fear the LORD and turn away from evil."

PROVERBS 3:5-7 (NLT)

Have you ever had a feeling that something was so very, very right, but when you did it, it ended up being so very, very wrong?

That's because feelings lie. They lie to you all the time! In fact, most of the wrong things you do actually feel right when you're doing them. Just a few months into a job, you ask yourself, "How did I end up here?" After six months in a relationship that once felt so right, you wonder, "What was I thinking?" A quick decision that seemed harmless at the time can leave you broken and scarred years later.

If you want fewer dead ends and difficulties in your life, depend on God's wisdom, not what your feelings say or what your gut tells you. How can you get God's wisdom? It's simple: Pray. Talk to God, and let him talk to you through his Word. The Bible says, *"If any of you lacks wisdom, you should ask God, who gives generously to all without finding fault, and it will be given to you"* (James 1:5 NIV).

God doesn't want you to make poor choices. He doesn't want you to hit dead ends or go through failure after failure. God wants you to succeed. You must not depend on your own understanding. Seek God's will because he wants to help you make wise decisions with your time, your money, and your relationships.

Everything You Need Comes from God

"My God will supply every need of yours according to his riches in glory in Christ Jesus."

PHILIPPIANS 4:19 (ESV)

Where do you put your security?

Putting your trust in your bank account, your job, or your investments is a recipe for heartache because you can lose all of those things.

You have to put your trust and security in something that cannot be taken from you: God! If you want God's blessing on your life, depend on his resources and not your own.

Your security shouldn't be in your job. Your job is a channel, but God is your source. If you understand this, you'll have less stress in your life.

If you turned on the faucet in your kitchen and no water came out, what would you do? Would you say, "Oh my, the world has run out of water—there's no water coming out of the

faucet, so there must not be any left in the whole world"?

Of course not. You'd know the problem is not with the source. There's plenty of water in the world. The problem is the channel. It's gotten blocked one way or another.

If one channel gets blocked in your life and the "faucet" stops working, God can turn on another faucet just as easily. If God closes a door in your life, he can open another door. And if another door closes, he can open a window, and you can crawl through it.

Jobs may come and go. Bank accounts rise and fall. Economies go up and down. Home prices can peak or hit bottom.

You can trust in God's unlimited resources for your security.

Your Mind Matters

"Fill your minds with those things that are good and that deserve praise: things that are true, noble, right, pure, lovely, and honorable."

PHILIPPIANS 4:8 (GNT)

What do you fill your mind with? The more you think about something, the more it takes hold of you. And when you think about things that aren't good for you, it's easy to fall into temptation.

Temptation begins by capturing your attention. What gets your attention arouses your emotions, causing you to act on what you feel.

Ignoring a temptation is far more effective than fighting it. The more you focus on things you know you shouldn't do, telling yourself, "I don't want to do this," the stronger it pulls you in. When your mind is focused on something else, the temptation loses its power. When temptation calls, don't argue with it—just hang up!

Sometimes this means physically leaving a tempting situation.

The Bible says, *"Run from anything that gives you evil thoughts"* (2 Timothy 2:22 TLB). This is one of the few times it's okay to run away. Turn off the television or screen. Walk away from a group of people who are gossiping. Leave the theater in the middle of the movie. To avoid being stung, stay away from the bees.

To reduce temptation, keep your mind occupied with God's Word, and you will be filled with good thoughts. You defeat bad thoughts by thinking of something better. This is the principle of replacement. You overcome evil with good (Romans 12:21).

Next time you are in the midst of temptation, what *"true, noble, right, pure, lovely, and honorable"* things can you think about instead?

Important Versus Necessary

"Dear Martha, you are worried and upset over all these details!
There is only one thing worth being concerned about.
Mary has discovered it, and it will not be taken away from her."

LUKE 10:41-42 (NLT)

Just because something is good doesn't always mean it is best.

Do you ever fill your life with so many good things—devotion to your family, church, career, and community—that you neglect your relationship with God? We shouldn't let the gifts become more important than the One who gives them! To fulfill God's destiny for your life, you actually don't have to do more; you probably need to do less.

Take Jesus' friends, Mary and Martha, for example. One day they invited Jesus over for dinner. Mary spent her evening listening to Jesus. Martha, on the other hand, was busy with hosting and worrying about the hors d'oeuvres and countless other details.

Martha got upset because she was doing all the work while her sister sat with Jesus. That's when Jesus gently corrected Martha: "My dear Martha, I see your hard work and I appreciate it. But it's distracting you from what I want most: your attention. All of your work is keeping you from what you need most: to sit at my feet and learn from me."

An honest look at both Mary and Martha reveals two great attributes: Martha's organized nature and Mary's relational nature, Martha's devoted service and Mary's devoted heart. It's not a matter of "wrong vs. right" but a matter of "important vs. necessary."

When your life is over, only one thing will really matter: Did you get to know the Son of God?

God Is Truth

*"[God] shows how to distinguish right from wrong,
how to find the right decision every time."*

PROVERBS 2:9 (TLB)

The way to discover the truth is to start with God, for he embodies truth. What is right and wrong is determined by the character of God himself. Dishonesty is wrong because God is honest. Unfaithfulness is wrong because God is faithful.

We learn the character of God through his Word. The Bible tells us what is true. Whether or not we like what it says is another matter. You can trust God's Word. In fact, to help you understand more about his character, God's Word—Jesus—became flesh in order to live among us (John 1:14).

Jesus not only tells us the truth; he is the truth. He says, *"I am the way and the truth and the life"* (John 14:6 NIV). He doesn't say, "I teach the truth," or "I point to the truth." He says, "I am the truth."

God's truth is universal and unchanging; it applies to everyone.

"Truth" that changes isn't truth, it's opinion. Truth is based on God's character, but opinions are based on an individual's comfort and personal desires. For example, adultery was wrong two-thousand years ago, it's wrong today, and it will be wrong four-thousand years from today. Truth is absolute.

Many people like to pick their "truth." You often hear people say there is a choice between different kinds of truth. They say, "Whose morality? Whose justice? Whose values?" Truth isn't relative; you don't get to choose what is true and what is false.

Every day, you have to choose if you are going to build your life on opinion or on the truth.

Your choice will dictate how you live, how you love, and, someday, how you die. But it's your choice.

How will you choose?

A Harvest of Blessing

"Let's not get tired of doing what is good. At just the right time we will reap a harvest of blessing if we don't give up."

GALATIANS 6:9 (NLT)

You're going to walk through different seasons in life and some of them will be difficult. The Bible says, *"There is a time for everything, and a season for every activity under the heavens"* (Ecclesiastes 3:1 NIV). Some seasons are for reaping, others for sowing.

When you plant a peach tree, you don't get fruit right away. The peaches come in over time. There's a waiting period. And when the peaches do come in, they ripen little by little; you pick only a few a day. If you pick too soon, you miss the flavor.

In the same way, you will also experience seasons of waiting. During these times, you may think nothing is happening. You may get tired of doing good. Be encouraged: God is still working, even if you can't see it. God promises that you will always harvest what you plant. And if what you plant is good, according to today's Scripture, you will *"reap a harvest of blessing."* God uses seasons of waiting to build your faith, to draw you closer to him.

But until then, until you see a little shoot stick up out of the ground, you need to trust that God is working— even when you can't see the fruit of your labor. Keep yourself from discouragement by trusting God. Don't give up. His promises are always true! Keep doing good, and in time, you will be blessed by God.

Bankrupt Without Love

*"No matter what I say, what I believe,
and what I do, I'm bankrupt without love."*

1 CORINTHIANS 13:3 (THE MESSAGE)

A life without love is wasted. You need to receive God's love so that it overflows and allows you to love others.

You need God's love because you aren't perfect. His love will never run out, no matter what you've done or will do. Consider King David: He was far from perfect! In fact, he made a series of bad choices. He lied, cheated, and committed adultery. He even had the husband murdered to cover up his sin.

David did many great things *for* God, and he did many things *against* God. Yet God called David a man after his own heart. How could God say that about a man like David? Because he knew that David's love for him was bigger than his mistakes. When David sinned against God, he admitted it and asked for mercy. How can you be after God's heart like David? Let God's love for you be bigger than your mistakes. Accept his perfect love by coming clean with your sins and asking for his forgiveness. Do this every day!

You need love in your relationships because it's the only way your relationships will last. People will sin against you and you'll sin against them, and the only solution to that pain is love. God's love also gives you the power to let other people off the hook when they sin against you. You've been forgiven by God, and now you are called to forgive others.

Today, how will you receive God's love so that you can love others?

August

OPEN DOORS

Live by God's Values

"[Moses] regarded disgrace for the sake of Christ as of greater value than the treasures of Egypt, because he was looking ahead to his reward."

HEBREWS 11:26 (NIV)

Everyone lives by a set of values.

If your values are based on circumstances, events, other people, and impulses, you will be tossed around. You'll be blown off course from God's purpose.

However, if your values are based on things that last forever—your relationship with God and with others—then, like he did with Moses, God will use you to make a difference for his kingdom!

Moses chose God's values over short-term, selfish thinking. He would have rather suffered for the sake of Christ than to have the temporary wealth and success of this world. Moses could have been a prince in Egypt, instead he was a shepherd in the desert for 40 years before God called him to lead Israel.

Moses looked to the future—all the way to eternity—to establish his values. He saw God's purpose for him by looking ahead, which empowered him to pass up the temptations and treasures surrounding him in Egypt.

Until you clarify your values, you can't live by them.

Today, you need to clarify your values by asking, "What's most important to me? What are the top values in my life? Do they align with who God wants me to be?" For example, if your values are integrity, humility, and generosity, write those down so you can have a reminder of how you want to live every day.

By clarifying your values, you are choosing God's purpose for your life.

What do you need to adjust in your life to bring it in line with God's values? Today is the day for you to choose to be who God wants you to be.

Forgiveness Is Unconditional

"Father, forgive them, for they do not know what they are doing."

LUKE 23:34 (NIV)

Forgiveness may be the most misused, misapplied, and misunderstood quality in our culture. There are a multitude of myths about forgiveness. Here are just a few: forgiveness must be asked for or earned, forgiveness minimizes personal pain and hurt, and forgiveness restores full trust and reunites a relationship.

Real forgiveness is unconditional. There's no attachment to it. You don't earn it, nor do you deserve it. You don't bargain for it. Forgiveness is not based on a promise to never repeat the offense again. You forgive because it follows Jesus' example. When Jesus stretched out his hands on the cross and said, *"Father, forgive them, for they do not know what they are doing,"* nobody earned it or asked for it. Jesus took the initiative and offered forgiveness.

Forgiveness also doesn't minimize the seriousness of the offense. When somebody asks for your forgiveness, you actually cheapen it if you say, "It's no big deal. It really didn't hurt." If it wasn't a big deal, then they don't need your forgiveness.

Forgiveness isn't the same as trust. When someone hurts you, you need to forgive them, but you don't need to trust them like you did before. You can't guard your heart if you trust people who aren't worthy of your trust.

On our own power, this kind of forgiveness isn't possible. But the power to forgive comes from Jesus. Remember God's unconditional love for you, and express that love to those who hurt you.

The Importance of Empathy

"All of you should be of one mind. Sympathize with each other. Love each other as brothers and sisters. Be tenderhearted, and keep a humble attitude."

1 PETER 3:8 (NIV)

In order to live in harmony with your spouse, your friends, or anybody else, you must have empathy. Not only do you need to be aware of what's happening in their lives, you need to develop a genuine concern for them. Empathy is important because it meets two of our deepest needs: the need to be understood and a need to have our feelings validated.

How do you become an empathetic person?

Start by slowing down so you can notice what's happening around you. Our culture teaches us to move fast, so we end up skimming relationally. You are skimming when you are hitting most of the high points and missing all kinds of details in the lives of people you care about most. When was the last time you allowed someone to share their heart with you? You can't sympathize if you aren't listening.

Once you've slowed down long enough to really listen, start asking thoughtful and specific questions. Most people hold their emotions pretty close, and they don't automatically share how they're doing. Use gentleness to draw them out. "I'm fine" is the standard answer, but that doesn't really tell you how they feel. Asking "How was today?" is better than staying busy. Asking "How was your conversation with Sue?" is even better.

The only way you are going to have the energy to be authentically empathetic is by staying close to God. If your emotional tanks get low, you'll be ruled by your own agenda. Selfishness pushes empathy into the background.

Ask God to help you slow down, ask good questions, and give you the strength to better love the people in your life.

The Purpose of Frustration

"When a fool is annoyed, he quickly lets it be known.
Smart people will ignore an insult."

PROVERBS 12:16 (GNT)

Some people are so frustrating, they will send you to your knees in prayer.

We all get frustrated by different things: a slow driver, a friend who never apologizes, and people who are rude and obnoxious. When you are frustrated, what's your first response?

Many people have developed unhealthy responses to frustration. They might avoid difficult people, but denial only delays the problem, not solve it. They might try to make frustrating people happy, but some people will never be happy. No matter what they do, it's never good enough.

How can you respond like Jesus?

God has put difficult people in your life to be "heavenly sandpaper." Although you are irritated, God is using them to take off your rough edges. God is more interested in your character than your comfort.

Consider your frustration as a learning opportunity.

Learn to look past their behavior to see where they are hurting on the inside. Hurt people will often hurt others. They're full of fear and insecurity. Maybe they're shouldering a pressure you don't know about. You can turn frustration into empathy with a little reflection.

Instead of dismissing these frustrating people from your life, look at them as a gift from God to help you become more like Christ. Frustration reveals something in you, and it can lead to a change of heart. Spend time in prayer asking God to help you have more patience and less words. Being frustrated doesn't give you permission to take it out on whoever caused your frustration. Frustration gives you the opportunity to show grace to others.

How will you handle your next frustration?

Be Willing to Be Interrupted

"Jesus told him, 'Go and do likewise.'"

LUKE 10:37 (NIV)

Love is often inconvenient.

If you want to serve like Jesus, be open to interruptions. This means holding on to your schedule with a loose grip. This may be difficult for you! For some people, just the thought of deviating from their plans leads to anxiety.

The reality is that people need you when they need you. Their hour of need won't fall neatly into the part of your schedule set aside for helping others.

Jesus taught that we should be like the traveling Samaritan. He allowed his schedule to be interrupted so he could care for a man left for dead.

Paul had plans to go to Rome and he eventually made it—as a prisoner! He was willing to have his plans interrupted to serve where God wanted him to serve.

Not every interruption is truly an interruption—not from God's point of view. He might be providing you an opportunity that you didn't plan for. Because God's plans are bigger than your plans, this is bound to happen! Next time you think, "I don't have time for this!" follow that with this quick prayer: "God, is this what you have for me to do?"

We can always find excuses not to help someone: *"I have my own problems," "I have a previous commitment," "I know someone else will help,"* and *"I have other responsibilities I can't sacrifice."*

God intentionally puts hurting people in your path so that you will learn to love like Jesus. Loving others can be more than inconvenient. God might be calling you to make a great sacrifice of your time, energy, or money. Today, are you ready for an interruption?

If the opportunity comes from God, it's not really an interruption; it's your destiny.

Tune into God's Voice

"God does speak—sometimes one way and sometimes another —even though people may not understand it."

JOB 33:14 (NCV)

Do you know how to tune into God's voice?

God speaks through the Bible; his will is found in his Word. It shows you the right steps to take, which is why you need to read God's Word every day.

God speaks through teachers. Have you ever been in a church service and felt like the teacher was delivering a message directly to you? There's no way the teacher could have known what you needed to hear, but the message was tailor-made for you by God. He uses the teaching of others to meet the needs of people who are listening.

God also speaks through impressions. Two extremes play out regarding impressions from God. The first extreme accounts for the people who don't believe God gives impressions at all—everything must be logical. The second extreme is about people who hold a mystical belief that every impression is from God. Find a healthy place in the middle and recognize that, for an impression to be from God, it has to match his Word.

God often speaks through circumstances. If you're going to live a life of significance, God has to make constant course corrections, and one way he does that is through the circumstances he brings into your life.

God does speak, so it's up to you to develop the ability to tune into his voice. Sometimes he will lead you in a way that you don't understand. Be patient and listen for his voice. God is faithful, and he will show you the way.

Bless Your Opposition

*"All the believers were together and had everything in common.
They sold property and possessions to give to anyone who had need."*

ACTS 2:44-45 (NIV)

No one sacrificed like the people in the early church. These early Christians didn't just give their money. They were radically generous with everything they had.

What would happen through our churches if we were just as generous? The Bible says we're stewards—or managers—of all that God has given us. We're responsible to use our resources and time in a way that impacts the Kingdom.

God doesn't give you resources just for your own enjoyment, but to make a difference in the world around you.

God's blessings are not meant to be hoarded. He blesses you so you can bless others. When you give to others you make room for God to give you even more.

That's a hopeful, encouraging truth to remember throughout the year. After all, generosity isn't something we only display at Thanksgiving or Christmas. Find ways to be radically generous every day. Make an impact on the people in your church, the people in your community, and the people God has strategically placed in your life.

Whose life can you bless today?

God Is Working While You're Waiting

"In the morning, LORD, you hear my voice;
in the morning I lay my requests before you and wait expectantly."

PSALM 5:3 (NIV)

When you ask God for help, you can wait with expectation.

You pray to a God who honors his promises. He is a good Father who always gives you what you need. When you wait expectantly, you demonstrate faith by believing God will do what he has promised.

Expectation isn't entitlement. Entitlement says, "I will get what I need from God because I deserve it, I've earned it. I've read my Bible five times this week and have been to church twice, so God has to give me what I need." Expectation says, "God will give me what I need because of who he is."

Waiting expectantly isn't easy, especially when you feel powerless. When you are trusting God to do the impossible—in your marriage, career, or relationships—and his timing feels too slow, it's hard to keep trusting him.

Don't be discouraged, and don't give up! Even though you don't know why God hasn't answered your prayers, you can trust him to keep his promise. God is always in control; he is never surprised and no one is more powerful than him. Your biggest problems are small to him.

While you are waiting, God is working. He is building your faith, teaching you his truth, drawing you closer to himself, and making you more like Christ. God knows what you need better than you do.

Follow David's example: Keep making your requests to God and waiting expectantly for him to answer.

God's Truth Will Set You Free

*"If you abide in My word, you are My disciples indeed.
And you shall know the truth, and the truth shall make you free."*

JOHN 8:31-32 (NKJV)

Nothing changes lives like the Bible. People struggling with addiction find sobriety, the broken find healing, the hopeless find hope in the Word of God. God's Word turns self-centered people into selfless servants, misers into givers, rebels into worshipers, and sinners into saints.

Laws can punish behaviors, but they cannot change human hearts. You can make laws to outlaw racism and bigotry, but no law can turn a bigot into a lover of people of other races. Only the truth of God's Word will set a hater free from his hatred. Only the truth of God's Word will set a doubter free from his doubts. Only the truth of God's Word will set a man or woman free from the prison of their past.

Secular universities all around the world have the second half of today's verse etched in stone on their buildings: *"The truth shall make you free."* But those same universities ignore the first part of the verse: *"If you abide in My word."* Your own opinions and the opinions of others won't set you free. Only the truth of God's Word will.

The fundamental question you must answer is this: What will be your authority in life? Will it be God's eternal Word or the world's ever-changing philosophies? Will it be what God says is true or public opinion? You need to decide, and you need to do it soon. Your life—and your freedom—depend on it.

Jesus Meets You in Your Storm

*"About three o'clock in the morning Jesus came toward them,
walking on the water."*

MARK 6:48 (NLT)

Jesus wanted to go off by himself to pray, so he sent the disciples ahead of him in the boat to cross the lake. It wasn't long before they were engulfed by a storm and blown off course.

Have you ever been blown off course by a storm? You thought you were following Jesus, but you ended up with unexpected troubles or at an unintended destination. Maybe you had no plans of being where you are today in your job, your marriage, or your finances. You've been blown off course by situations you couldn't control, and you've given up hope of getting back on track.

Maybe you are wondering whether you can even survive.

When you're at your moment of desperation, what does Jesus do? For his storm-tossed disciples, Jesus came to them—"walking on the water"! He didn't tell the disciples to come to him. He knew they couldn't get to him, so he went to them. When you're at that point of desperation, Jesus comes to you too.

Jesus did not stand on the shore and shout instructions. When you're in a storm, you don't need advice. This is the heart of the Gospel: God doesn't stand on the shoreline telling you what to do. He comes out and meets you in your pain, your fear, your depression, and your discouragement. What a loving God!

You may feel abandoned right now, but you're not. You might not be able to fix your problems, but you can fix your eyes on Jesus.

Get Refueled God's Way

"Because of the LORD's faithful love we do not perish, for His mercies never end. They are new every morning; great is Your faithfulness! I say: The LORD is my portion, therefore I will put my hope in Him."

LAMENTATIONS 3:22-24 (HCSB)

What do you do when you are drained?

Emotional exhaustion isn't foreign to people in the Bible—Job, Elijah, Naomi, David, Jeremiah, and even Jesus experienced it. When Jeremiah wrote the book of Lamentations, Jerusalem had been captured, and the Israelites were in exile. Everything Jeremiah held sacred had been ruined.

Jeremiah was emotionally exhausted! For an entire book of the Bible, Jeremiah released his frustrations and expressed his emotions to God. In the midst of his complaints, he focused on these aspects of God's character: steadfast love, unfailing mercy, great faithfulness, and kindness.

Jeremiah chose hope over despair, and his hope was not disappointed.

When life overwhelms you, don't pretend it's not happening. Denial won't do you any good. Be honest with yourself and express your feelings to God. You can do this without letting your problems become your main focus. Instead, fix your eyes on God by remembering who he is and what he's done for you.

Emotional exhaustion is similar to being really hungry. You need to eat something healthy, not the empty calories that come from junk food. Chocolate may sound good when you are starved, but it won't give you what your body needs. Similarly, God made your emotions, and he's the only one who knows how to bring you restoration when you need it most.

Make it your habit every morning to be renewed by God's mercies. God's faithfulness is the fuel you need.

How to Fight Spiritual Warfare

"For our struggle is not against flesh and blood, but against the rulers, against the authorities, against the powers of this dark world and against the spiritual forces of evil in the heavenly realms."

EPHESIANS 6:12 (NIV)

There is more to the world than what you can see with your eyes or touch with your hands.

The spiritual battle is real, and so is our enemy: Satan. As believers, he has lost the war for our eternal salvation. But in the present, he is working to make us ineffective for Kingdom work. To fight the spiritual war, you need to do two things on a continual basis.

Consistently take every thought captive. The battlefield for spiritual warfare is primarily in your thought life. Our enemy is the father of lies. Some things sound true on the surface, but in the light of truth they don't stand up. We need God's truth to transform Satan's lies.

In addition, put on God's armor. In Ephesians 6, Paul says that just as the Roman soldier is dressed for the battle, we also need to be appropriately dressed for our spiritual battle. You can prepare yourself by praying:

"Lord, help me resist the enemy. I want to put on the belt of truth to fight the devil's lies. I want to put on the breastplate of righteousness to protect my heart. I want to put on the shoes of peace to tell others the Good News. I want to hold up the shield of faith to block the devil's arrows—life's setbacks and temptations. I want to put on the helmet of salvation to protect me from doubts about Jesus and my salvation. And I want to take the sword of the Spirit to help me trust in his Word. Amen."

You Can Fight the Feeling

"It was faith that made Moses leave Egypt without being afraid of the king's anger. As though he saw the invisible God, he refused to turn back."

HEBREWS 11:27 (GNT)

Do you ever feel lazy?

Sometimes we just want to lie on the couch and be entertained. We don't feel like doing anything productive, especially if it involves dealing with another problem.

Here is the truth: You don't want to be controlled by apathy.

Just because you don't feel like doing something, doesn't mean you shouldn't do it. For example, you may not always feel like praying or reading your Bible. Does this mean you don't need time with God? Of course not. You need time with God whether you feel like it or not. Maturity means living by your commitments, not your feelings.

In the same way, you don't become a godly person by doing only what you feel like doing. Godly men and women choose to develop habits that produce godliness. Do you know anyone who eats well and exercises consistently? They don't always feel like eating the right thing or working out, but they live by their commitments—and their persistence pays off.

How do you develop godly persistence? The key is to look to God for direction rather than your feelings. Moses is a great role model for godly persistence. For 40 years, he led a group of crying, squabbling, complaining people around the desert while they questioned his leadership over and over. Yet he never gave up because he kept his eyes on God.

The pursuit of godliness will require a commitment that's stronger than your feelings.

Choose Faith over Fear

> *"'Be quiet!' many of the people yelled at him. But he only shouted louder, 'Son of David, have mercy on me!' When Jesus heard him, he stopped and said, 'Tell him to come here.'"*

MARK 10:48-49 (NLT)

Fear can paralyze your potential, prevent you from reaching out for help, and prohibit you from growing closer to God. If you want to jump-start your faith, you will have to learn how to face your fears so they don't control you.

When you choose fear over faith, your spiritual life gets trapped in a rut because the fear of emotional pain replaces the hope of God's promises. Fear keeps you from trying to do anything new for God, and therefore limits your commitment to serve him.

Bartimaeus, the blind man Jesus encountered in Mark 10, had to face his fear of rejection if he wanted to reach Jesus. When he shouted out to Jesus, many of the people yelled, "Don't do that. Be quiet. Don't make a scene. Surely Jesus isn't interested in you. He has more important things to do."

Bartimaeus chose to live by faith rather than fear. So he continued to shout out—even louder.

To get closer to Jesus, you will need to turn your back on your fear. Your faith isn't dependent on what others think about you. Your faith isn't even dependent on what you think. All that matters is what God thinks.

If your fears start saying, "God isn't interested in you," reject them as lies. God sent his Son to save the world. Jesus cared about Bartimaeus, and he cares about you.

God's love for you is perfect, complete, and unconditional.

Is there any fear in your life that you need to stand up to?

What Do You Want from Jesus?

"Jesus asked him, 'What do you want me to do for you?'
The blind man answered, 'Teacher, I want to see.'"

MARK 10:51 (NCV)

After Bartimaeus chose faith over fear, Jesus asked him an important question, "What do you want me to do for you?"

Why do you think Jesus asked that question? The answer seems obvious. Jesus had the power to heal, and Bartimaeus needed his blindness cured.

Jesus asked the question for Bartimaeus' benefit—and ours. It allowed Bartimaeus to publicly announce his faith—that he trusted in Jesus' ability and willingness to heal him. Bartimaeus believed Jesus wasn't just a teacher, but that he was also God. Before Jesus, no prophet from Israel had ever cured blindness. The blind man was trusting Jesus to do something that had never been done before. That's faith!

Here's the amazing thing: Jesus asks you the very same question, "What do you want me to do for you?" This isn't a question of entitlement; it's a question that builds faith because it forces you to look inward and examine your expectations of Jesus.

If you don't trust God to work powerfully in and through your life, chances are, he won't.

God wants to work in your life. He has big plans, and he wants to use you to make a difference in the world. Do today what the blind man did long ago: Cry out for help. Take an honest look at what is broken in your life, and ask Jesus for hope and healing.

In faith, what do you want from Jesus?

Living Guilt Free

"He does not punish us for all our sins; he does not deal harshly with us, as we deserve. He has removed our sins as far from us as the east is from the west."

PSALM 103:10, 12 (NLT)

God gives you what you need, not what you deserve.

We deserve judgment for our sins because we are guilty for doing bad things, but Jesus took the punishment we deserve. He has removed them *"as far as the east is from the west."* Earth has a north pole and a south pole, but there is no end from east to west. God has taken your sin and wiped it out!

King David committed adultery, and then, to cover it up, he had the woman's husband murdered. Can you imagine the guilt he carried? The far reaching effects of adultery and murder are devastating. David didn't deserve forgiveness or mercy from God. David knew he was wrong, and he also knew that God is a merciful God.

David prayed: *"Have mercy on me, O God, because of your unfailing love. Because of your great compassion, blot out the stain of my sins. Wash me clean from my guilt. Purify me from my sin"* (Psalm 51:1-2 NLT).

If you are struggling with a sin right now, read Psalm 51. Read it slowly, and read it several times. Make it your prayer and meditate on the truth. God is in the business of forgiveness; he can purify, cleanse, and restore you.

Follow David's example. Admit your guilt to God and ask for his mercy. He will forgive you because he is good, not because you are good enough to earn it. God has forgiven you, so accept his forgiveness and forgive yourself too.

The Crisis of Control

"This left Jacob all alone in the camp, and a man came and wrestled with him until the dawn began to break. When the man saw that he would not win the match, he touched Jacob's hip and wrenched it out of its socket."

GENESIS 32:24-25 (NLT)

For many people, wanting to be in control is their biggest struggle in life. That was Jacob's problem—he tried controlling his life to such an extent that one night he went one-on-one with God and wrestled an angel all night long.

Think about the biggest problem you've got right now, and it most likely boils down to these two questions: "Will I trust God?" and "Will I obey God?" No matter what your problem is—financial, physical, relational, social, or vocational—your biggest problem is not your problem. The real problem is whether you choose to obey and trust God.

God doesn't want your life to be painful, but he often allows an uncontrollable crisis in your life in order to get your attention. Jacob walked with a limp his entire life, which was a constant reminder of his struggle. Do you think God had his attention?

How does God use a crisis? You are more likely to change when the pain you feel exceeds your fear of change. You don't change when you see the light; you change when you feel the heat. All of a sudden, you're flat on your back and forced to look up.

Where are you struggling with God? What will it take for you to trust and obey him in every area of your life?

Put Christ at the Center of Your Life

"[God] will give you all you need from day to day if you live for him
and make the Kingdom of God your primary concern."

MATTHEW 6:33 (NLT96)

You create balance in your life by learning and living out the principles in God's Word.

It all starts by building your life around Christ. Therefore, put him at the center of your life, and he will teach you how to be balanced.

Think of your life like a wheel. At the center of the wheel is the hub. And out of that hub are all the spokes of life which represent your relationships, family, career, finances, dreams, goals and every other area of your life.

What does your life revolve around right now? Whatever you think about the most is what you center your life around.

If you have a solid center, you're going to have a solid life. But if you've got a weak, flimsy center, you're going to crack at the edges. Have you heard the expression, "I feel like I'm coming unglued"? If you've felt that way, it means you have a faulty center. It means something other than God has taken first place in your life. Whatever it is, if it's not God, it's not strong enough to hold you together.

The core of your life will provide the power you need. Power always emanates from the hub outward. If you don't have God at the center of your life, you've got a power shortage! Nothing else has enough power to help sustain you through all the unforeseen crises that you're inevitably going to experience.

Put Christ at the center of your life, and he will give you stability, balance, and power.

God Has a Special Assignment for You

"Many Samaritans from the village believed in Jesus because the woman had said, 'He told me everything I ever did!'"

JOHN 4:39 (NLT)

What excuses have you been making to avoid being used by God?

It doesn't take years of following Jesus to do what God put you on earth to do. No matter what you've done, God has a special assignment for you. In fact, it doesn't even take a day of "good" living. God can use you the moment you put your trust in Jesus—like he did with the woman at the well in Samaria.

What started out as a simple request for a drink of water, became the longest recorded conversation Jesus had with an individual, a conversation in which Jesus offered the woman, not well water, but living water—the kind that leads to eternal life.

Not only did Jesus initiate this conversation, he knew going into it she has had five husbands and wasn't even married to the one she woke up to that very morning. Jesus knew beforehand about her rather complicated past, yet he still sought her out!

The woman then left her water jar beside the well, ran back to her village, and told people about Jesus—and *"many Samaritans from the village believed in Jesus."*

Are you ready for your special assignment? God doesn't need you to get it together first. When you look at the Bible, you'll see that God has used all kinds of "misfits": Jacob was insecure, Leah was unattractive, Moses stuttered, Samson was codependent, Rahab was immoral, David had an affair, Jonah was reluctant, John the Baptist was eccentric, Peter was hot-tempered, Martha worried a lot, Zacchaeus was unpopular, and Thomas had doubts.

God had an assignment for all of them. He has one for you, too, if you will stop making excuses.

Jesus Came for the Brokenhearted

"He has sent Me to heal the brokenhearted."

LUKE 4:18 (NKJV)

Have you ever had a broken heart?

Doctors today say a broken heart is a medical reality with measurable physical effects. After experiencing stress or serious trauma, some of the hormones released by the brain actually weaken the tissue of the heart. This results in chest pain as the normal rhythmn of the heart is interrupted. It's called "broken heart syndrome."

Emotionally, a broken heart can come from disappointment, rejection, or resentment. When things don't turn out as we plan, it hurts. We are wounded in the wake of rejection or careless words. When the attack comes from a close friend, the pain is all the more deeper.

Pain is real, and you don't have to hide or deny it. You can stop pretending it's not there and deal with it. You need to face it head on so you can find healing for your broken heart.

Here's the good news: Jesus came to heal the brokenhearted. God the Father sent his Son to live a perfect life, die an unjust death, and defeat death so that our broken hearts might be healed. You don't need to hide your brokenness from Jesus; it was his mission to come and heal you!

When your heart is broken, it won't get better on its own.

When you hold onto your personal brokenness, you are missing out on God's best for your life. You become a shadow of who you are supposed to be. The longer you wait, the deeper the shadow becomes.

Jesus came to heal your broken heart. When will you let him?

It's a Matter of Trust

"I want you to trust me in your times of trouble,
so I can rescue you and you can give me glory."

PSALM 50:15 (TLB)

When you are in trouble, where do you put your trust?

Maybe you are counting on your skills, money, friends, or power to get you through the trouble. Whatever it is, if you aren't trusting your Creator, then you are trusting something he made—and it wasn't designed to hold your trust.

We love to overcome our problems on our own because it feeds our ego.

Sometimes we don't trust God because we can't see him, and he doesn't always speak to us directly. We hide behind an excuse that says, "If God would show himself to me, I'd trust him more." The truth is, you trust in things you can't see—all the time. You can't see a cell phone signal, but you trust it. You can't see the WiFi, but you trust it to get you on the internet.

Trusting your phone is easy, but trusting God—especially in times of trouble—is really difficult. That's because trusting God means you need to stop relying on lesser things like money or friends. WiFi won't ask you to change your life, but God loves you enough to help you become more like Jesus. It's a better life, but it's not easy.

Are you willing to trust in the One who is unseen but more reliable than anything in all of creation?

"Dear God, forgive me for trying to handle problems on my own. I am not big or powerful enough, but you are. Show me where I need to trust you and give me the strength to hold on only to you. I give you my life. Amen."

The Power to Say No

"You are not controlled by your sinful nature. You are controlled by the Spirit if you have the Spirit of God living in you."

ROMANS 8:9 (NLT)

You have compulsions—habits, lusts, drives, desires, attractions—that make you feel like you have no choice but to act upon them. Sometimes you feel like you just can't help yourself, that it's impossible to say "no."

As a believer in Jesus, you have access to the Holy Spirit, which gives you the power to say "no." You will still be tempted; you will still have sinful desires—but you are no longer controlled by them. God's power lives in you so you can be controlled by the Spirit.

You may be tempted to think, "If it's natural, why should I limit it?"

Many things come naturally, but that doesn't mean they are good. For example, for some of us, it's really easy to be lazy. We get out of bed in the morning, hoping we can take the path of least resistance all day long. That's a natural desire, but it's not good.

It's natural to be self-centered. But if you don't limit that desire, it will damage your relationships. Self-centered parents raise self-centered kids. Self-centered friends are surrounded by people who only look out for themselves.

Jesus was the opposite of selfish: *"For even the Son of Man did not come to be served, but to serve, and to give his life as a ransom for many"* (Mark 10:45 NIV). Learning to say "no" to our natural, selfish desires is difficult. Without the power of the Holy Spirit, it's actually impossible.

Where do you need to start saying "no" in your life?

Jesus Knows Your Name

"Jesus looked up at Zacchaeus and called him by name, 'Zacchaeus!' he said."

LUKE 19:5 (TLB)

Zacchaeus had been ridiculed and rejected his entire life—first for his appearance and then for his sinful ways. But Jesus called him by name. Imagine the shock Zacchaeus must have felt! How did Jesus know his name?

God knows your name. He knows where you are. He knows what you're going through, why you're going through it, and how you feel about it. He knows you better than you know yourself. He cares about you personally.

The name Zacchaeus means "pure one," which is surprising given that he was a corrupt government official. As a tax collector, he gathered more taxes than Rome required, so he got rich off of the excess. Zacchaeus was a Jew working for Rome—he was taking advantage of his own people! In the gospels, tax collectors were often grouped with "sinners." In calling Zacchaeus by name, Jesus said, "Hey, Pure One, I'm coming to your house today." Jesus was affirming the potential he saw in Zacchaeus.

You may be afraid to get close to Jesus because you think he's going to scold you for everything you've done wrong. But that's just not true. Jesus wants to affirm you. He wants you to know how much he loves you.

Consider this: When Jesus died on the cross, he stretched out his arms, and the soldiers put nails through his hands. The scars on his hands are a sign of God's unfathomable, everlasting love for you.

Your Faith Can Move Mountains

"Have faith in God! If you have faith in God and don't doubt, you can tell this mountain to get up and jump into the sea, and it will. Everything you ask for in prayer will be yours, if you only have faith."

MARK 11:22-24 (CEV)

Faith opens the door to miracles.

God has set up the universe in a hierarchy of laws, and the law of faith is a higher law than the laws of nature. That's where miracles come in. When people have faith in God, it can actually do more than the laws of physics.

Does God still perform miracles today? Absolutely! God is working in your life and all around the world—every minute of every day. His power has never diminished and it will never run out. Faith says, "God, I am trusting that you can move any mountain to accomplish your will."

Ask yourself this question: "What's the mountain in my life that needs moving?"

Many of us believe our mountains are unmovable. The truth is, things will never change if you don't believe they will. What makes you so certain that your mountain won't move? You limit God's power when you believe the lie that a mountain is too big for him to move. When you underestimate what God wants to do in your life, you hinder his work: *"[Jesus] did not do many miracles there because of their lack of faith"* (Matthew 13:58 NIV).

God is calling you to exercise your faith in him, and your faith will supersede the law of nature. This has been proven over and over again in the past, and God will continue to move mountains in the future.

Choose to Trust God

"It was by faith that Noah built a large boat to save his family from the flood. He obeyed God, who warned him about things that had never happened before."

HEBREWS 11:7 (NLT)

Faith is acting in obedience, even when you don't understand what God is asking of you. This is the kind of faith that Noah had, and God wants us to have the same faith.

When God says, "Love your enemies," and "Forgive the people who hurt you," that's not easy! There are a lot of commands in the Bible that seem difficult, unreasonable, unrealistic, unachievable, or even impossible. When God says things like, "You should save sex for marriage," he's not being mean. He says it because he knows what's best for you.

Every time God tells you to do something, it's a test of your faith. The question is this: "Do you trust God, or do you trust your own way? Do you trust the Word, or do you trust the world?"

As a kid, did your parents ever ask you to do something that seemed unreasonable? When you asked them why, they would say, "Because I said so!" God will say the same thing to you throughout your life. He'll say, "I want you to do this." When you ask him why, he'll say, "Because I said so."

Faith is believing when you don't see it, but it's also obeying when you don't understand it. If you do not learn to obey, you'll miss so many blessings in life that God has in store for you.

What is God asking you to do that may seem unusual—even impossible? Learn to do what God asks, and watch how he'll bless your life.

Mouth Management

"Lord, help me control my tongue; help me be careful about what I say."

PSALM 141:3 (NCV)

How does God help us manage our mouth? By going directly to the source: your heart.

Have you ever said, "I don't know what got into me! I'm not that kind of person"? Well, the truth is, it wouldn't be coming out of your mouth if it wasn't in your heart first. In other words, it's not your mouth that gets you in trouble, it's your heart! Whatever's inside of you is what comes out. The Bible says, *"Whatever is in your heart determines what you say"* (Matthew 12:34 NLT).

Your words demonstrate your heart's condition. That means that someone with a harsh tongue is demonstrating an angry heart. Someone who brags a lot is revealing an insecure heart.

A person who is over talkative has an unsettled heart. Critical words reveal a bitter heart.

On the other hand, when you share encouraging words with others, it reveals a joyful heart. When you offer gentle words to people when they're down, it shows you've got a loving heart. If you say kind and comforting words to people, it shows you've got a heart of peace. What you say shows what you're like on the inside.

Contamination can only be eliminated at the source. When God helps you control your mouth, he changes you from the inside out. God specializes in heart transplants.

What do your words reflect about the condition of your heart?

The Only Way to Be Free

"I am the door; if anyone enters through Me, he will be saved."

JOHN 10:9 (NASB)

Would you like to have more freedom in your life?

Until you learn to make the most of your opportunities, you will lack the freedom God has planned for you. You will encounter many doors in your life. You'll find doors to happiness, sadness, success, and failure.

Some doors are traps, and others are opportunities.

The Bible has a lot to say about doors. In fact, when the Bible talks about a door, it is often a metaphor for opportunities. Your freedom in life largely depends on which doors you decide to walk through.

You will often go through the wrong doors or miss the right ones. However, there is one door you just can't afford to miss: the door to freedom. Freedom is a big deal to God. He doesn't want you enslaved to guilt, resentment, grief, the past, the future, or anything else.

God wants you to be free from the effects of sin.

The biggest prisons in life aren't physical. They're the prisons erected in your mind. You might be trapped in a destructive relationship, crippling debt, or an unbreakable habit.

No matter what kind of prison you're in, you need a way out. You can't enter the doors of opportunity God has planned for you until you escape your prisons. They are holding you back from the freedom God wants for you. Jesus is the only door to freedom. Accept his free gift of salvation in faith. And when you follow him, he will release you from the chains of anxiety, fear, lust, and anything else that is holding you back.

He's the one door you don't want to miss.

The Value of Memorizing Scripture

"The whole Bible was given to us by inspiration from God and is useful to teach us what is true and to make us realize what is wrong in our lives; it straightens us out and helps us do what is right."

2 TIMOTHY 3:16 (TLB)

In order to become spiritually mature, develop the habit of memorizing Scripture. God doesn't want you to remain a spiritual baby. He wants you to live the blessed life you're meant to live.

Here are some important reasons for keeping God's Word in your heart.

You can use it to overcome temptation. There may not be a Bible nearby when you're tempted, but you'll always have God's Word with you if you've memorized it. When Satan tempted Jesus in the wilderness, Jesus' only defense against this attack was the Word of God. If Jesus knew a better way to fight temptation, he would have used it.

You can use it when you need comfort. When you're under stress or in a crisis, you can find comfort from God's Word by recalling Scripture you've stored in your mind. God's truth will offer you comfort in the moment you most need it.

You can meditate on Scripture wherever you go. If you've memorized Scripture, you can think about it when you get into bed at night or as you drive to an appointment. You can meditate on God's Word because you've memorized it. And the practice of meditation will bring you peace.

In other words, memorizing Scripture allows you to always have God's Word with you, to encourage and empower you, regardless of your setting or circumstances.

God Has a Plan for You

*"All the days planned for me were written
in your book before I was one day old."*

PSALM 139:16 (NCV)

Your life is not an accident. You were created for a purpose and have a God-designed destiny that only you can fulfill.

Before you were born, God shaped you to have a unique mixture of spiritual gifts, passions, abilities, personality traits, and experiences. There's no one else like you in the world. In fact, the Bible says you are God's original masterpiece, custom designed for a specific purpose. It's an eternal purpose, and God is preparing you for it during your life on earth.

God wants you to fulfill your destiny—even more than you do! However, your destiny is your choice. God will not force it on you. He allows you to make choices that are not necessarily part of his will. If you choose to chase pleasure, popularity, position, or possessions instead of God, you'll miss his plan and waste your life. Jesus said, *"What good is it for someone to gain the whole world, yet forfeit their soul?"* (Mark 8:36 NIV).

It's never too late to align your life with God's will. Even if you've made a mess of your life, God can turn disaster into destiny. All you have to do is turn from your old ways and pray, "God, I want your purpose for my life." No matter what you've done or how far you've strayed from his path, God will realign you to his purpose.

Faith Is Thanking God in Advance

"When you pray and ask for something, believe that you have received it, and you will be given whatever you ask for."

MARK 11:24 (GNT)

When you need something, do you turn to God first, or do you look elsewhere and only come to God when everything else has failed? If turning to God isn't your first option when you need help, it's because you don't really believe that he will deliver.

Think about it this way: If someone handed you a check right now for a thousand dollars, would you wait until you cashed it to say, "Thank you"? No! You'd thank that person right away. Yet the thousand dollars wouldn't really be yours until you actually cash the check; the check is really just a promise of money. When you are given the check, you can genuinely say thanks, believing that the promise is credible and that the person has enough money in the bank to cover the amount of the check.

Faith puts trust in God's promises. Faith doesn't have to wonder if God is trustworthy; it makes the request and assumes God will listen. Faith thanks God in advance for his answer.

When you thank God after he answers, that's called gratitude—and it's important! Gratitude isn't faith. Faith looks forward and trusts in God. Gratitude looks back at what God has already done. Gratitude builds faith. If you are having a hard time trusting in God's promises for the future, look back on what he's already done in your life. God has done great and wonderful things in the past, and he will continue to do great and wonderful things in the future.

God will listen to you when you are desperate. But you don't have to wait until then! In your hour of need, make him your first option, not your last.

A Fresh Start Begins with Repentance

"Let us test and examine our ways. Let us turn back to the Lord. Let us lift our hearts and hands to God in heaven and say, 'We have sinned and rebelled.'"

LAMENTATIONS 3:40-42 (NLT)

The path to a fresh start and a clear conscience begins with repentance.

What does it mean to repent? Literally, the word means to turn back and go in another direction. Repentance begins with reflection and awareness. Do a gut-level, honest evaluation of your life. You look inside to identify what areas of your life are no longer aligned with God's will. Then, you admit your sins to God and surrender your life to him. Repentance says, "God, I'm sorry for what I've done against you. Help me to live according to your will, not mine." That's it! Repentance isn't difficult to understand, but it is difficult to do!

When we think about our sin, we often rationalize it. That means we tell ourselves "rational lies," like, "It was no big deal," "It happened so long ago," "It was just a stage I went through," or "Everybody does it." If you want a fresh start, you cannot rationalize away your sins. You cannot minimize it, excuse it, or blame others. That is not true repentance.

The greatest barrier to your fresh start with God is you. Nobody else is standing in your way. You just need to get honest with yourself and God. God wants to heal the hurts, bad habits, and hang-ups in your life, but he's waiting on you to acknowledge your sins and humbly return to him.

Are you ready for a fresh start?

September

OPEN DOORS

Bring Balance to Your Life

"Spend your time and energy in the exercise of keeping spiritually fit."

1 TIMOTHY 4:7 (TLB)

You will lose your passion for life and for God if you are either overworked or underworked.

Life is a series of seasons. You need a healthy rhythm between rest and work. Too much of either will cause you to lose your passion. Depending on your personality, you may lean toward one extreme or the other.

One extreme is the people who are always giving out. They are always helping, sharing, volunteering, serving, working, and being generous. They never take time to recharge, which eventually leads to compassion fatigue. What is compassion fatigue? You just stop caring about God, other people, and in extreme cases, you stop caring about yourself. You are burnt out from too much work and service to others.

The other extreme is the people who are always taking in, but never giving out. They go to endless amounts of Bible studies, Christian concerts, and conferences. They listen to sermons and Christian podcasts, doing all they can to learn and grow, but they aren't really helping anybody. This may come as a shock: Bible study without ministry is extremely dangerous. The more you know about God's plan for your life, the more responsible you are to God.

Do you lean one way or the other?

Balance goes deeper than work and rest. You need to balance God's five purposes for your life. You need to worship God privately and with others. You need to connect with other believers and spend time alone with God to grow. You need a ministry where you are using your abilities to serve others. You also need to be mission-minded when you share your faith with people who don't know Jesus.

What do you need to do to bring balance to your life?

Forgive Because You're Forgiven

"Remember, the Lord forgave you, so you must forgive others."

COLOSSIANS 3:13 (NLT)

God calls you to forgive the people who have hurt you. This isn't easy, but you have to learn how to forgive others.

First and foremost, forgive those who've hurt you because God has forgiven you. To be a forgiving person, you need to first accept the forgiveness of God through Jesus Christ. The Bible says that God came to earth in human form to offer forgiveness for everything that's ever been done wrong. The payment for your sins has already been made in Jesus. That's Good News, and it's the source of your power so you can forgive others.

You should also forgive those who've hurt you so that resentment will not control you. Resentment makes you miserable. It keeps you stuck in the past, and when you're stuck in the past, you are controlled by the past. Perhaps you are allowing people who hurt you 10, 20, or even 30 years ago to still hurt you to this day. Don't let that happen. They can't hurt you anymore, so just let it go.

Another reason to forgive those who've hurt you is because you will continue to need forgiveness for yourself. Forgiveness is a two-way street. You cannot receive what you are unwilling to give. Jesus teaches us that our relationship with him is hindered when we won't forgive others. Living in unforgiveness is hypocritical, we've been forgiven by Jesus and we will need more of his forgiveness in the future, you must learn to forgive others.

Today, who do you need to forgive?

Feed Your Mind with God's Word

"I will not set before my eyes anything that is worthless.
I hate the work of those who fall away; it shall not cling to me."

PSALM 101:3 (ESV)

Just like water and air pollution cause a lot of problems, so do the worthless things we allow to fill our heads. It's called mind pollution. What you feed your mind is just as important as what you feed your body. Which of the following mental "food groups" do you usually choose?

Mentally toxic foods are poisonous thoughts like bitterness, envy, lust, or anger. These thoughts actively destroy your mind and will derange, degrade, or demoralize you.

Mental junk food has no nutritional value. It will distract you from what's important, but it won't hurt you, but it definitely won't give you the wisdom you need to make good decisions. Most of our media—TV programs, news shows, social media feeds, etc.— fall into this category.

Brain food is the good stuff. It educates you in areas like math, history, English, philosophy, and geography. You need to fill your mind with brain food. It'll make you a well-rounded person.

The Bible is superfood. God's Word will teach you what you won't find anywhere else. It answers fundamental questions like, "Who am I? Where did I come from? Where am I going? Does my life matter? Is there a purpose to my life? Am I significant?"

The Bible is the only place to get true answers to life's most important questions. Consider cutting your mental junk food in half and put that time into reading the Bible and talking to God in prayer.

Enjoying God's Gifts

"If God gives us wealth and property and lets us enjoy them, we should be grateful and enjoy what we have worked for. It is a gift from God."

ECCLESIASTES 5:19 (GNT)

Are you so busy getting more stuff that you don't enjoy what you already have? God has blessed us richly, but we miss out on contentment when we fall into the trap of "when and then" thinking. We think: "When I get a raise, then I'll be content." "When I get a bigger house, then I'll be content." "When I get married, then I'll be content." "When my kids go off to school, then I'll be content."

The truth is: You are as content as you choose to be.

Contentment doesn't come from having a problem-free life. If you are not enjoying God's gifts now, you won't enjoy them later. Contentment has nothing to do with your circumstances because it has everything to do with your attitude.

Contentment never comes from having more. Why would that make you content, if you're not content with what you have now? Until you learn how to thank God for what you have, you will always want more.

Everything good in your life comes from God. *"Whatever is good and perfect is a gift coming down to us from God our Father"* (James 1:17 NLT). Take a moment to consider all of the good things in your life. Do you spend more time asking God for more or thanking him for what you have? "Thanks" is always a better prayer than "More."

Enjoy your God-given gifts with gratitude, and your desire for more will diminish.

Make Every Step Count

*"All athletes are disciplined in their training. They do it to win
a prize that will fade away, but we do it for an eternal prize. So I
run with purpose in every step. I am not just shadowboxing."*

1 CORINTHIANS 9:25-26 (NLT)

Every step in your journey with Jesus should be taken with purpose and intentionality. There's a heavenly prize ahead—an eternal reward that awaits those who honor God in everything they do.

Living a life *on purpose* requires self-discipline. This means you won't be able to do everything that other people do. God's plan is different from the world's plan. Being a disciple of Jesus often means taking the more difficult path.

Olympic runners must give up all kinds of stuff in order to go for the gold. They must go to bed at a certain time, eat a certain way, and train at a certain time. They must count the cost of what it will take to win. Then they make the necessary sacrifices, denying their natural urges and inclinations. The rigorous training is never the focus; their sights are set on the prize.

The spiritual life requires discipline.

Paul says every step must be purposeful. Finishing the race God has marked out for you requires a steady commitment and long-term thinking. It requires you to take an honest look at your weaknesses in light of God's strength, asking him to keep you from veering away from his plans and purposes.

Don't be tempted by shortcuts. They aren't short; they lead to delays and self-destruction. Stay on the straight and narrow path and keep pressing toward your goal. Remember the example of Jesus, who was not distracted by the things of this world and made every step count, for he knew of the joy ahead!

What Does God Think of You?

"You are a chosen people. You are royal priests, a holy nation, God's very own possession . . . You can show others the goodness of God."

1 PETER 2:9 (NLT)

If you don't feel good about yourself, how can you reflect God's goodness to the world?

You need more than the "power" of positive thinking. What God thinks about you weighs far more than a single positive thought. Every day, you need to remember how precious his thoughts are about you, and consider the following truths:

God accepts you entirely. Everyone needs acceptance, but how much of your life do you spend trying to earn acceptance from others? God has settled this issue. What Jesus did on the cross made you completely acceptable to God—no matter what you've done in the past or will do in the future.

God loves you unconditionally. God doesn't say, "I love you if . . ." He loves you, period. You can't make God love you more or less; his love is already perfect. His love is not based on your performance, but rather on his character.

God forgives you completely. Many people live with deep feelings of shame and guilt. Romans 8:1 says, *"There is no condemnation for those who belong to Christ Jesus"* (NLT). You belong to Jesus by believing in him. Let go of your guilt—God has. He doesn't rehearse your sins; he forgives them.

God values you immeasurably. Value is determined by what a person is willing to pay for something. Jesus Christ paid for you with his life. That means you have immeasurable value.

God has chosen you to belong to him. As a "royal priest," you represent him to the world. You are a trophy of grace on display so that people might see his goodness.

Give the Gift of Your Attention

"Do not be interested only in your own life,
but be interested in the lives of others."

PHILIPPIANS 2:4 (NCV)

We live in a world where technology leaves us continually distracted. We no longer pay attention to the people around us like we should.

When you walk into a meeting, how many people are looking at their phones and texting? The same thing happens at restaurants, even when families are spending time together. It's not just the kids, adults have the same problem struggling to be present. You see it every day, people with their heads down looking at a screen or with their headphones on, keeping them from hearing other people.

If you want to have happier relationships, you need to learn the lost art of paying attention. You can develop this habit by taking an interest in others.

The greatest gift you can give somebody is your attention. Why? Because your attention is your time, and your time is your life. You're never going to get it back, and that's why it is so precious when you give it.

This is a simple but powerful tool in growing strong relationships. Anyone can learn to take an interest in others! Are you interested in what your kids are interested in? Do you listen to what your spouse has to say? Do you give your coworkers your full attention when they speak to you? Do you notice your neighbor as you walk by him in the morning?

Today, give others the gift of your attention.

The Path of Everlasting Life

"Search me, O God, and know my heart; test me and know my anxious thoughts. Point out anything in me that offends you, and lead me along the path of everlasting life."

PSALM 139:23-24 (NLT)

The psalms are not only God's Word to us, they should also be our words back to him. When you make this psalm your sincere prayer, God will speak to you, leading you closer to him.

God already knows everything about you, but giving him consent to know you allows you to gain new personal insights that would otherwise be unknown. When you pray, *"Search me, O God,"* you are asking him to tell you who you really are. It's like saying, *"Here I am God, I want to be an open book. I know I have blind spots, and I'm asking you to show them to me."*

As God brings things to your mind, write them down. Why is this important? Nothing in your life will become dynamic until it becomes specific. Your thoughts will become more clear when you put them into words. With clarity, you can take action.

God will tell you what you need to hear. He will reveal your anxieties—areas of your life where you need to trust him. If you are anxious about your job, you need to trust God for his provision. If you are anxious about the results from a medical exam, you need to trust God for his peace and strength.

God will also reveal your faults and sins. Confess these back to God and ask for his forgiveness.

When you are uncertain, ask him for guidance, and he will lead you *"along the path of everlasting life."*

Be honest with God, and listen to what he tells you.

Stand Strong

*"Put your trust in the Lord your God, and you will stand your ground.
Believe what his prophets tell you, and you will succeed."*

2 CHRONICLES 20:20 (GNT)

The best way to make your problems bigger is to focus on your issues rather than trusting God.

When you try to fight the battles that belong to God, not only will you burn out, but you will also lose. You weren't designed to stand alone; you don't have the strength. When you are worn out, you finally say to God, "I'm sorry. I can't handle this situation, and I've tried everything. I need to give it to you because it's bigger than me."

You don't need to wait until you are worn out to trust in God.

When you are feeling the pressure, you can stand your ground by trusting in God's strength rather than your own. You may be able to stand on your own for a while, but eventually, you will fall. If you want to stand strong, you need God.

Standing strong is an attitude of quiet confidence in the character of God. You will be successful when you put your trust in what he says to you through his Word and the Holy Spirit. When you get with God, you'll never have to give up ground because he is your strength.

When the burden is overwhelming, you may be tempted to cave in under the pressure. God doesn't want you to back down from difficult situations or sacrifice your integrity. He wants you to trust him through the challenges and learn from them. If you run from them, you'll miss out on learning from God. Chances are, you'll need to repeat that lesson.

God is committed to your success, but you need to trust him and his Word so you can stand your ground.

Stay Focused

*"Anyone who lets himself be distracted from the work
I plan for him is not fit for the Kingdom of God."*

LUKE 9:62 (TLB)

God has an amazing life planned for you, but Jesus made it clear that you need to stay focused.

The devil is committed to keeping you "out of the game." He doesn't want you doing Kingdom work. Keeping you distracted is one of the methods he uses to make you ineffective.

Would you agree that we are flooded with distractions in our world today?

Take people-pleasing, for example. When we are distracted by pleasing others, their plans become more important than God's plans. We become consumed by thinking about what others want and expect from us rather than focusing on God's will.

Your hobbies become a distraction when they develop into an obsession. There's nothing wrong with having a hobby—until it becomes a top priority in your heart. Some things aren't necessarily bad, they just aren't good. If a hobby or a habit isn't helpful, it's probably a distraction. Do you want what's good, or do you want what's best for your life?

Getting caught up in the past can be a distraction in a couple of different ways. You might get stuck by reminiscing over the "good ol' days," ignoring your God-given opportunities in the present. On the other hand, you might be overburdened with regret and unable to move forward. In any case, the past is a prison when it keeps you from focusing on God's work for today.

Pleasing others, prioritizing hobbies, and being stuck in the past certainly aren't the only distractions. What distractions are standing in your way of staying focused on God's plan for you?

Life Is Passion

"[Jesus said,] Love the Lord your God with all your heart and with all your soul and with all your mind and with all your strength."

MARK 12:30 (NIV)

Nothing great is ever accomplished in life without passion. The creative force behind all great art, drama, music, architecture, and writing is passion. Without passion life becomes boring and monotonous.

Passion is what mobilizes armies into action. Passion causes explorers to boldly go into the unknown. Passion keeps scientists up late to find the cure to a dreaded disease. Passion transforms a good athlete into a record-breaking athlete. Passion makes the impossible, possible.

One day, a man walked up to Jesus and said, "Lord, what's the most important thing in the Bible?" Jesus said that nothing else matters in life if you don't love God passionately. God wants you to love him *"with all your heart and with all your soul and with all your mind and with all your strength."*

God wants you to love him with everything you've got. That's passionate love.

In our world, it's become acceptable to be passionate about anything except God. It's fine to be passionate about movies, sports, politics, fashion, and restaurants. The moment someone is passionate about their relationship with God, they get criticized. You could go to a concert, political rally, or sporting event and get excited and shout until you become hoarse from yelling. But if you get too emotional about your faith, you'll be labeled a fanatic.

It's also easier to be passionate about other things because they won't challenge your life like God will. However, passionately loving God and following his ways will radically transform you.

What's your life's passion?

You Don't Have to Live with Guilt

*"A man who refuses to admit his mistakes can never be successful.
But if he confesses and forsakes them, he gets another chance."*

PROVERBS 28:13 (TLB)

God is ready to give you another chance.

He is *always* ready to give you another chance. This is who God is; it is an unchanging truth about his character. This is good news because everyone needs another chance.

Would you agree that you aren't perfect? Everyone feels guilty because no one is always good. We are all irresponsible and make mistakes. Sometimes the mistakes create devastating consequences.

How do you typically handle your guilt? If you don't handle your guilt the way God intended, it will destroy your confidence, damage your relationships, and keep you stuck in the past. It can even hurt you physically.

You need to give your guilt to God.

You weren't designed to hold on to it. Your guilt ought to drive you closer to God, not further away from him. God doesn't want you living with your guilt—that load is too heavy. God wants you to admit your mistakes and abandon them completely. You can tell God because he already knows everything about you and still loves you unconditionally.

God wants you to live with a sense of promise and hope, but you won't have this until you confess your guilt to him. When you do, you will experience a forgiveness that is instant, free, and complete.

The Problem with Stuff

*"What do you benefit if you gain the whole world but lose your own soul?
Is anything worth more than your soul?"*

MATTHEW 16:26 (NLT)

What you love reveals a lot about you. How much do you love your stuff?

The purpose of life is not to collect more stuff. One problem with possessions is that the more you have, the more work and effort it takes to maintain, clean, protect, and repair them. More stuff results in a more complicated life, which doesn't translate into more happiness.

Yet we collect more things because we think it'll make us happy.

How much more do you need in order to be fulfilled? You may have more stuff than your parents did. In fact, we have an entire industry that didn't exist 50 years ago: personal storage units. We have accumulated so much stuff that we can't keep it in our homes! We pay rent every month to hold all the extra stuff that has become important to us. After a while, your stuff dominates your life.

To discover how important your stuff is to you, ask yourself this question: How do I feel when my things are taken away? If your heart is in your stuff, you'll be devastated when it is gone. You *"lose your soul"* when you no longer own your stuff, but rather it owns you. The most important things in life are not your things!

God designed you for a higher purpose—to love him and to love others. Our treasures on earth can be taken away, but treasures in heaven are secure for eternity.

Extra Grace Required

"Ask God to bless those who persecute you
—yes, ask him to bless, not to curse."

ROMANS 12:14 (GNT)

We all have EGRs—people who come with Extra Grace Required—in our lives. They annoy us, anger us, frustrate us, and test us. But they also help us grow. God calls us to bless people who cause us the most trouble. How much more is this true for those who only annoy us?

Do what's right, no matter what the EGRs in your life do. If they insult you, treat them with kindness. If they wear on your nerves or they're too slow for your pace, treat them with patience.

You cannot control what other people think about you. You cannot control what other people do to you. But you do have 100 percent control over how you respond.

You might be completely within your rights to retaliate, but Jesus calls you to take the higher ground, for it is where you're given a clear perspective. When you take the high ground, you can see past a person's actions to their pain. When you take the high ground, you rise above the irritation and the conflict, choosing to keep the peace. You might have the perfect comeback to put them in their place, but Paul tells us to lift them up, not to cut them down.

Maybe you are thinking, "I don't have anybody persecuting me." Cross out the word "persecute" and replace it with "irritate." Ask God to bless the people who irritate you. Instead of asking God to judge them, ask him to bless them. This is what real love looks like. Real love doesn't just love people who are lovable; real love loves the unlovable. Real love is patient with the irritable people in your life.

God empowers us to love even those we find hard to love.

Jesus Rescues the Humble

*"I am poor and needy; please hurry to my aid, O God.
You are my helper and my savior; O Lord, do not delay."*

PSALM 70:5 (NLT)

Is it easy for you to ask for help?

The Bible is full of situations where people needed to be rescued: Adam and Eve, Joseph, Moses, Jonah, Peter, Paul—just to name a few. They all needed a rescuer, a savior, because their strength was not enough to overcome their problems. Not all of them found it easy to ask for help because they were filled with too much pride. Some of them were unwilling to give up their pride, so God put them in impossible situations so they could see their own pride.

Pride keeps you from asking for help.

Pride says, "I've got this! I don't need help! I am good enough on my own." Truth is, you can't handle everything.

You need help from God. This may be difficult because you don't want people to think you're weak or foolish or somehow less perfect than the image you project.

Humility isn't afraid to ask for rescue.

Your deepest troubles can only be solved by God. When you turn to Jesus, you can trust that he will rescue you. He came to earth to save all humanity through his death and resurrection.

This means you have to admit you need rescuing. You will have to echo the psalmist's prayer, *"I am poor and needy."* It takes honesty and humility to admit your need like David did.

God is ready to help you. But first, you must surrender your pride.

Plant a Seed in Faith

"Unless a kernel of wheat falls to the ground and dies, it remains only a single seed. But if it dies, it produces many seeds."

JOHN 12:24 (NIV)

What does a farmer do with a barren field? He just starts planting seed because he knows that nothing is going to happen until seed is in the ground.

Do you have a barren field in your life? You might be waiting on God for a job, a spouse, a financial windfall, or some other opportunity. Has it occurred to you that God might be waiting on you to plant a seed first? Everything in life starts as a seed—relationships, businesses, and even churches. Nothing happens until a seed is planted.

Why does God require you to plant a seed first? Because planting is an act of faith. You take what you have, and you give it away. That takes faith! It also brings glory to God. It's the principle of sowing and reaping: Whenever you have a need, plant a seed.

Start by taking what you have and giving it away. If you need more time, give more time to your loved ones. If you need more money, give money to someone who needs it. If you need more energy, spend energy helping somebody else. If you need more wisdom, share the wisdom you have with others. If you need meaning and significance, give your life away to Jesus!

It may not make sense to give away something you need more of, but that is exactly the kind of attitude God wants to bless. It's one of the best ways to produce fruit in your life.

God's Plan for Your Life

"Each one, as a good manager of God's different gifts,
must use for the good of others the special gift he has received from God."

1 PETER 4:10 (GNT)

The person God made you to be determines what he intends for you to do. You will understand the purpose for which you were created when you understand the kind of person you are.

God is consistent in his plan for each of our lives. He would not give us inborn talents and temperaments, spiritual gifts, and all sorts of life experiences and then not use them! By reviewing and studying these factors, we can discover the destiny God has for us—the unique way God intends for us to serve him.

You are only responsible for the gifts God gives you. So, if you aren't artistically gifted, you are not expected to paint pictures like Rembrandt. When you get to heaven, God isn't going to compare you to anyone else, but he will ask you: What did you do with what you were given?

Esther used God-given abilities to fulfill her destiny. She was intelligent, well-liked by others, and had the courage to speak up when others wouldn't. Because of these qualities, she won favor with the king, which put her in a position to save her people.

Paul was a gifted teacher, leader, developer of others, and tent maker. God used his gifts to travel the world, planting churches, writing letters, and supporting himself with his trade. God used him to write more than half of the New Testament!

Just as God gave Esther and Paul gifts for a purpose, God has done the same with you. If you want to discover your destiny, look to see who God made you to be. The key to living a productive and fulfilling life is using your gifts to serve God by serving others.

The Joy of Your Salvation

*"Restore to me the joy of your salvation
and grant me a willing spirit, to sustain me."*

PSALM 51:12 (NIV)

What's the easiest thing for you to lose? It's not your keys, glasses, or even your phone.

The easiest thing for you to lose is your joy. It can be gone in an instant. All it takes is a phone call, an email, or even a look of disapproval. Joy is a serious issue—and not just because it's easy to lose.

When God's people aren't filled with joy, it makes God look bad. Throughout your life, you will face countless joy stealers. Three common culprits are an unbalanced schedule, unused talent, and unconfessed sin. Do you feel like you aren't as close to God as you used to be? Has your faith become more of a routine, like you are going through the motions? You can tell you've lost your joy when you have a short fuse and feel ready to give up.

It's actually easy to get your joy back. To recover your joy, you need to pray the same prayer as David. Admit that you have lost your joy and that God is the only one who can restore it. To reclaim your joy, pray this prayer:

"God, I don't want to live a joyless life. I need your help. I have let anxiety and hurt and resentment and confusion and many other things steal my joy. Thank you for sending Jesus to be my Savior. Fill me with your grace, so I can let go of all the pain. I don't understand it all, God, but I want to find my joy only in you. I want your joy to be my strength. Amen."

God Is Always Right on Time

"'Lord,' Martha said to Jesus, 'if you had been here, my brother would not have died. But I know that even now God will give you whatever you ask.' Jesus said to her, 'Your brother will rise again.'"

JOHN 11:21-23 (NIV)

Have you ever struggled with God's timing? The truth is, God is never late or in a hurry. His timing is always perfect.

Lazarus lived in Bethany with his sisters, Mary and Martha. When Lazarus became gravely ill, they asked Jesus to come to them. Jesus was just a few miles from Bethany, but he took three days to get there. During that time, Lazarus died. As you could imagine, Martha struggled with Jesus' timing.

When we look at the Gospel of Luke, we learn that Martha liked to be busy—even to the point of doing work rather than listening to Jesus. It's not surprising that she felt like Jesus was slow in responding.

Jesus wasn't late! Jesus did what the Father wanted him to do. Jesus had work to complete before he went to Bethany. God's goal was not to heal Lazarus but to raise him from the dead. Jesus did a miracle to build peoples' faith in him. Jesus walked up to Lazarus' tomb, told someone to roll the stone away, and said, "Lazarus, come forth!" And that's exactly what Lazarus did!

Sometimes God lets a situation get so bad that only a miracle will do. That's when it's time to hold on and keep your faith. Trust that God's timing is perfect. Keep praying, serving, and believing.

God is always right on time.

Joy Through Serving

"I will rejoice even if I lose my life, pouring it out like a liquid offering to God, just like your faithful service is an offering to God. And I want all of you to share that joy."

PHILIPPIANS 2:17 (NLT)

There are two secrets to joy and both involve serving others.

Get your mind off of yourself. The more you focus on yourself, the more miserable you will become. To find real joy, you must shift your focus from inward to outward. Change "it's all about me," to "it's all about serving others." Instead of focusing only on your personal needs, take time to recognize the needs of others.

How can a person find joy by helping others? This is counter-intuitive and countercultural. Everything in society says it's all about you, but that mentality couldn't be more wrong. It's not surprising that most people lack feelings of significance; it's the result of being too selfish. The truth is, *helpful people are happy people.* When you pour your life into others, the result is joy for you and for them. This joy is contagious, prompting them to serve others too.

Use your gifts to help others. Eric Liddell, an Olympic Gold Medalist, famously said, "God made me fast. And when I run, I feel his pleasure." God gifted Eric beyond his running ability. A year after winning his gold medal, Liddell became a missionary in China. He didn't have any regrets from leaving behind fame and fortune; he knew a life serving others counted far more than just running races. He understood God gave him his gifts not to enrich himself, but to serve others and share his faith. Here's the point: God blesses you so you can bless others.

Have you lost your joy? Think about how you might serve the people in your church and your community, and make a plan to do it!

God Can Restore You

"If you return to me, I will restore you so you can continue to serve me."

JEREMIAH 15:19 (NLT)

No matter how far you are from God, restoration is always an option. As a member of his family, you are always welcomed back with open arms. When you are ready to return to God, he's willing and able to make things right.

In the Parable of the Lost Son, the son rejected his father. He asked for his share of the inheritance, left his family, and set off to live a wild life. When his money ran out, he hit rock bottom. Eventually, he came to his senses; he returned home in humility, to the arms of a loving father.

After following Jesus for more than three years, Peter denied knowing him—not just once, but three times!

Yet Jesus restored Peter and affirmed his leadership in the church.

Jonah ran from God's plan for his life. He got on a ship that was literally headed in the opposite direction. In the belly of the big fish, Jonah cried out to God, and he was restored. God then used Jonah to change the entire city of Nineveh.

You may think God's forgotten you, but he hasn't. You may feel like you've drifted too far away from him, but that's not true either. *"No matter how deep the stain of your sins, I can take it out and make you as clean as freshly fallen snow"* (Isaiah 1:18 TLB).

Do you need to be restored? In humility, return to God.

276
A YEAR OF DAILY DEVOTIONS

Invest in Eternity

"Tell them to use their money to do good. They should be rich in good works and generous to those in need, always being ready to share with others. By doing this they will be storing up their treasure as a good foundation for the future so that they may experience true life."

1 TIMOTHY 6:18-19 (NLT)

You've probably heard the expression "You can't take it with you"—but you can "send it ahead" by investing in people's eternal destination.

God wants you to use some of the money he gives you to help bring others to Jesus.

You might save to go on a mission trip or support someone else to go. Consistent tithing to your church allows them to reach your community. Send a child or teenager to camp, so they have an opportunity to hear the Gospel and respond.

We spend our money on all kinds of things that don't have long term influence. But helping others find Jesus is the best use of your money and resources.

When you die and get to heaven, you will encounter friends who say, "Thank you for investing in me. I'm in heaven because of you! I'm not your friend for life; I'm your friend for eternity. I'm in heaven because you cared enough. You bought me a Bible. You bought me a ticket for that life-changing event. You gave me a book that pointed me to Jesus."

Others will say, "You spent your money to help spread the Good News to my village, even though you'd never seen us before. Because you gave, I became a follower of Christ. I'm in heaven because of you!"

How will you invest in eternity?

God Is on Your Side

*"For God is working in you, giving you the desire
and the power to do what pleases him."*

PHILIPPIANS 2:13 (NLT)

No matter what you face this week, you don't have to face it alone.

God is with you, working powerfully in your life. The word "working" in Greek is the word energeo, from which we get the word "energy." God is the energy driver in your life. You don't have to rely on willpower, and the truth is, willpower isn't enough.

God's energy is transforming you from the inside out. This means he gives you the right desires in your heart and mind so that you do the right thing with your actions and words. This is the life he created you to live.

God is also for you. God is your ally. In fact, he is committed to your success. Some people think God is like an angry parent who is mad at them all the time. That couldn't be further from the truth. He's not mad at you, he's mad about you.

Since God is for us, there is no challenge we can't overcome. God is bigger than any problem you will face. He can overcome a toxic relationship, a mountain of debt, a failing marriage, an overbearing boss, a challenging teenager, or a terminal illness.

No one and no thing is bigger than God. And he is right by your side.

Make this your prayer today:

"God, thank you for being on my side. I need your help because I can't do it all on my own. I don't know what today will bring, but I know you are in control. Help me to trust you more than I trust anything else. Amen."

God Gives Great Dreams

"Now glory be to God, who by his mighty power at work within us is able to do far more than we would ever dare to ask or even dream of— infinitely beyond our highest prayers, desires, thoughts, or hopes."

EPHESIANS 3:20 (TLB)

God's work in your life will be bigger than anything you can imagine. God will give you a big dream—a new picture for who you can be and the work he wants you to do. When you say "yes" to God, you're saying "yes" to making an impact in the world that's immeasurably more than you can ask or imagine.

In the Bible, there are many examples of God giving someone a dream about the future. God gave Noah the dream of building an ark. God gave Abraham the dream of being a father to a great nation. God gave Nehemiah the dream of rebuilding the wall around Jerusalem. God gave Paul the dream of telling the world about Jesus.

How do you know when a dream is from God? How can you be sure that your dream isn't just something you've thought up yourself?

If your dream is from God, it will be so big that you couldn't possibly do it on your own.

Without God, *some people* can do really amazing things: They can set a world's record, invent something ingenious, raise great kids, be successful in business, show great care to those in need—and the list goes on.

With God, *every single person* has the potential to outshine all of these amazing accomplishments. When God's mighty power is at work in his faithful servant, there is no limit to what can happen.

What's the dream God has given you?

Dreams Are Activated by Decisions

"What good is it, my brothers and sisters, if someone claims to have faith but has no deeds? . . . In the same way, faith by itself, if it is not accompanied by action, is dead. But someone will say, 'You have faith; I have deeds.' Show me your faith without deeds, and I will show you my faith by my deeds."

JAMES 2:14, 17-18 (NIV)

When God has given you a great dream, it will require you to surrender your life to him in new ways. The pursuit of that dream will draw you closer to him. After God gives you a dream, it needs to be followed by a decision. It's your choice: Will you follow God's plan or will your life remain unchanged? God isn't going to build your dream for you.

James teaches us that faith is a verb. It's active and not passive because it's something you do. When God gives you a dream, he shows you where you have to trust him. You have to decide to turn that dream into a reality.

A great illustration of this spiritual principle is an acrobat swinging from a trapeze, high above the ground. The most thrilling moment, for the crowd and the acrobat, is when he lets go of one bar to reach the other.

Faith decisions are like this, you have to let go of the old in order to grab onto the new.

If you don't let go, you'll swing back and forth until you finally stop, at which point you'll be hanging in the air. Then, the only way out is down!

Where is God asking you to trust him? You are only a decision away from activating the dream he has for you.

When God Delays Your Dream

"But these things I plan won't happen right away. Slowly,
steadily, surely, the time approaches when the vision will be fulfilled.
If it seems slow, do not despair, for these things will surely come to pass.
Just be patient! They will not be overdue a single day!"

HABAKKUK 2:3 (TLB)

After you make a decision to follow your dream from God, you can expect some kind of a delay.

It's human nature to hate waiting. We don't like to wait in a doctor's office, in traffic jams, at restaurants, or grocery lines. Worst of all is waiting on God.

When our dream is delayed, it causes us to forget many things. We tend to forget our dream. We forget what God has done in our lives and his goodness to us in the past. We forget God's power and that his presence is with us.

When a delay occurs in your life, don't start acting like God's never done anything for you. Has God done things for you in the past? Take some time to write those down so that you can remember them and give thanks to God for them. You can count on him to do it again tomorrow and the next day and the day after that.

Expect your dream to be tested with a waiting period. Why does God make you wait? It teaches you to trust in him. You learn that his timing is perfect. God is never late and he's never early. Delays are discouraging, but remember this: God's delay never diminishes or destroys his dream for your life. God's delay will build your faith.

A delay is not a denial. Children must learn the difference between "no" and "not yet"—and so must you. Many times, when we think that God is saying "no," he is really saying "not yet."

Difficulties Develop Your Dream

"This means tremendous joy to you, I know, even though you are temporarily harassed by all kinds of trials and temptations. This is no accident—it happens to prove your faith, which is infinitely more valuable than gold."

1 PETER 1:6–7 (PHILLIPS)

If your God given dream is in a season of delay, God may allow some difficulties to mature your faith. This prepares you for when your dream is fulfilled.

You'll face two types of difficulties: circumstances and critics. This is a natural part of the broken world that we live in. God uses these things to grow us closer to him when facing adversity and opposition.

When Moses led the people of Israel out of Egypt into the desert toward the Promised Land, he had one problem after another. First, there was no water. Then, there was no food. Then, there were a bunch of complainers. While Moses was talking to God on Mount Sinai, the Israelites decided to worship a false god—they made a golden calf.

Moses was doing what God wanted him to do, but he still had problems. These problems shaped the people and got them ready for their dream.

Joseph had a dream of becoming a ruler, yet he was sold into slavery and thrown into prison on a false charge, where he languished and was forgotten.

God does this because he is building your faith. When you finally come to a place where the difficulties become overwhelming, where you've reached your limit, where you've tried everything and exhausted all your options, it is then that God does a mighty work through you.

When Your Dream Feels Dead

"Abraham, when hope was dead within him, went on hoping in faith . . .
He relied on the word of God."

ROMANS 4:18 (PHILLIPS)

How do you know when hope has died in your life? You start using the word "never." I'm never going to get married. I'm never going to graduate. I'm never going to get well. I'm never going to get out of debt. I'm never going to be able to let go of my past. I'm never going to be able to heal from all of that shame and heartache. I'm never going to be able to change into the person God created me to be. I'm never going to see this situation turn around.

"Never" is the warning light that tells you your hope has died.

When you are at a dead end, you need the Bible. Read it, study it, memorize it, and meditate on it. The Bible teaches you who God is and what he's promised. When you are at a dead end, you need God more than anything else.

When you rely on God, he will encourage your heart and revive you. You will give up despairing because even though your life is out of your control, it's not out of God's control.

A dead end is a test of your faith.

You may be at a dead end now, and it seems there is no way out. The way through is to cling to God and his promises. Remember, things are never as bleak as they seem. You're seeing the situation from a human viewpoint rather than God's viewpoint.

God is your provider; he supplies you with everything you need—even when it feels like your dream is at a dead end.

Say Goodbye to Shame

"If God says his chosen ones are acceptable to him, can anyone bring charges against them? Or can anyone condemn them? No indeed!"

ROMANS 8:33-34 (CEV)

Would you agree that you aren't perfect?

Some mistakes are so big, they lead to extreme feelings of guilt and shame. Although these feelings were created to drive us toward God, at times they make us avoid God because we feel ashamed. Shame is the awareness of our sin, and unconfessed sin will build up a barrier between you and God.

The shame says, "I'm not good enough for God, so why would I want to spend time with a God who's simply going to remind me of all the ways I've failed?"

God completely accepts you—right now, just as you are. He loves you unconditionally. The more you understand and accept his love, the more your life will be changed.

You may have spent your entire life trying to gain the approval of others.

It has influenced how you dress, how you talk, and how you live. When you understand that God loves you unconditionally, you realize this: You don't have to earn God's approval.

Because God's love sets you free from sin, you no longer need to carry your shame. In Jesus, you are made right before God and no longer condemned.

Let God break the grip of shame on your life. Pray to him, *"God, I'm asking for your forgiveness. What I did was wrong, I admit it, and I want to change."*

When you know God loves you, you can lay down your guilt before the cross and pick up his forgiveness. Rejoice today that you can rest in the perfect love of your Father.

God Will Deliver You from Trouble

"My soul is in deep anguish. How long, LORD, how long?
Turn, LORD, and deliver me; save me because of your unfailing love."

PSALM 6:3-4 (NIV)

David was a king after God's heart, but he often found himself surrounded by his enemies. Some of these circumstances created intense agony in David's soul. God used these situations to grow his faith. David viewed his troubles as opportunities to cry out to God for help and deliverance.

You may not be in deep anguish right now, but it's only a matter of time until your problems become so overwhelming that you will call on God for help. His love is unfailing, and God will deliver you.

God will bring deliverance by changing your circumstances. Sometimes God delivers you by miraculously altering your situation. For the Israelites, trapped between an angry army and an impassable sea, God split the Red Sea and then closed it back up again.

That will happen many times in your life, but it's not going to happen all the time.

God also uses personal deliverance. Instead of changing the circumstance, God changes the thing that needs the most change: you. God will change you on the inside, giving you a new dream, a new attitude, or a new perspective. For example, God may teach you more patience so you become less angry. When God delivers you from trouble, he is working in your life to make you more like Jesus.

God's ultimate deliverance is heaven. God has not promised to remove all of your pain or solve every problem. We live in a broken world, but the ultimate deliverance will come one day in heaven, where there is no more pain, sorrow, and suffering.

October

Hurry Is the Death of Prayer

"Be still in the presence of the Lord, and wait patiently for him to act."

PSALM 37:7 (NLT)

You can't hear God speak if you don't slow down long enough to listen. Hurry is the death of prayer! You've got to be quiet and wait patiently.

One way to do this is to wake up earlier and start your day with God. You'll be able to spend time with God without distractions tempting you to rush off and tackle your to-do list. Consider it the most important appointment of your day.

If you were told that tomorrow at 4:00 a.m. the Queen of England wanted to meet with you privately, you probably wouldn't go to bed tonight. You'd get all spiffed up with a new outfit and fresh haircut. You'd probably arrive 30 minutes early. Every other appointment on your calendar would take a backseat to your one-on-one appointment with the Queen!

The Creator of the universe wants to meet with you tomorrow morning! You don't even have to dress up or leave your home, but you do have to plan for it. That means you have to stop doing something in order to start doing what God wants. You have to decide what's more important: another 30 minutes of sleep or time with God?

No doubt that your day is filled with many important responsibilities, commitments, and activities. Your time with God is your most important appointment. Why? Because it will give you the insight, strength, and encouragement you need to fulfill God's purpose for your life.

God's Grace Will Get You Through

*"My purpose in writing is to encourage you and
assure you that what you are experiencing is truly
part of God's grace for you. Stand firm in his grace."*

1 PETER 5:12 (NLT)

Today, do you need encouragement?

If you feel like giving up, God is with you. He understands your situation completely because Jesus felt like giving up too. He will help you stand firm with his sustaining grace. If you stumble, he will lift you up.

You don't deserve it, and you can't earn it. His grace is a free gift.

God's sustaining grace gives you wisdom when you're tempted. The Bible promises that God will provide a way of escape when you're tempted. It may mean turning off your favorite show. It may mean leaving a situation. It may mean changing the way you're thinking. God will provide a way for you to escape temptation.

God's sustaining grace gives you energy when you're tired. Have you noticed the easy thing and the right thing are not always the same thing? God gives you the power to do the right thing when you're exhausted.

God's sustaining grace gives you comfort when you're troubled. God is with us through the suffering and the pain. These seasons are temporary, and eventually you will be fully restored. God will use you to comfort others out of the comfort you have received from him. God's sustaining grace will work in you, and then it will work through you.

Everything you are experiencing in life—both the highs and the lows—is under God's control. He is the One who is able to sustain you through his grace.

Your Mission Is Urgent

"We must quickly carry out the tasks assigned us by the one who sent us. The night is coming, and then no one can work."

JOHN 9:4 (NLT)

Your mission—the "tasks" assigned to you by God—has eternal significance because it will impact the eternal destinies of other people.

There are many priorities in your life, but none of them have eternal consequences like your mission does. Your mission is more important than any job, achievement, or goal you will reach during your life on earth. Nothing you do will ever matter as much as helping people establish an eternal relationship with God.

Our mission requires urgency, not just because it's important, but also because our time is limited. Here's the truth: Eternity without God is real; hell is not a myth. People who don't choose to live with Jesus in this life won't live with him in the next.

The clock is ticking on your life mission, so don't delay!

You were made for a mission. Where is God calling you to be the light in our dark world? Get started on your mission of reaching out to others. We will have all of eternity to celebrate with those we have brought to Jesus, but we only have our present life in which to reach them.

This does not mean you have to quit your job to become a full-time evangelist, missionary, or pastor— unless that is God's calling in your life. God wants you to share the Good News where you are. As a student, mother, preschool teacher, salesperson, manager, or whatever you do, you should continually look for people God places in your path with whom you can share the Gospel.

Wisdom Looks for the Lesson

"Instruct the wise and they will be wiser still;
teach the righteous and they will add to their learning."

PROVERBS 9:9 (NIV)

How do you typically respond to negative feedback?

After a pastor preached his first sermon at his new church, a guy walked over to him and said, "Pastor, that sermon stunk." The pastor was trying to be reasonable and open about it, and asked, "What didn't you like about it?" He replied, "In the first place, you read it. Second, you read it poorly. Third, it wasn't worth reading in the first place." Ouch!

If you want to be wise, you need to learn from others—even when they offer critical feedback. This isn't easy to do! Most of us are sensitive to receiving negative opinions. If somebody makes a suggestion, we often take it personally and get defensive. But a wise person can learn from anyone, even if their feedback is negative.

You can't teach yourself everything. Proverbs 12:15 says, *"A fool thinks he needs no advice, but a wise man listens to others"* (TLB). If something is true, listen and learn from it. If it's false, ignore it and forget it. The truth is, you have blind spots—everyone does. The only way you'll learn about them is from someone else telling you what they are.

Avoid being easily offended by others so you don't shut the door on learning something new.

Negative feedback can be painful, especially when it's personal. It's tempting to get defensive, but you'll become wise if you look for the lesson instead.

No Matter What

"If you openly declare that Jesus is Lord and believe in your heart that God raised him from the dead, you will be saved. For it is by believing in your heart that you are made right with God, and it is by openly declaring your faith that you are saved."

ROMANS 10:9-10 (NLT)

God wants to make you right with himself. How does he accomplish this?

God knows you can't make yourself perfect. Heaven is a perfect place without sadness, evil, or injustice. Here's the problem: You are sinful, and sin can't exist in the presence of God, which makes going to heaven by your own efforts impossible.

Therefore, God sent Jesus to pay for your sins so you could be declared righteous. The Gospel is called Good News because it means every sin you've ever committed or will commit has already been paid for by Jesus Christ on the cross. Through Jesus, you can be made right with God.

You have to accept by faith what Jesus did for you. When you confess your sins and believe in Christ, God promises that you will be forgiven and will become part of his family in heaven.

Today is the day to settle this. If you aren't sure you're going to heaven when you die, please pray this prayer:

"Dear God, thank you for making me and having a plan and purpose for my life. Today I confess my sins. I have wronged you, and I ask you to save me—not based on what I've done but based on what Jesus Christ did for me. I put my trust in your Son, Jesus. I put my trust in your grace, mercy, and forgiveness. I want Jesus to be the Lord of my life. Amen."

How to Worship When You Are Wounded

"Sing to the LORD! Praise the LORD! For though I was poor and needy, he rescued me from my oppressors."

JEREMIAH 20:13 (NLT)

Everybody has been wounded in life in different ways—not just physically, but also emotionally, spiritually, and relationally. In fact, those wounds are deeper than physical wounds. You don't remember the physical bumps, bruises, and scars you got growing up, but you do remember the verbal put-downs: "You're not going to amount to anything," or "You're no good." Those wounds stick with you.

The prophet Jeremiah knew what it was like to be wounded by others. He courageously shared God's Word with many people, only to be laughed at. Yet what did he do? He praised God, thanking him for his goodness.

The point is, there are a lot of things you can praise God for even when your life seems bleak. When you've been wounded emotionally, spiritually, or relationally, you can still do what Jeremiah did: Worship God in response to who he is, not in response to your circumstances.

Maybe you don't have a lot of reasons to be happy right now, but you do have every reason to worship God with joy. Worship him because he is compassionate, merciful, loving, and faithful; his love never runs out.

The next time you're overwhelmed by ridicule or rejection, be overwhelmed instead by the greatness of God and his love for you—which will move you to worship when you are wounded.

Seek First to Understand

"Be full of sympathy toward each other, loving one another with tender hearts and humble minds."

1 PETER 3:8 (NLT96)

Being a peacemaker requires sympathy and empathy.

When you're trying to resolve a conflict with someone, the starting point is to listen carefully so you can empathize with their feelings. Sympathy is saying, "I'm sorry you hurt." Empathy says, "I hurt with you."

When you value a relationship, work toward empathizing with the other person's doubts, fears, and interests. Their doubts may not be your doubts but try your best to empathize with them anyway. You may not have the same fears, but show sympathy and seek to understand their concerns. Whatever they are interested in, show interest in it too.

When somebody is hurting you, they don't need a lecture; they need a listener. The reason people hurt others is because they're hurting inside. That's why you have to look beyond the hurt that you're experiencing and ask, "What is hurting them inside that's causing them to hurt me?" This is hard work, because when you are angry, you are naturally focused on yourself. In order to be a peacemaker, you have to make a mental shift.

When you sit down with a person you've had conflict with, take the lead and say, "We're not going to avoid it anymore. We're not going to just appease each other and pretend everything is okay. Let's deal with it." One of the real values of conflict is that when you resolve it, it always creates greater understanding. The very thing that you think is often going to separate you, will actually bring you closer and make your relationship stronger.

In order to get to the issue and become a peacemaker, learn to sympathize and empathize with others.

Love Turns Work into Ministry

"Our people must learn to spend their time doing good, in order to provide for real needs; they should not live useless lives."

TITUS 3:14 (GNT)

Work is important, but the reason why might surprise you.

If you're a believer, the way you approach work should be totally different from the way everybody else approaches work. Many people watch the clock, eager for the day to be over. Their work is endured and rarely enjoyed.

The truth is, work isn't a necessary evil. Actually, it's a gift from God. We were created for work because work is about doing good and providing for real needs.

You don't have to be a pastor or missionary to do ministry. The parable of the Good Samaritan (Luke 10:25-37) is about a man who wasn't a religious leader, yet he did good while working. As he was traveling, he saw a person in need, helped him, and carried on with his business.

No matter what kind of work you do, you serve God by serving others. In fact, service is the pathway to real significance. It is through ministry that you discover the meaning of your life.

God wants to work through you to serve others. The key is not what you do, but how you do it. When you do your work with an attitude of love, your work becomes a ministry. When you see your work as an opportunity to serve God, your attitude will change.

How would your attitude at work be different if you viewed it as a ministry?

Don't Doubt Your Salvation

"I write these things to you who believe in the name of the Son of God so that you may know that you have eternal life."

1 JOHN 5:13 (NIV)

As a believer, you don't need to live in fear or worry. God doesn't want you to wonder whether or not you'll be in heaven with him. God does not want you to doubt your salvation.

The apostle John made it clear: If you believe in Jesus, you can know for certain that you have eternal life. In this life, God won't answer every one of your questions. But the question about your eternal security is answered with a resounding "yes!"

What does it mean to believe in the Son of God? The best place to turn is John 3:16 because the entire Bible can be summarized in this single verse. In fact, its very structure illustrates the Gospel. The word "Son" is in the middle of this verse, making it a bridge. The first twelve words are all about God, and the last twelve words are all about you.

"For God so loved the world, that he gave his only begotten Son, that whosoever believeth in him should not perish, but have everlasting life" (John 3:16 KJV).

In God's plan, Jesus is the bridge between God and you. God is on one side, humanity is on the other, and Jesus Christ came to earth to bring them together. He's the bridge over troubled waters. He's the mediator between God and man. Jesus came to bring us into relationship with God.

This is the most important message in the history of the world.

Your salvation is based on God's promises and his character, so you can live in the freedom and security of eternity.

Develop an Active Faith

"I pray you may be active in sharing your faith, so that you will have a full understanding of every good thing we have in Christ."

PHILEMON 1:6 (NIV)

What if you had the cure for cancer and didn't tell anyone about it?

Followers of Jesus have something even more important to share than a cure: salvation. *"For it is by grace you have been saved, through faith—and this is not from yourselves, it is the gift of God—not by works, so that no one can boast"* (Ephesians 2:8-9 NIV). In Jesus, your past is forgiven, you have a purpose for living, and your future is secure in heaven.

Would you agree that the world is less than perfect? The solution is Jesus. God is calling you to actively share your faith.

Maybe you feel like you're in a spiritual slump. Sharing your faith deepens your understanding of all the good things you have in Christ. It's important to remember all the ways God has blessed you in order to get out of a spiritual rut.

You might think, "I'm not a pastor or a missionary," and you rationalize slipping into a passive faith. In God's family, it's true that everyone has different roles. Yet, everyone is called to have an active faith.

What does an active faith look like? Praying for the people you know who don't have a relationship with Jesus. Telling others your story—how you came to know Jesus and how your life was transformed since that day. Inviting them to attend church with you. Asking them about their beliefs. Giving them a Bible or a Christian book about what it means to follow Jesus. God will tell you how to share your faith; your responsibility is to be willing.

Who is going to be in heaven because you lived an active faith and shared it with them?

You Don't Need to Pretend Anymore

"I have gained perfect freedom by following your teachings."

PSALM 119:45 (CEV)

Everywhere you look, you can find people who like to pretend.

It's not a game; they aren't children who are playing make-believe. They're adults pretending to be someone other than themselves in order to get the approval of others. Seeking approval typically plays out in one of two ways.

Some are trying to meet the expectations of someone else, and that means they're allowing their purpose in life to be defined by someone other than God. This is a dangerous way to live because people's expectations are inconsistent.

Other people are trying to meet their own unrealistic expectations of perfectionism. That's when you think you must be perfect to be loved and accepted. Inevitably, we fall short of being perfect, so the only option that makes sense is to fake it.

Are you pretending? Maybe you've been pretending for so long that you don't know who the real you is anymore. You're wearing a mask, and it's wearing you out. Everyone else thinks you've got plenty of money, success, and happiness.

When you stop to think about it, you know the truth: You're exhausted.

What's the antidote for pretending? Stop focusing on what others think and start focusing on what God thinks.

Only one person knows you completely and still loves you unconditionally: God. He knows your purpose because it's what he's created you to do. Living for God rather than the approval of others simplifies your life.

Enjoy the peace of living for an audience of one.

God Will Make a Masterpiece

*"GOD always does what he says, and is gracious in
everything he does. GOD gives a hand to those down on
their luck, gives a fresh start to those ready to quit."*

PSALM 145:13-14 (THE MESSAGE)

God is gracious in everything he does—you can build your life on that promise. But God never said that everything in your life will be good. We live on a broken planet, and terrible, heartbreaking things happen every day.

Your body is broken; it doesn't always work the right way. Your mind is broken; it doesn't always think the right way. The weather is broken, the economy's broken, and relationships are broken.

God has not promised perfection—not until heaven, where there will be no sorrow, sadness, sickness, or suffering. You can't expect heaven on earth because the earth is filled with brokenness.

Sometimes the brokenness of the world leads to bitterness in the heart. We know things could be better, that they should be better, but they aren't.

This might describe your life right now. Maybe you're so bitter you want to quit. But remember this: God has a good plan for your life.

Have you noticed that when you make a cake, most of the ingredients on their own don't taste good? Flour, by itself, does not taste good. Raw eggs, vanilla, and salt taste terrible on their own. However, when they are all mixed together, you can create a tasty masterpiece.

When you let God work all the "ingredients" of your life together—the good and the bad—he will make a masterpiece. God takes the bitter, puts it in the batter, and makes you better.

Don't quit! God is greater than all of the bad things that happen. Allow God to give you a fresh start. He can use everything in your life—even the bitter and broken things.

Make Your Suffering Significant

*"We can rejoice, too, when we run into problems and trials,
for we know that they help us develop endurance."*

ROMANS 5:3 (NLT)

Redemptive suffering is when someone suffers for the benefit of other people. It's what Jesus did for you. When he suffered and died on the cross, he wasn't paying for his sins because he didn't have any. He was paying for our sins.

When you experience suffering, you decide if it will be redemptive or not.

You may have heard the story of Joseph from the Old Testament. His brothers were jealous, so they sold him into slavery. Later, he was unjustly accused and thrown into prison. God was working in his life, and he eventually became the second-in-command in Egypt.

Years after their betrayal, Joseph confronted his brothers and said, *"You intended to harm me, but God intended it all for good. He brought me to this position so I could save the lives of many people"* (Genesis 50:20 NLT).

You might be in the middle of a season filled with problems and trials. The world may mean you harm, but God will use everything for good. Joy is possible during seasons of pain. Joy in life depends on what you know, not what you experience. Our trials develop us so we can help others.

God will never waste a hurt. God will work in your life so that he can work through your life to impact others.

Praise God and rejoice during a trial, because suffering will build your endurance and help others in their pain.

You're Never Persuasive When You're Abrasive

"A wise, mature person is known for his understanding. The more pleasant his words, the more persuasive he is."

PROVERBS 16:21 (GNT)

If you were in the market for a new car, wouldn't you rather talk to a salesperson who was present and available for questions than to an obnoxious one? That's not even a choice! When you are making an important decision, you don't want someone in your face pushing their agenda.

It takes wisdom and maturity to speak persuasively. The key is to use pleasant words so that you don't offend others.

Proverbs 25:15 says, *"Gentle speech breaks down rigid defenses"* (The Message). How do you get through to a family member whose guard is always up? Use words that are pleasant and gentle. Do everything you can to keep from offending them. You can do this by making the effort to understand where they are coming from. Empathy always wins.

We are often abrasive when we are angry. Anger doesn't have to result in sin. Take some time to calm down so that you can speak with gentleness.

If you want to help people live for Jesus, talk to them in a gentle way. If your approach is "Let me tell you all the things that you're doing wrong," you'll build all kinds of barriers. Be persuasive by using words that build up and encourage. People already feel guilty, they don't need you to make them feel worse.

You're never persuasive when you're abrasive.

To Serve Others, Open Your Eyes

"Look out for the good of others."

1 CORINTHIANS 10:24 (NCV)

In order to help others, you need to slow down to actually see people. You need to do more than just notice and acknowledge them. You need to be fully present so that you can truly see them. If you don't take the time to look at others, you'll never know how to be sensitive to their needs.

There are people all around you who need your encouragement.

If you were to take a cross-country trip, you would have several options for travel. A plane would get you there the fastest, but you wouldn't see much of the country. You could take a train or even a car, and both would give you opportunities to see more than by flying. If you really wanted to take in as much as possible, you'd walk.

The slower you go, the more you see.

Looking out for others is a choice you need to make—it won't happen automatically. You need to ask God to give you the "spiritual radar" to be on the lookout for people around you who are hurting emotionally, spiritually, or physically.

It's not always easy to see the needs of other people. Sometimes we are too focused on our own problems to see when others are hurting. At times we lack awareness because our schedule is overloaded.

The truth is, you were created to serve God by helping others. In doing so, you are fulfilling the law of Christ. But you can't help someone with their burden if you don't see it.

If you care, you'll be aware.

What's So Good About the Good News?

"Go into all the world and preach the Good News to everyone."

MARK 16:15 (NLT)

Every Christian is called to share the Good News. It's the story of God's gift of salvation through the Crucifixion and Resurrection of Jesus Christ. You may be thinking, "My friends and the people I work with aren't interested in the Good News."

You're dead wrong! Though they may not be interested in religion, they are interested in the Good News. The problem isn't their lack of interest; the problem is that you may have forgotten how good the Good News really is.

When you've been a Christian for a while, it's easy to forget how miserable you were when you lived with no hope. You forget what it was like to not know where you'll go when you die. You forget what it was like to live with guilt, fear, regrets, bitterness, and boredom—a life before Christ that lacked meaning, purpose, and significance.

As you share the Good News, you'll discover that most people think they have to work really hard and be really good to get God's approval. They think they've got to be religious by keeping a lot of rules. If that's what the Good News is, no wonder they don't get excited about discussing it.

But here's the truth about the Good News: You are able to enter into a relationship with God by trusting in Jesus Christ—not through a religion of rules, regulations, and rituals.

God says you get to know him just by trusting him. If you trust his Son with your life, you get forgiveness for your past, a purpose for living, and a home in heaven forever.

Think about the people you come into contact with every day. Who needs to hear the Good News?

We're in It Together

*"People should be concerned about others
and not just about themselves."*

1 CORINTHIANS 10:24 (GW)

We are all interconnected because that's the way God designed us.

Like ripples in a pond, every decision you make affects someone else. First, it changes you, and then you influence other people. In most cases, the impact can be positive, but every time you're irresponsible, it hurts someone else too.

The choices you make influence your family and friends, neighbors, and coworkers. For instance, when someone in your family is dealing with a problem, it's not just their problem; it's the family's problem. When dad's under stress, it affects everybody in the family. Every decision has consequences.

Imagine you go out on a rowboat with a friend. It's a good-sized boat, and you each have plenty of your own space. You row out to the middle of the lake and just relax for a while. Then your friend starts drilling a hole in the bottom of the boat in their side. You say, "What are you doing? You can't do that!" Your friend says, "Don't worry about it. It's my life. This is my side of the boat, and I'm not drilling it on your side." You respond, "But you don't understand: We're in the same boat. If the boat goes down, we're both going down with it."

When we are irresponsible, the two most common excuses we give are, "Nobody will know about it," and "It won't hurt anybody." You're wrong on both counts. Until you learn how to be concerned for others, and not just yourself, you will continue to rationalize your poor decisions.

You need to be responsible because your decisions will impact others.

God Is Good and Loving

*"Surely your goodness and love will follow me all the days of my life,
and I will dwell in the house of the LORD forever."*

PSALM 23:6 (NIV)

Do you believe that God is good and loving?

Knowing the truth about God corrects our thinking. This is important because there are many misconceptions about God. He's not an angry judge, ready to punish us. God is not like a vending machine, where we can choose what we want to get from him. He isn't a bad father who is distant and uncaring.

Believing the truth about God will clarify your prayers. The sincere, heart-felt acceptance of God's goodness and love will lead to prayers that are more powerful, passionate, and purposeful.

Living in view of the truth about God will change your perspective. When bad times come, you will be comforted because God is always good and loving. You will also remember to put your hope in the promise of heaven.

When good times come, you will be thankful to God because he has blessed you out of his goodness and love. No matter how many blessings you have, you won't love the gifts more than the gift giver.

God's goodness and love are not abstract concepts, for they meet us in our everyday lives. David said they will *"follow [you] all the days of [your] life"* because God wants you to experience and love him for who he really is.

Serving Is the Key to Better Relationships

"Your attitude must be like my own, for I, the Messiah, did not come to be served, but to serve, and to give my life as a ransom for many."

MATTHEW 20:28 (TLB)

The root of most relational problems is self-centeredness. When you want it your way and the other person wants it their way—and neither of you will budge—the result is conflict. You need a new perspective.

Perspective comes from serving. When you are committed to helping others, because of what Jesus has done in your life, your mindset will change—and your relationships will get better.

God wants you to learn how to be unselfish. It's a lifelong course of study! Unfortunately, so many people spend their entire lives without even enrolling in the class. You can change that and learn to be unselfish by acting like Jesus.

Next time you read about the life of Jesus, notice how he dealt with others.

He always put others before himself. When you take on his attitude, you live your life not for your benefit—but for the benefit of others. Jesus consistently modeled this throughout the Gospels.

Learn to put the needs of others before your own. This attitude requires humility, and it isn't easy. But it's the only antidote to selfishness.

When you serve, you'll not only become more like Jesus, you'll actually become more respected and loved by your friends. People want to be around those who are serving others—this character trait is attractive because it's uncommon.

Jesus teaches us that serving is the key to better relationships.

You Can Be Right with God

"The Good News shows how God makes people right with himself."

ROMANS 1:17 (NCV)

Righteousness is a big word in the Bible. It's used hundreds of times. God loves righteousness and God is righteous. He leads us in paths of righteousness and will one day judge the world in righteousness. What does this important word really mean? Righteousness means being right with God.

This is the Good News: God made us right with himself through Jesus' death as payment for our sins. A convicted criminal begs on his knees before the king, but a redeemed criminal is able to stand upright because he is no longer guilty.

Why should you care about being right with God?

Righteousness is the way you get to heaven. God wants you to be in heaven with him, but we can't be righteous on our own—we need Jesus. *"Indeed, there is no one on earth who is righteous, no one who does what is right and never sins"* (Ecclesiastes 7:20 NIV). God isn't going to force you into heaven; you have to choose to love him back. Once your life here is done, you won't have a second chance to decide where you'll spend eternity.

Righteousness is also a lifestyle. Once you have been made right with God, he wants you to live an upright life. The righteous life is one that pleases God. Why should you care about living righteously?

Life is about getting to know God. It's not about acquisition, achievement, or finding pleasure. Those things don't bring life. Real life is only found in living according to God's will.

God is calling you to righteousness. How will you respond?

Don't Wait for Perfect Conditions

"If you wait for perfect conditions, you will never get anything done."

ECCLESIASTES 11:4 (TLB)

Is your spiritual life in a rut? Do you feel like you aren't getting anything done or moving in the right direction?

If you are waiting for perfect conditions, you'll be waiting forever! Stop procrastinating and get started today. There will never be an ideal time for you to get control of your calendar, your circumstances, or your relationships.

Sure, there are seasons in life when you need to pause. There are times you need to be still, especially before you make a big decision. However, waiting on God doesn't mean wasting the opportunities he's provided. When you know what God wants you to do, you need to get started on it.

If you're thinking, "When things settle down, then I'll start a daily quiet time, spend more time with my kids, join a small group, restore that broken relationship, or work on my goals."

You need to realize the truth: Things will never settle down.

Life is like a train that runs on two tracks, with good things and bad things happening simultaneously. Life's circumstances are never all good or all bad. You can't wait for perfect conditions; they are a myth, for they give a false hope that will never come, not on this side of eternity.

Don't waste another minute waiting for ideal circumstances to come your way. Just get started today!

How to Live by God's Power

"For the Kingdom of God is not just a lot of talk;
it is living by God's power."

1 CORINTHIANS 4:20 (NLT)

Talk is cheap. Why? Because anyone can learn the right things to say.

It's easy to fall into an attitude that says, "Never let them see you sweat." And so we project a false image to the world. When you go to church or show up to small group, you can sound as if everything in your life is great, but are you really living by God's power?

Imagine waking up in the morning, and as you think about the challenges of your day, you were reminded that you didn't have to face it all alone. You can live by God's power, and it is more than sufficient for your needs.

God's power created the universe and it is greater than life and death.

His power can handle any challenge or issue you are facing. God cares about your big problems and your small problems because they are all small to him. God's power is available to you by believing in Jesus. The more you live according to his Word and trust in his promises, the more you will be living in God's power.

God is not interested in you becoming more self-reliant. He is calling for your surrender; he wants you to be dependent on him. We don't have enough power to handle everything life throws at us. We can try, but we'll end up frustrated, exhausted, and unfulfilled.

Today, will you choose to live by God's power?

Acceptance Doesn't Mean Approval

*"Accept each other just as Christ has accepted you
so that God will be given glory."*

ROMANS 15:7 (NLT)

One way to love others is to accept them as Jesus has accepted you.

Jesus didn't wait for you to clean up your act before inviting you into his family. Jesus accepted you just as you were. Accepting others is difficult, especially when there's a difference in personality or a relational conflict. When you struggle with accepting others, remember how Christ has accepted you. Do you want to show great love? First recognize your own "many sins," and ask God for his forgiveness every day.

There is a big difference between acceptance and approval. You are called to accept everyone, but you are not called to approve of what everyone does. It doesn't matter *what* people have done, *who* they've done it with, *how* long they've done it, or *where* they've done it. You are called to accept them. God loves you, but it doesn't mean he approves of everything you do. God always begins with acceptance. After the gift is received, he helps us to become more like Jesus. When we accept others, God gets the glory.

This means God gets all the credit! You might have a difficult time talking to others about Jesus, but you can show your faith by accepting them unconditionally. When people outside of God's family experience radical acceptance, they get to see just how good God really is. What a powerful statement in our divided world!

Everyone is looking for acceptance; offer it freely as Jesus did to you.

God Wired You to Make a Difference

*"I glorified you on earth by completing down
to the last detail what you assigned me to do."*

JOHN 17:4 (THE MESSAGE)

Jesus came to earth with a mission. God has a mission for your life, too.

God has given you unique talents and abilities to benefit others, and he's gifted others with talents and abilities to benefit you. If you don't share your talents with those around you, they will be cheated. If they don't share their talents with you, you'll miss out.

For instance, you can be grateful for people who are talented in areas you're not. If you struggle with money management and filling out your tax return, isn't it great that God created people who are good at math and accounting? You can also be grateful for people who have mechanical skills, particularly if you don't even know what a carburetor is.

If you make the best chocolate chip cookies in your neighborhood, then God gave you that gift to share with others. Maybe you're a great teacher, but how can you use that talent if you don't teach others?

Everything in our society says, "It's all about me." Yet nothing could be further from the truth! God is calling you to use your gifts to help others. Jesus glorified God by fulfilling his mission. God wants you to follow his example.

How has God gifted you? How can you use your gifts to be a blessing to others?

Grateful Prayer Brings Peace

"In all your prayers ask God for what you need, always asking him with a thankful heart. And God's peace, which is far beyond human understanding, will keep your hearts and minds safe in union with Christ Jesus."

PHILIPPIANS 4:6-7 (GNT)

How much peace do you have in your life?

True peace comes when you ask God for what you need with a thankful heart.

You can trust God to meet all of your needs! Time and time again, God demonstrated in the Bible that he is our Provider. He has provided for our physical, mental, emotional, and spiritual needs.

We get frustrated when we don't get everything we want, but we can trust God to give us everything we need.

You need to pray with an attitude of thankfulness. Parents understand the power of gratitude. They want to hear their children say "thank you" when they give them what they need. Your heavenly Father also wants you to ask for what you need—*with a grateful heart.*

Gratitude keeps our requests from becoming demands because thankfulness is the antidote to entitlement.

The way to pray is to be specific with your requests and your gratitude.

Instead of asking God, "Will you help me today?" pray, "Help me have a good attitude when I see Cindy today." Instead of saying to God, "Thank you for everything," tell God exactly why you are grateful: "Thank you for my family because they are a great support."

God promises you a peace that is far beyond human understanding—nothing the world offers can even come close. To receive God's gift of peace, you must ask for help, with a grateful heart.

Be a Blessing

"I will bless you . . . and you will be a blessing."

GENESIS 12:2 (NIV)

Some people are like reservoirs. They collect God's blessings without letting them overflow to others. Other people are like a pipeline. They receive God's blessings and say, "God, help other people through me."

God gives you far more blessings when you're like a pipeline than when you're like a reservoir.

The Bible teaches that we are blessed so we can bless others. The purpose of our blessings is not to feel good, be happy, and live comfortably. God will do good *in* your life so he can do good *through* your life.

The more you bless and help other people, the more God blesses your life. You cannot out-give God. The more you try to bless other people around you, the more God says, "I'm going to pour blessings on you."

How do you bless others? You don't need to figure out by yourself, you can follow God's example. Anything God has done good in your life, you can reflect that good to others. God has forgiven you, so you can bless others with forgiveness. God pays attention to you, so you can bless others with your attention. God has given you material blessings, so you can pass that on to others who are in need. Everything good in your life can be passed on to others—you can be a pipeline of blessings from God to others!

This is one reason it's important to remember and think about how God has been good to us: so we'll be encouraged to do good to others in the same way.

Blessing others is a mindset, a lifelong habit to practice and develop. The more God blesses us, the more he expects us to help others.

Today, are you going to be like a reservoir or a pipeline?

Change Is a Choice

"Put on your new nature, and be renewed as you learn to know your Creator and become like him."

COLOSSIANS 3:10 (NLT)

Change requires a choice. It's not enough to dream about changing. In order for you to actually change, you need to make a decision and commit to it.

Are you going to be any different in six months or a year from now? Are you going to be healthier, stronger, and more mature? Are you going to be in less debt? Are you going to be more like the person God wants you to be?

It will only happen if you choose to change; it isn't going to happen accidentally. Your life doesn't have an autopilot that will passively lead you to become more like Jesus. You have to put in the effort to work alongside the Holy Spirit. This means you'll have to let go of some old things in order to grab hold of the new.

Take eating and exercise for example. There comes a time when you have to let go of that donut and grab hold of an apple. Or you may need to say "no" to binge watching "just one more episode" and say "yes" to a workout.

You're only one decision away from starting a new habit.

You may be stuck in the middle because you haven't let go of the old patterns, habits, and ways of thinking. The Bible says to throw them off and trust that God is changing you from the inside out with his Holy Spirit.

God is waiting on you to say, "Yes, Lord, I'm willing to make these changes."

What's the next decision you need to make?

Meekness Does Not Equal Weakness

"Blessed are the meek, for they will inherit the earth."

MATTHEW 5:5 (NIV)

The Bible lists many benefits of meekness: The meek will be satisfied; God will guide them; they will become wise; they will be filled with fresh joy.

The problem is that we misunderstand the term. Most of us don't really know what meekness means. In fact, we often confuse it with "weakness." Nobody wants to be weak, so they think they don't want to be meek.

The truth is meekness and weakness are at the opposite ends of the spectrum. In fact, the Greek word for meekness means "strength under control." It's used to describe a wild stallion that has been tamed. That stallion still has all the strength it had when it was wild, but now its strength is under control. It is strength bottled up for the master's use. God doesn't want you to be weak, but he does want you to be meek.

Here's a simple definition of the word meek: Let go and let God. Let go of controlling your life, and let God have control. It is surrendering, submitting, and agreeing to what God wants to do in your life. It's letting God be God.

There isn't a phrase that will do more for your health physically or emotionally than "let go and let God." If you'll begin to practice it in your life, it will relieve stress, eliminate worry, defuse anger, and dissolve resentment.

Where do you need to let go and let God?

Wisdom Is a Lifestyle

"Who is wise and understanding among you? Let them show it by their good life, by deeds done in the humility that comes from wisdom."

JAMES 3:13 (NIV)

What comes to your mind when you think of wisdom?

Wisdom has nothing to do with your intelligence or education. It has everything to do with your relationships and your character. Wisdom is a lifestyle; it's more than words or wishes.

Solomon could have asked God for anything, but he asked for wisdom. God was so impressed with his request, he said, "Solomon, I'm going to grant it. You're not only going to be the wisest man in the world; you will also be wealthy, famous, and powerful." Wisdom is the key to everything else you want in life.

Many of society's high achievers are viewed as smart and successful—or "wise" in what they do—but they lack humility. The "wisdom" of the world leads to pride, which says, "Look at everything I have done!"

Many people have a misunderstanding of humility. They think that humility means putting yourself down, saying, "I'm no good. I'm not worthwhile. I can't do anything right." That's not it at all.

Humility doesn't mean thinking less of yourself; it means thinking of yourself less.

Humility is being honest about your weaknesses and recognizing your strengths as gifts from God. Not only was Paul honest about his strengths, he was also honest about his weaknesses. In fact, he was so honest, he wrote them down for posterity. You can read about them 2,000 years later. He said, "I'm weak in this area. I have this problem." Your strengths enable you to fulfill God's purpose for your life, and your areas of weakness keep you dependent on him.

You need to make wisdom your lifestyle. God wants you to have a good life filled with good deeds that are done in humility.

How to Love the Unlovable

"Be joyful. Grow to maturity. Encourage each other. Live in harmony and peace. Then the God of love and peace will be with you."

2 CORINTHIANS 13:11 (NLT)

You likely have people in your life who get on your nerves. They might be selfish, prideful, obnoxious, or even offensive, but their effect on you is the same: You dread interacting with them.

Are you ready for a hard truth? God wants you to live in harmony and peace with others—even the difficult people in your life. When it comes to personal relationships, God says, "Don't be so easily offended. Learn to get over it so you can live in harmony with others."

But this isn't easy! How can we be kind and compassionate toward difficult people?

No one is perfect, and that includes you. You'll be able to love the unlovable if you remember that there are times when you are unlovable, too! If you expect perfection from people, not only is this irrational, but you're going to get frustrated. The Bible basically says, "Cut them some slack so you can keep the peace."

Another key to loving the unlovable is to look past their behavior and see the pain and insecurity motivating their actions. Everyone has a past that prompts their present behavior. That doesn't excuse their actions, but greater understanding paves the way for greater compassion and empathy.

You will always have people in your life who annoy or offend you. As a follower of Christ, you are called to live in harmony with them, forgiving them because God has forgiven you.

Where Is God Working?

"When the LORD saw Moses coming to take a closer look, God called to him from the middle of the bush, 'Moses! Moses!' 'Here I am!' Moses replied."

EXODUS 3:4 (NLT)

What commands your attention?

Every year, companies spend billions of dollars in order to capture your focus. They appeal to every emotion possible: fear, happiness, desire, lust—because they know that if they have your attention, they have you. When your thoughts are dominated by movies, politics, the news, and the infinite scroll of your social media, you're not the best version of yourself.

What if your attention was on God?

One day, Moses was tending his father-in-law's sheep—he'd been doing it for 40 years. When he led the flock into the wilderness, Moses saw a burning bush—and decided to go check it out.

When God saw Moses approaching, he called to him: "Moses! Moses!" The bush wasn't even burning up! More than the flames, what made the bush extraordinary? God called to him from the middle of it, to which Moses replied, *"Here I am!"*

God is waiting for you to move in close before he calls you by name.

What does this mean for you? In the midst of your routine, when you least expect it, God will surprise you with an invitation to come to him. But you will have to be on the lookout for him.

There are many times in the Bible when people ignored God's call because they were too distracted by other, less important things.

Be on the lookout for God, and when he calls your name, respond like Moses and say, *"Here I am."*

November

God's Recipe for Significance

"Speak up for those who cannot speak for themselves, for the rights of all who are destitute. Speak up and judge fairly; defend the rights of the poor and needy."

PROVERBS 31:8-9 (NIV)

How do you use your influence?

Our natural inclination is to first help ourselves and the people we love. However, God is calling us to go beyond our instincts. He wants us to help the people who need it most—those who have no voice, no one to defend them, and no access to the basic necessities of life.

Think about how radical this command is: Help people who can't help you back.

This is true servanthood, and it's God's recipe for significance. When you help the poor, you will honor God and be blessed. You will also gain respect from others, which will open up doors of opportunity to serve the poor even more.

If someone asked you, "Does God have favorites?" you'd probably say, "No. He treats everybody equally." You'd be wrong because the Bible clearly states that God does have favorites. God favors the poor. They are the ones who get stomped on, get ignored, and get bypassed. God says if you care about my favorite people, then I'm going to take care of your needs. God blesses those who bless the poor.

In fact, God says the acid test of your faith is not how many Bible verses you memorize or how often you say, "Praise the Lord!" The acid test of your faith is how you treat people in unfortunate circumstances.

Take a moment to do an inventory of your influence. How can you help those who can't help themselves?

Your Faith Keeps You Going

---

*"We are pressed on every side by troubles, but we are not crushed.
We are perplexed, but not driven to despair. We are hunted down, but never
abandoned by God. We get knocked down, but we are not destroyed."*

---

2 CORINTHIANS 4:8-9 (NLT)

Faith unlocks the promises of God and gives you the power to hold on in tough times.

But it's important to understand that just because you have faith, God won't necessarily take you out of difficult circumstances. He may leave you in the circumstances to grow your faith.

Corrie ten Boom was a young Dutch Christian. She helped many Jews escape the Holocaust during World War II; for that reason, she was sent to a Nazi concentration camp. She said the people in those camps who refused to give up were the ones with deepest

faith. Why? Because faith gives you the power to hold on in tough times.

It's this resilience that gives you the ability to bounce back and to keep going. Nobody goes through life with an unbroken chain of successes. Everybody experiences failures and makes mistakes. The resilience that comes from faith gives you the ability to keep going because you believe God can do something at any moment to change the direction of your life. It means you faithfully believe that he will give you exactly what you need—when you need it—as you rely on him to accomplish his purposes in your life.

Be Wise with Your Words

"The tongue is a small thing, but what enormous damage it can do. A great forest can be set on fire by one tiny spark. The tongue . . . can turn our whole lives into a blazing flame of destruction and disaster."

JAMES 3:5-6 (TLB)

When we don't have self-control in our life, we're vulnerable to all kinds of problems.

Anything out of control in your life can harm other people and damage your close relationships. Uncontrolled anger, lust, addiction, spending, drinking, or ambition can create enormous problems. But the greatest destroyer of relationships is an uncontrolled tongue.

The average person has 30 conversations a day. That means you will spend one-fifth of your life talking. At some point, your mouth will probably get you into trouble. The odds are against you!

James compares the tongue to a tiny spark because that's all that is needed to create a great forest fire. A careless word can ignite your relationships and make them all go up in smoke.

Have you ever met a verbal arsonist?

Their words are dangerous. They use words of discouragement, disappointment, accusation, criticism, sarcasm, condemnation, or attack . . . the list is endless. Gossip is especially destructive because it spreads like an airborne virus. Careless words have destroyed careers, friendships, and families.

Instead, use your words to build others up. Catch people doing something right and tell them about it. Affirm their character when they make difficult decisions. Lift them up with words of encouragement. Building others up with your words isn't difficult, but in our world, it is uncommon.

You reflect God's glory in a dark world when you control your mouth and build others up.

You Have Just Enough Time to Do God's Will

"In the beginning God created the heavens and the earth."

GENESIS 1:1 (NIV)

If you feel overworked, overloaded, and overscheduled, this may be the most significant truth you'll ever read: *You have just enough time to do God's will.*

As the Creator of the heavens and the earth, God's presence and power are unparalleled; his planning is perfect.

If you don't think you have enough time in your day, one of two things is true: Either you're doing things God doesn't intend for you to do, or you're doing things God intends, but in the wrong way. God wouldn't give you a list of things to do, and then not give you the time to do them.

If you feel like you don't have enough time, either you're trying to do too much, or you're wasting time. Either way, you aren't living according to God's plan; you are following your own plans.

Sometimes we try to do too much because of "when and then" thinking. We believe *when* we achieve a particular goal, *then* we will be happy. The happiness lasts about three seconds, so we jump back on the hamster wheel to chase after the next thing we think will make us happy.

God made you, and he knows what you were made to do.

When we waste our time, typically it's because we aren't doing what God has called us to do, in the way that he wants us to do it. Your time is limited; once it's spent, you won't get it back. It's not enough to do what God wants; you also have to do it in the way God wants it done.

Are you worn out, burned, or stressed out?

What needs to change?

Act on Your Dreams

"Be careful how you act; these are difficult days. Don't be fools; be wise: make the most of every opportunity you have for doing good. Don't act thoughtlessly, but try to find out and do whatever the Lord wants you to."

EPHESIANS 5:15-17 (TLB)

Everyone has a dream. Desires and ambitions are a natural part of life. The question isn't whether you have a dream, but rather, "What are you doing with your dream?"

Most dreams never come true. It has nothing to do with how smart, outgoing, or spiritual you are. Usually, your dreams don't come true because you're unwilling to take the necessary risks to reach them. When you play it safe, you aren't making *"the most of every opportunity you have for doing good."*

The Bible shares a sad, one-sentence commentary about a king who failed to achieve an important ambition in his life: *"Jehoshaphat built a fleet of trading ships to go to Ophir for gold, but they never set sail—they were wrecked at Ezion Geber"* (1 Kings 22:48 NIV).

While it's a tragedy for your ship to never come in, it's a greater tragedy for you to build a ship and never set sail. King Jehoshaphat built an entire fleet of ships to go after gold, and not one of them got out of the harbor. Evidently a storm came up and, while these ships were in the harbor, they were slammed against the rocks and were destroyed.

Some people spend their whole lives waiting for their ship to come. But God is waiting for you to sail your ship out of the harbor.

Ask God what he wants to do with your dreams, trusting that he is with you all the way. He wants you to live a life where you take risks based on faith, sailing toward the dreams he's given you.

What Prayer Isn't

"One day Jesus was praying in a certain place. When he finished, one of his disciples said to him, 'Lord, teach us to pray.'"

LUKE 11:1 (NIV)

Frustrations with prayer are usually caused by misconceptions about prayer.

God's Word shatters the common myths about prayer. Prayer is not a magic wand. Prayer isn't an instant fix that will change all of your circumstances. God loves you unconditionally, but he doesn't respond to your prayers with "Your wish is my command." We serve God, not the other way around.

Prayer is not a fire extinguisher with a sign that says, "Break glass in case of emergency." It's easy to pray on the bad days—when you need help. You also need to pray on the good days. Prayer isn't the last option after you've tried everything else; it ought to be your first choice.

Prayer isn't a tug of war, where if you win, then God will listen to you.

God wants to listen to and answer your prayers. This misconception turns prayer into a transaction, where you beg, bribe, and bargain: "God, if you do this, I will do that." God doesn't want your prayer to resemble a transaction, but instead be the catalyst for transformation.

Prayer is not a ritual to relieve guilt. You don't need to say the same prayer over and over again to remove your guilt. Prayer is not a punishment for sin. It's a privilege, not a duty. Prayer ought to be joyful—even in the difficult times—not a way to pay penance to God.

Prayer is simply a conversation with God. Talk to your heavenly Father. Tell him what's on your heart and you will receive the mercy and grace that you need today.

God's Love for You Will Never End

*"The mountains and hills may crumble,
but my love for you will never end."*

ISAIAH 54:10 (GNT)

You don't need to ever doubt God's love for you.

His love for you is perfect and complete. You don't need to earn it—you can't! You don't need to worry about losing his love—you can't do that either! God's love for you is eternal and inescapable. It's not possible for him to love you any more—or any less. God's love is not based on who you are or what you do; his love is based on who he is.

His love for you is unconditional. You are completely accepted by God, just as you are. Many people spend much of their lives trying to earn acceptance from their parents, peers, those they respect and envy, and even total strangers. God has already settled the issue of your acceptance. What Jesus did on the cross made you completely acceptable to God—no matter what you've done or will do. God doesn't say, "I love you if . . . " or "I love you because . . ." He says, "I love you—period!"

You're immeasurably valuable to God. If you ever question your value to God, look to the cross. An object's value is based on what someone is willing to pay for it. The Father paid for you with the death of his Son; could there be anything of greater value than that?

You will have seasons of doubting God's love for you—this is a natural part of growing to spiritual maturity. When this happens, remember that God loves you even if you don't feel it. In his eyes, you have immense value, and his love for you is unconditional and perfect.

Tell It Like It Could Be

*"[God] speaks of future events with as much
certainty as though they were already past."*

ROMANS 4:17 (TLB)

If encouraging words fill people with life, why are negative words more common?

It doesn't take any skill or discernment to tear someone down. Negative people will often justify their choice of words by saying, "I just tell it like it is." However, this kind of talk doesn't work to create lasting change. There's a better way: You can give people hope, not by telling them "like it is," but by telling them "like it could be."

When Abraham was 99 years old, God said to him, "Abram, I'm going to change your name from Abram to Abraham," which means "the father of a great nation." Abraham actually responded with laughter because he didn't have any children.

God sees the bigger picture. Eventually, Abraham's descendants became the nation of Israel. When God tells us something that seems impossible, we need to trust him because nothing is impossible for God. But there's another lesson to learn: We need to speak words of hope and truth. We need to help people see that a better future is possible. You can encourage others by saying: "I'm praying for your success; I know you'll give it everything you've got, and I'm here to cheer you on—and God is for you, too!" or "I love your humility in seeking help from others. It's refreshing to see someone be eager to learn."

It takes practice, but sharing words of hope sends a loving message that says, "I care about you. I believe in you and you, matter to me."

God's Solution to Temptation

"We capture every thought and make it give up and obey Christ."

2 CORINTHIANS 10:5 (NCV)

Here's the secret to overcoming temptation: Don't fight it—refocus.

The Bible doesn't tell you to resist temptation. It tells you to resist the devil, and that's a whole different issue. The key to overcoming temptation is not to push back. It's to change your focus altogether. Why? Because whatever you resist, persists. Whatever gets your attention, gets you.

The battle for sin always starts in the mind. Temptation follows a predictable pattern: attention, activation, and action. Your mind gets fixated, your feelings kick in, and then you act on it. However, if you're focused on God's truth, you're not allowing your mind to drift into areas it has no business going.

It's true in every area of life—good or bad. If you focus on godly things, you'll be pulled in God's direction. If you focus on ungodly things, you'll be pulled in the opposite direction. Whatever you focus on gets your attention—and you.

The key is to change your mind. Don't try to fight a temptation; instead, turn your mind to God's truth.

The problem is, capturing every thought and turning it to Christ isn't easy. It takes practice. You can't always control your circumstances, and you can't always control the way you feel, but you can choose what you think about. And that will change the way you respond to temptation and help you overcome it with God's help.

Pray for It Before You Pay for It

"Until now you have not asked for anything in my name. Ask and you will receive, so that your joy will be the fullest possible joy."

JOHN 16:24 (NCV)

Are you in financial need and waiting for God to help?

God has promised to meet your financial needs. He's just waiting for you to ask for his help! God says you don't have because you don't ask!

One of the reasons we see so few miracles in our lives is because we just don't ask for them. Instead of living a life based on Christ, we live a life based on credit. When we have something we need, instead of stopping and asking God for it, before we even think about asking God for it, we just use that credit card. We trust credit instead of Christ.

If you want to see God work in your life, pray for it before you pay for it. Do you pray about major purchases before you make them? Or do you just take care of it with your credit card? Every time you use that credit card before praying about it, you're short-circuiting a possible miracle in your life. Before you charge a purchase, why don't you ask God about it first?

God is not going to give you everything you pray for, so don't be surprised. But there are some things he does want to give you, just to do a miracle in your life. Many people have never had a financial answer to prayer because they've never prayed for it specifically.

Do you know why God wants you to learn to ask for things in prayer? So he can provide them, and so you'll be full of joy. God is a loving Father. He's not some ogre sitting in the sky, waiting to make your life a bummer. He wants to bless your life! You just have to ask.

Serving Leads to Significance

"If one of you wants to be great, you must be the servant of the rest."

MATTHEW 20:26 (GNT)

Do you want to be great?

In our world, there is no shortage of people who want to be great—either in their own eyes or in the eyes of others. Who wouldn't want to be admired? Or have power, success, or material possessions?

There's nothing wrong with wanting to be great. When you recognize that God created you to have a thirst for greatness, ambition is a good thing. God wants you to be great, that's the way he created you! God doesn't make junk. Wanting to be great is an expression of the wonder God has placed within you.

Our problem is not our desire to be great; the problem is that we don't know how to get there.

Jesus tells us the way: To be great, we must serve others. Jesus didn't just teach about servanthood, he demonstrated it. He went to the cross as the ultimate act of service: He gave his life as our ransom, paying the price we never could.

Serving isn't easy! But it makes a big impact. Serving looks to the needs of others, and then compassionately meets those needs. You need to make serving a habit that stays with you all day long. Develop eyes that are always on the lookout for ways to help others. Additionally, find a way that you can serve at your church or in your community. Giving back is personally rewarding! You are never more like Jesus than when you are serving others.

Are you ready to be great? Get ready to serve.

Always Speak the Truth

"Someone who holds back the truth causes trouble."

PROVERBS 10:10 (GNT)

Are you ever tempted to hold back the truth?

When it comes to avoiding conflict, many people find it easy to rationalize holding back on telling the truth.

When you don't have honesty in a relationship, you are "hiding" and "hurling." First, you hide your true feelings, even from the people who are closest to you. As you continue to hide, you approach the relationship with hidden agendas— these are expectations that you don't communicate. This makes your actions difficult to understand because the other person has no idea where you are coming from.

Holding everything on the inside isn't healthy either. Eventually all of it erupts like a verbal volcano. When this happens, you hurl insults and shaming statements. If you didn't hold back the truth in the beginning, you never would have reached this point.

When you hide and hurl, you destroy intimacy and end up with superficial relationships. You don't want that.

In the end, people will appreciate your honesty, even if it results in conflict. Here's why: Confrontation is painful, but truth comes out of conflict. Conflict can actually be a bullet train to true intimacy and connection.

If you don't deal with it now, you will deal with it someday. You are only postponing the inevitable crisis. The longer you put off a problem, the worse it gets. You've got to risk honesty if you care about the relationship.

Have you been "shading" the truth in any of your relationships? What will happen in the long run if you don't come clean now?

You Grow Spiritually in Community

"Let us think of ways to motivate one another to acts of love and good works. And let us not neglect our meeting together, as some people do, but encourage one another, especially now that the day of his return is drawing near."

HEBREWS 10:24-25 (NLT)

Why is it important for you to go to church every week?

You don't need church to make God love you more or to make him more willing to forgive you. God won't answer more of your prayers because you show up to a building every week.

You need to go to church because you need the motivation and encouragement that comes from being with other believers. You also need to be motivating and encouraging to others. Maybe you had a great week, and you don't "need" church. Who's going to miss out on the encouragement you provide?

Haven't you ever been on the edge of hopelessness, where just a warm smile or an encouraging word made all the difference in the world?

You need to gather with other believers so that you can both receive and give encouragement. This is what it means to be the church, the bride of Christ.

Here's the truth: Christians need one another to grow. You can't develop a deep faith in isolation. Many people think spiritual growth is a private matter, but God calls believers to live out their faith in community.

If you think you can grow spiritually on your own, you've made an idol out of individualism.

How can you get your heart ready for church this week?

How God Feels About You

"Long before he laid down earth's foundations, [God] had us in mind, had settled on us as the focus of his love."

EPHESIANS 1:4 (THE MESSAGE)

Before God created the universe, he thought of you.

The Bible says the entire universe was created so God could love us. We are *"the focus of his love,"* unlike the rest of creation—unlike animals, angels, stars, or anything else. You were created to be loved by God.

If you grasp that profound truth and let it sink into your soul, you will find great strength, confidence, and peace. God created the entire universe in a specific way to support the existence of human beings, so that he could create you and love you.

The most important thing you can *know* is that God created you to love you. The most important thing you can do is to know and love him back.

Loving God back is your number one purpose in life.

The tragedy is that most people go their entire lives missing their purpose. They know all kinds of things— stock quotes, sports scores, the latest technology, etc.—but they don't know God. They miss out on discovering the depth of God's love and all the blessings he has in store for them.

You may know *about* God, but do you know him personally? Do you have a friendship, a meaningful relationship with God? Like in any relationship, you must spend time with the other person in order to know them deeply and establish a meaningful connection.

Why You Need Others in Tough Times

"Because you are praying for me and the Spirit of Jesus Christ is helping me, I know this trouble will bring my freedom."

PHILIPPIANS 1:19 (NCV)

When you experience a setback, your natural response may be to withdraw, to build a wall around yourself, and to push people away. There's a better way.

When setbacks weaken your faith, allow other people to trust God for you. You need a church family to help support you, pray for you, and encourage you.

Paul was strengthened by the Holy Spirit and by the prayers of others. You need to be connected if you want people to pray for you!

When you're in the midst of troubles, redirect your attention away from bitterness. Join with others who can encourage you to trust in God and help you praise him for what he has done in your life.

Where do you find that kind of support?

You can find it by joining others for worship at a local church. Worshiping God with other people will give you a new and needed perspective on your setbacks. You can also get involved in a small group Bible study. Most churches are too big for you to build relationships by only attending worship services. You need a group of about a dozen people, where you not only study the Bible, but also share your struggles and pray for each other.

You won't find a comeback on your own. You need God's people to build you up and help you keep your focus on God.

Choosing Your Standard

"They are hopelessly confused. Their closed minds are full of darkness; they are far away from the life of God because they have shut their minds and hardened their hearts against him. They don't care anymore about right and wrong."

EPHESIANS 4:17-19 (NLT96)

Where do your core beliefs about what's right and wrong come from?

Your core beliefs determine your convictions, and your convictions determine your conduct, and your conduct determines your character. Your beliefs actually matter because they translate into your character.

Before you determine who you want to be, you need to figure out what you believe. Your values will impact your stress level, your success, your salvation, and many other significant areas of your life.

If you want to build a lasting life of success and significance, you must build it on lasting values. Our society is in a stage of moral decline. This crisis can be seen in politics, business, entertainment, education, and religion.

What is the cause of the decaying of values in our society? Truth decay. The fact is, we no longer value the truth. Instead, two insignificant things have become more important than the truth: convenience and pragmatism. The first says, "Is it easy?" and the second says, "Does it work?"

This represents a major shift in values. Every generation needs to know the difference between right and wrong. Without the truth, there are no standards by which you can evaluate your life.

Are your core beliefs based on God's Word, or something else?

Pray in Jesus' Name

"And I will do whatever you ask in my name, so that the Father may be glorified in the Son. You may ask me for anything in my name, and I will do it."

JOHN 14:13-14 (NIV)

God wants to answer your prayers, but he wants you to ask in Jesus' name.

What is so special about praying "in Jesus' name"? Some people think it's a spiritual sign-off, like adding "10-4, good buddy" to signal the end of a prayer.

Other people think praying "in Jesus' name" is a kind of mystical password that gets you access to God: "Here are all my requests. By the way, here's the codeword: 'In Jesus' name.'"

What's the real reason God wants you to ask in the name of Jesus? It's because he wants to answer your prayers. In fact, the only way to get your prayers answered is to depend on Jesus. There is no other way! Every blessing God gives you is a result of being united with Christ.

When you come to God with your requests, you can't ask on your own merit. You must come on the merit of Christ—and pray: *"Father, I'm coming to you because your Son said to. I'm coming because of what Jesus Christ has already done for me on the cross. He's promised that I can ask in his name, so that's what I'm doing right now."*

If you've got the right attitude, it's not necessary to say "in Jesus' name" at the end of every prayer, but it's always a good idea. Why? Because it reminds you why you have the right to pray—because Jesus is your mediator and has made a way for God to hear and answer your prayers.

Don't Let Gossip Destroy Your Relationships

"A gossip betrays a confidence, but a trustworthy person keeps a secret."

PROVERBS 11:13 (NIV)

People often think of gossip as one of those "little" sins. But when God talks about gossip, he lists it with sexual immorality and murder because it is so destructive to relationships. Gossip can tear apart friendships, families, and churches.

Gossip is talking about a situation with somebody who is neither a part of the solution nor the problem. Gossip makes people feel better about themselves and feel morally superior to others.

The book of Numbers shares a story about a family who struggled with gossip. Miriam gossiped about her own brother, Moses. Not only did she openly criticize him for who he married, but she also questioned God's decision in choosing Moses as leader.

When God told her what she had done wrong, he immediately gave her leprosy.

Do you know what God did next? He invited Moses to pray for Miriam's healing—the person who gossiped against him.

Some of you have been deeply hurt by things said around the office or by a broken confidence between a friend or a family member. Here's what God says to you: "Pray for the person who gossiped against you so that you can be released from the hurt in your life."

Or maybe you've been the one gossiping. This story in the Old Testament reminds us how serious gossip is and how hurtful it can be to people, whatever side of it you're on.

Resentment Is a Killjoy

"Watch out that no bitterness takes root among you, for as it springs up it causes deep trouble, hurting many in their spiritual lives."

HEBREWS 12:15 (TLB)

Nothing destroys a relationship faster than resentment.

We hurt each other in relationships, sometimes intentionally, and often unintentionally. Either way, the result is conflict and hurt feelings. It's a fact of life. What you do with that hurt determines whether you're joyful or miserable.

You've probably heard someone say, "I just don't love him anymore. I just don't have any feelings for her anymore." That's a sign that resentment is involved because resentment eats up emotional energy. You resent the fact that they hurt you and eventually you have no emotional energy left and feel empty inside. Resentment says, "I won't forgive you." Resentment is a killjoy in relationships.

You may feel cheated in a relationship. You're thinking,

"This is not what I expected." The fact is that any relationship, or any marriage, is built on two very imperfect people trying to work on issues together. If you expect perfection and don't work on your unrealistic expectations, you're going to lose your joy.

If you hang on to resentment, it will always hurt you more than anyone else. Resentment is self-destructive and counterproductive. It doesn't just hurt your human relationships, it also infects your relationship with God.

Resentment is like a weed—the longer you wait to deal with it, the more work it will take to uproot it. Start early when resentment is just a seed!

Ultimately, when you refuse to forgive others, you are only hurting yourself.

Managing Your Choices

"I have the right to do anything," you say—but not everything is beneficial. "I have the right to do anything" —but I will not be mastered by anything."

1 CORINTHIANS 6:12 (NIV)

Some things are not necessarily wrong, they're just not necessary. Many of the choices you make in life are not between good and evil. The choices you make in life are between what's good and what's best. Everything is permissible, but *"not everything is beneficial."* Most of the decisions you make are morally neutral. So when making a choice, the question is: "Will this help me, or will this hinder me in pursuing my life purpose?"

For example, you could spend your entire week watching television. That might not be morally wrong, but it's definitely a waste of time. When you waste your time, you're wasting your life.

Until you figure out why God put you here on earth, you really have no basis by which to make decisions. Until you know your purpose, all the other

decisions have no context by which you can determine, "This helps me move toward my goal in life. This helps me become what God wants me to be and this doesn't."

Discernment is a key to success in life because you don't have time for everything. The better you become at prioritizing what matters most, the more effective you're going to be.

You don't have time to do everything in life. The good news is, God doesn't expect you to do everything. The even better news is, there are only a few things worth doing. To really make an impact with your life, figure out what's important and what's not, what's essential and what's trivial, and then make a decision based on what's the best use of your life.

God Will Meet Your Needs

"Since [God] did not spare even his own Son but gave him up for us all, won't he also give us everything else?"

ROMANS 8:32 (NLT)

When you were a kid and needed something, you probably asked your parents. Sometimes what you needed was expensive, but you never worried about where they would get the money to pay for it. That wasn't your job! Your job as their kid was to simply ask.

When it comes to your heavenly Father, it's not your job to figure out how God is going to provide for you. Your job is to just ask. God is interested in every area of your life. He already knows what you need, but he still wants you to ask him for it.

The biggest tragedy that could ever happen to you is separation from God. But God has already taken care of that problem. If God loved you enough to send Jesus to die for your sins, don't you think he loves you enough to help you with your finances? Don't you think he loves you enough to help you with your health, your relationships, your career decisions, and your deadlines?

As God sees it, there are no big problems. Nothing is too hard or too expensive for your heavenly Father to provide. Thank God for the gift of salvation through his Son, and start asking him to align your wants, wishes, and desires with his will.

Your Life Is a Test

"Nothing in all the world can be hidden from God. Everything is clear and lies open before him, and to him we must explain the way we have lived."

HEBREWS 4:13 (NCV)

Life is a test of your responsibility.

God created you and has a plan for your life. He's given you everything you need to succeed, and he is testing your responsibility. The decisions you make in your life influence your eternity.

Life here on earth is the warm-up act for eternity. It's the dress rehearsal. God is testing your level of responsibility for what's going to happen later on. God put you on this earth primarily for two reasons: to get to know him personally through his Son, Jesus Christ, and to develop your character.

God is interested in your character because it's the only thing you're going to take with you when you die. God is evaluating your responsibility, and the Bible says that we will be rewarded in eternity according to our responsibility and our relationship to Christ here on earth.

One day God is going to do an audit on your life. He's going to ask, "What did you do with what I gave you? How did you use your time, money, and influence for my purpose?" One day you will be held accountable to God for how responsibly you lived your life.

God has seen everything you've ever done. We can rationalize our irresponsibility by thinking, "Nobody will ever know." Truth is, God knows. And his opinion is the only one that really matters.

Jesus Is Praying for You

"Who then is the one who condemns? No one. Christ Jesus who died—more than that, who was raised to life—is at the right hand of God and is also interceding for us."

ROMANS 8:34 (NIV)

Consider the fact that God knows everything.

He knows the past, the present, and the future all at once. He already knows what's going to happen in your life this afternoon, next week, next month, next year, and for the rest of your days. He's never confused or surprised.

Did you know that this also means he can pray for your life before anything happens?

The night before Jesus went to the cross, he was with his disciples. Peter was bragging and saying, "Lord, I would die for you!" Jesus loved Peter, but he knew Peter was impulsive. He also knew Peter was going to deny him three times before the next morning. Jesus told Peter that he had already prayed for his trials before he experienced them.

Jesus has already prayed for what you're going to go through this year.

In fact, right now Jesus is in heaven, praying for his family. He is interceding for you, meaning he is talking to God on your behalf. This is the Good News: You don't have to represent yourself before a Holy God because his Son does this for us. You are no longer condemned for anything you've done (or ever will do) because you've accepted God's free gift of salvation through faith.

The Bible says no matter what you go through today, next week, or next year, Jesus is praying for you. He is on your side. You aren't alone—even if you feel like it—you've never been alone.

Working Together
We Accomplish More

"Two people are better than one, because they get more done by working together."

ECCLESIASTES 4:9 (NCV)

God put you on earth to complete a mission. There are some things you can't do on your own because God designed you to work with others.

When you work as a team with other believers, you increase the amount of work you can get done for the Kingdom. You're able to share the workload, resources, finances, and abilities. Plus, it's more fun to get the job done with a team of believers who love and support each other. When you have a church family, celebrations are multiplied and struggles are divided. That's good math!

Picture it this way: When it snows, each flake that falls to the ground is fragile. It can get blown about by the wind or easily be stepped on. When snowflakes stick together, they can be shaped into snowballs. When more snowflakes stick together, the snowball can become so big, it stops traffic.

Working together, we can make a big difference when we simply do our part.

Did you know that our work on earth is actually preparing us for eternity? The Bible tells us that God's servants will serve him in heaven, and it will bring us much joy. Working alongside others changes our character in ways that will never happen when we work alone.

As you walk through life, remember that you're not supposed to do everything on your own. You need other people to walk alongside you— and other people also need you. As you share the burden of your work with fellow Christians, you'll find that you actually accomplish more for the glory of God.

Make Time to Serve

"If you think you are too important to help someone, you are only fooling yourself. You are not that important."

GALATIANS 6:3 (NLT)

God is much more impressed with your service than your status. If you can get over your ego—by giving it up to God—you will accomplish a lot for the Kingdom.

Did you know that you can serve anywhere you want? It doesn't have to be only at your church. Opportunities to lend a helping hand are all around you. Are you good at plumbing, gardening, auto repair, housekeeping, or accounting? Use the skills you already have to help others in practical ways. Don't make serving others more complicated than it really is.

Helping others is as simple as keeping your eyes open for their needs, and then doing something about them. Every need presents an opportunity to show God's love in a tangible way. God is counting on you to step up and share his goodness by helping others.

Consider your workplace. Five days a week, you are around people who are hurting. Behind some of those smiles and polite conversations, people are weighted down by unimaginable burdens. When your eyes are open to the needs of others, God will show you when and how he wants you to help.

It's difficult to serve at home, but that's where it'll make a huge impact. Families that serve one another can handle anything!

There's always an excuse not to help others. If you don't have time to help others, then you are too busy. God did not put you on earth to live just for yourself. Following Jesus means a life of service. If you think you are too good to help others, *"you are only fooling yourself."*

Begin praying for God to open your eyes so you can help others.

If You're Wise, You Won't Disguise

"But the wisdom that comes from heaven is first of all pure;
then peace-loving, considerate, submissive, full of mercy
and good fruit, impartial and sincere."

JAMES 3:17 (NIV)

One of the qualities of wisdom is sincerity.

A "What you see is what you get" attitude is rare in our world. Most people spend a lot of time and effort propping up false images of themselves to impress others. The results typically fall flat, as people just pretend to be impressed.

In ancient Greek theater, just a few actors would often perform the entire play by repeatedly changing parts. They would hold masks in front of their faces for each part, so one person could play five or six different parts. The actor was called a hypocrite. Their real identities were hidden by several different false personas.

Masks are great for entertainment but terrible for relationships.

If you're wise, you won't be a hypocrite. You won't wear masks in order to project something that you're not. You're well aware of your weaknesses, and you don't try to hide them. Pretending that you've got it all together fools nobody.

Wisdom is genuine and authentic; it's expressed with integrity.

People appreciate honesty because it's refreshing. When you start telling people about your weaknesses, they won't be shocked. They probably already know what they are. In fact, they might find your honesty encouraging and get inspired to share some of their own weaknesses with you. When your wisdom is sincere, you connect with others.

Today, commit to living a transparent life before God and others.

Lean on God's Promises
When Troubles Come

"When neither sun nor stars appeared for many days and the storm continued raging, we finally gave up all hope of being saved. After they had gone a long time without food, Paul stood up before them and said: ... 'But now I urge you to keep up your courage, because not one of you will be lost; only the ship will be destroyed.'"

ACTS 27:20-22 (NIV)

When everything in your life is falling apart, you can trust God's promises.

The apostle Paul and his shipmates were battered by a storm, and it looked like all hope was lost. God had told Paul they would be safe, so he told the others to take courage and trust God. Paul didn't place his faith in the ship or the captain. Though Paul knew the storm would destroy that boat, he believed that the promises of God would last.

Paul trusted God's promises as his anchor.

When you are in a storm, do you put your trust in a puny lifeboat? Maybe you think your personality can get you through. Perhaps your looks have always been the key to your success. Are you convinced your money can buy you out of the problem?

Someday, all of those things will perish and let you down. The only safe place to be in the middle of a storm is directly in the center of God's will. Paul's shipwreck story has an incredible ending: The ship was destroyed, but the people made it safe to shore. God's promises always come true.

In the middle of your storm, lean on God's promises.

God Wants You to Forgive Others

"Be kind and tender-hearted to one another, and forgive one another, as God has forgiven you through Christ."

EPHESIANS 4:32 (GNT)

You will never have to forgive anybody more than God has already forgiven you.

You must forgive because resentment is self-torture. Holding on to resentment destroys your relationships with others, robs you of joy and peace, and interferes with your relationship with God.

You only make yourself miserable when you refuse to let go. Your past is in the past; learn from it, but don't linger there. It cannot hurt you anymore unless you make the decision to hold onto it. For your own sake, forgive those who have hurt you.

If you don't forgive others, you will become a prisoner of your own unforgiveness.

You also must forgive because you need God's forgiveness every day. You cannot receive from God what you are unwilling to give to others. Jesus said, *"If you forgive those who sin against you, your heavenly Father will forgive you. But if you refuse to forgive others, your Father will not forgive your sins"* (Matthew 6:14-15 NLT).

You are going to be hurt in life. And when you are hurt, you have only two options: You can rehearse it over and over again or you can release it once and for all. Rehearsing it only continues the cycle of pain. Releasing the pain through forgiveness is the path to inner peace.

When you find it difficult to forgive others, take a good look at your own life to see where you need God's forgiveness. When you make it a habit to confess your sins to God, you'll find it easier to forgive others. The pain still hurts, but you won't be a prisoner to your past.

The Problem with Procrastinating

"All hard work brings a profit, but mere talk leads only to poverty."

PROVERBS 14:23 (NIV)

God wants you to act—today!

Whether it's a project you've been postponing or a relationship you've been neglecting, now is the time to take action. No matter what the reason is for your delay—laziness, perfectionism, wounded pride, fear, or indecision—stop procrastinating and get to work!

Delay always has a cost and the Bible is very clear about the destructive consequences of procrastination in our lives.

Procrastination wastes opportunities. God wants you to make the most of every opportunity, not some or even most, but every opportunity. When you procrastinate, life speeds by and you miss out on the options God is putting in front of you. There is a time limit on your life, once you waste a day, you are never getting it back.

Be a good steward of your life and make the most of every opportunity.

Procrastination causes you problems. The Bible says that a lazy person has trouble all throughout their life. What happens when you put off filling your car with gas? Even more tragic is when you postpone going to the doctor. Problems rarely take care of themselves, the longer you wait, the harder your life becomes.

Procrastination leads to pain for others. Did you know that at its core, procrastination is unloving? Showing real love to people takes commitment, time, and energy. Real love is hard work! When you put it off, you damage your relationships. This is why a lot of marriages fall apart. Both people are unwilling to put in the effort to make it work.

Jesus Means God Saves

"She will bring a son to birth, and when she does, you, Joseph, will name him Jesus—'God saves'—because he will save his people from their sins."

MATTHEW 1:21 (THE MESSAGE)

What does Jesus save us from?

The term "sin" is tossed around so often that, for many people, it has lost some of its meaning. They view sin as a personal list of things they shouldn't do. When you decide for yourself what is wrong and what isn't, you tend to look at your list and think,
"If I just don't do these things, then I'm a good person."

However, sin isn't subjective—everyone doesn't get to create their own definition of sin. As the all powerful Creator of the universe, God defines sin.

Sin is not a list of do's and don'ts, it's much deeper than that. Sin declares independence from God and it's rooted in pride—thinking you know better than God about what is right and wrong.

Sin is an "I" problem—"I want to be my own boss. I don't need God." Sin tells God, "I know what will make me happy more than you do, so I'm going to do what I want to do with my life, not what you put me on earth to do."

Every one of your problems is caused by sin. Sin causes confusion in your life. It causes guilt, shame, regret, bitterness, resentment, and grudges. Sin causes worry, fear, anxiety, depression, discouragement, emptiness, despair, and conflict between you and other people. You are separated from God by your own sin.

The Bible says that Jesus came to remove that separation by saving you from your sins. No matter what you've done, Jesus wants to give you a clean slate. His ability to save you from your past is more powerful than anything you ever did in your past.

What does Jesus save you from? Sin, and everything that follows in its wake.

December

OPEN DOORS

Jesus Is Worth the Journey

"When Jesus was born, some wise men from the east came to Jerusalem."

MATTHEW 2:1 (NCV)

Searching for truth isn't a part-time job. It takes everything you have.

Jesus was born in Bethlehem, which is just six miles from Jerusalem. At the time of Jesus' birth, Jerusalem was the spiritual center of the world. All kinds of spiritual activity was taking place in Jerusalem. All of the major religious leaders of the world were in Jerusalem, but none of them were seeking Jesus. King Herod missed baby Jesus. So did the business leaders of Bethlehem. You too, can have Jesus right in your midst and still miss him if you're not looking for him.

The wise men looked for Jesus. They were willing to make a four to five-month trip across a scorching hot desert to find Jesus. They were serious about seeking God and were willing to do whatever it took to find him.

You can't let anything get in the way of your search for God. It's the most important thing you can do in your life.

Jesus said that the Kingdom of Heaven is like a pearl that is so valuable, we would have to sell everything we have to get it. It seems the wise men from the East understood this long before Jesus ever spoke the parable.

They were willing to give up the comfort of their homes for a long, tough journey because they wanted to worship him.

What do you need to give up in order to worship Jesus?

Dedicate Everything to God

"For the dedication of the new wall of Jerusalem . . . They were to take part in the joyous occasion with their songs of thanksgiving and with the music of cymbals, harps, and lyres."

NEHEMIAH 12:27 (NLT)

Whatever God builds (or rebuilds) in your life must be dedicated to him—this means you declare it for God's glory.

If you want something to succeed, you must dedicate it to God. To have a strong family, business, or church life, you must dedicate it to God. Without dedication, what you've built begins to decay. With dedication, it continues to stay strong.

Dedication is a vital step for those who want to see God's work remain. Far too many people trust God to restore a relationship or career, only to take it back into their own hands once the hard work of rebuilding is done. In their desperation to avoid failure, they trust God, but once the crisis passes, they begin to trust themselves again.

The people of Israel went through this pattern repeatedly. They would trust God; things would improve; they would take it back to themselves; things would fall apart; and they would have to trust God again.

The key to not seeing that pattern happen is found in *dedicating* it all to God. Look at Nehemiah—he knew the wall wouldn't be truly completed until it had been dedicated. The dedication was not some nice little celebration ceremony at the end of the project; it was an all-important part of the rebuilding, which recognized who would get the credit for its usefulness—God.

It's out of your dedication of whatever God has put into your hands that you recognize why it's there and what it can be used for. Make dedication a part of your everyday life.

Only Trust God

> *"The poor, deluded fool feeds on ashes. He trusts something that can't help him at all. Yet he cannot bring himself to ask, 'Is this idol that I'm holding in my hand a lie?'"*

ISAIAH 44:20 (NLT)

Your trust is powerful. Whoever or whatever you trust will influence, guide, and direct the trajectory of your life. If you want to know your future, look at what you are trusting today.

When you put your trust in people or things to meet a need that only God can meet, you are setting yourself up for disappointment and frustration—and ultimately, self-destruction.

God wants to be the top priority in your life. Not only does he deserve that spot because he is your Creator, but also because he will never let you down. When something takes God's rightful place in your life, that thing becomes an idol. Whatever is in first place in your life is your god. Our society says your god can be anything

you want it to be. If it is not God, you have just built an idol.

We can make idols out of anything, even the good things in our life.

We bow down to idols all the time with our careers, relationships, and even our families. We act as if that's what gives us meaning, significance, and self-worth. Only God can give us our purpose, but creating idols gives us a sense of control.

When you serve an idol, not only will you be disillusioned, you will also drift off the course God has for your life.

Trust in the One who made you, loves you, and is always working for your good.

Don't Let Your Anger Lead You into Sin

"If you are angry, be sure that it is not out of wounded pride or bad temper. Never go to bed angry—don't give the devil that sort of foothold."

EPHESIANS 4:26-27 (PHILLIPS)

It is not a sin to get angry. It all depends on how you deal with it.

The problem is, most of us express our anger in ways that take us further away from our goal instead of moving us closer to it.

Don't suppress your anger. You know it's there, but you just bottle it up. Anything under pressure will eventually explode. You can only suppress your anger temporarily, at some point, it'll come out when you least expect it.

When you repress your anger, you don't just push it down, you totally deny it. You say to yourself, "I am not angry. Everything is fine." When you repress it long enough, it can lead to depression. Don't let that happen:

Talk to God because he can handle your anger.

Don't express it in inappropriate ways. Some people pout, and everyone around them has to walk around on pins and needles to avoid making them more upset. Others become sarcastic. It may feel good in the moment, but you hurt people with your words. Some people manipulate and their goal is "Don't get mad, get even."

How you express your anger is a learned behavior—that means it can be unlearned.

So what do you do? You confess your anger to God and admit how you're feeling. Share if you are frustrated, afraid, or threatened. The more honest you can be, the easier it will be to deal with the root causes of your anger.

Living with Responsibility

"Live life, then, with a due sense of responsibility, not as men who do not know the meaning and purpose of life but as those who do."

EPHESIANS 5:15 (PHILLIPS)

God created you and gave you the ability to choose how you respond in life.

You can respond in many different ways to stress, success, problems, crises, and opportunities. It all comes down to your choice. Most of what happens in your life is out of your control. You didn't choose when or where you were born. You also don't choose many of the circumstances and events that happen to you. But you do have the freedom to choose how you respond—and you are responsible for the consequences.

If you want to do something great with your life, you have to learn responsibility.

There's been a dramatic decline in the acceptance of personal responsibility in our society. People don't want to accept responsibility for anything anymore. In fact, we want to avoid all of the negative consequences for our decisions by accusing others and excusing ourselves.

Many of the persistent values today are the antithesis of personal responsibility.

We hear a lot today about rights but not so much about responsibilities. We hear a lot about entitlement, but we don't hear much about obligations. The entitlement mentality says, "The world owes me a living." Someone with a victim mentality believes, "None of my problems are my fault. In fact, they're all your fault." None of these values will challenge you to grow in character and self-discipline as much as personal responsibility does.

Today, how can you take greater responsibility in your life?

How to Bear Fruit That Lasts

*"You did not choose me, but I chose you and appointed you
so that you might go and bear fruit—fruit that will last."*

JOHN 15:16 (NIV)

When you read Jesus' words in John 15, you will discover that "fruit" is a metaphor for a life that pleases God. Your most important success comes from bearing fruit for Jesus because it will last for eternity.

Most of what you do on earth won't last. Ten years after you die, no one will remember the accomplishments you made in your career. Nobody will care what movies you saw, what books you read, or how you spent your free time.

In God's family, he wants you to make a real difference in the world. You have the potential to make an eternal impact.

Producing lasting fruit happens when you remain in Jesus: *"Yes, I am the vine; you are the branches. Those who remain in me, and I in them, will produce much fruit.*

For apart from me you can do nothing" (John 15:5 NLT). We remain in Jesus by knowing and doing his Word.

Producing lasting fruit makes God look good. When you live like Jesus is telling you to live, the people around you will notice. When they know that Jesus is the reason for your lifestyle, they will have more respect for God.

Producing lasting fruit means loving people. God wants you to invest in others because nothing is more important than helping people determine the destiny of their lives. When you love others, they will be more open to saying "yes" to Jesus' love.

How will you go and bear lasting fruit today?

Jesus Came for You

"God showed how much he loved us by sending his one and only Son into the world so that we might have eternal life through him."

1 JOHN 4:9 (NLT)

You've probably heard the saying: "Jesus is the reason for the season."

That is true! Christmas is not about a Santa; it's about a Savior. In the midst of all the busyness that comes with this time of year, it's hard to keep Jesus at the center—but that's where he belongs.

There's a deeper truth: You are also the reason for the season. Jesus came to earth because you needed him. God sent his Son to do something you could never do on your own: pay for your sins. If you didn't need it, God wouldn't have done it. If you didn't need the certain hope that Jesus Christ offers, he wouldn't have wasted the effort.

You need Jesus.

Your sins have made a relationship with God impossible. That's why Jesus came to earth—to save you from everything you've done wrong, so that you could be forgiven and restored into a right relationship with God.

Why would God give up his divine privileges, his glory and honor, to come for your rescue? Because he loves you. He loves you more than you will ever understand. There's no way you can fathom how much God loves you. Trying to understand God's love is like an ant trying to understand the internet—ants don't have the capacity. No one will ever love you as much as God does.

God's Christmas gift to you is eternal life. His grace is truly a gift because it's free. Your job is to accept this gift through faith.

Love God with All Your Heart

"The most important commandment is this: . . .
'You must love the LORD your God with all your heart,
all your soul, all your mind, and all your strength.'"

MARK 12:29-30 (NLT)

God is very clear about the way you ought to love him. He wants you to love him passionately—*"with all your heart, all your soul, all your mind, and all your strength."* In fact, Jesus says that's the most important commandment.

You have the ability to love God with all your heart because you were made in the image of God. God gave you emotions because he has emotions. For instance, the Bible says God feels joy, grief, and pain among other important emotions.

Your ability to feel is a gift from God. It is your emotions that allow you to love and create, to be faithful, and loyal, kind, and generous, and to express the way you feel about the good and bad in life. Your emotions may not always seem like a gift, but even the negative ones have a purpose in your life.

There are two extremes to avoid: emotionalism and stoicism. Emotionalism says the only thing that matters in life is how you feel because your feelings control everything. On the other hand, stoicism says feelings aren't important at all, and the only things that matter are your intellect and your will.

God doesn't want you on either extreme. You're to love him with all your mind, not just your heart and emotions. You're to love him with all your heart, not just through your thoughts and logic. Your love for God is meant to be multifaceted; you're to love him with all the heart, soul, mind, and strength that you have.

Reflect Before You React

"Patient people have great understanding, but people with quick tempers show their foolishness."

PROVERBS 14:29 (NCV)

Do you need more patience?

You can't talk about patience without talking about anger. The Greek word for patience is *macro thumos. Macro* means "long or slow," and *thumos* means "heat, energy, anger, or wrath." A person with patience is slow to get angry.

Anger is not wrong. In fact, God gave you the ability to get angry. Sometimes anger is the appropriate response to a situation. God has given you the capacity to get angry, but it must be managed. Anger out of control is highly destructive in your relationships, but anger in control is an asset when it leads to positive changes. For example, controlled anger can move you to speak out about an injustice.

You have far more control over your anger than you think you do. It's difficult to control your anger because of the overpowering adrenaline rush—the chemical reaction that happens in your body. The key is for you to decide in advance how you're going to handle it. You've got to learn to be patient to have healthy relationships.

Many people, especially Christians, often think that they are being patient if they deny their anger. That's not patience, that's called denial. Patience is not just pushing anger down and pretending it doesn't exist.

Have you noticed that you can't think clearly when you're angry?

Patience engages your mind and leads to greater understanding. Next time you start to get angry, look at the situation from as many angles as possible. Resist your natural urge to act impulsively. Instead, make the decision to reflect before reacting.

Have a Conversation with Your Creator

"I love the LORD because he hears my voice and my prayer for mercy. Because he bends down to listen, I will pray as long as I have breath!"

PSALM 116:1-2 (NLT)

How do you grow a deep relationship? Unlike a casual conversation that begins with—"Hi. How are you?" and quickly ends with "See you later!"—significant relationships require serious conversations.

Relationships don't stand still, meaning that they either grow or decay. If you want a relationship to grow, you need to have significant conversations on a regular basis. This won't happen without intentionality and self-discipline.

The same is true in your relationship with God. It's either growing or decaying, and this is determined by the quality and consistency of your communication with him.

Communication is how you get to know others. To get to know God, what do you talk about?

Anything. You can talk to God about your hopes, dreams, fears, anxieties, goals, ambitions, hurts . . . anything you'd tell a close friend, you can tell God. He wants to hear everything you care about. You can share the things you are embarrassed about, the things you're proud of, and the things you're ashamed of.

You can talk to God about every part of your life.

If you don't feel close to God because your Christian life has become routine, dull, joyless, and lifeless, there's a simple remedy: Start talking with God again. Don't let prayer become a duty or obligation. It's a privilege! The Creator of the universe wants to listen to you, in fact, he's waiting to listen to you right now.

Limiting Your Freedom

*"Be careful, however, that the exercise of your freedom
does not become a stumbling block to the weak."*

1 CORINTHIANS 8:9 (NIV84)

Sometimes there is a legitimate reason to limit your freedom in Christ.

When exercising your freedom hurts someone, you need to show restraint. For example, you are free to say whatever you want, but that doesn't mean it's always best to say what's on your mind. You need to show some discernment, and think before you speak so you don't hurt someone.

In the early church, Christians were debating about eating meat that was offered to idols. In those days, the pagan temples would sacrifice animals and then sell the meat at a discount.

Some Christians got the idea, "We don't believe in those gods. That meat is just as good as any other meat and it's a bargain." So they started buying all this discounted meat, believing they were being good stewards of their money.

Other Christians thought, "That was partaking in the pagan religion and we used to be members of that group. We can't eat that meat." Their goal was to be holy—set apart for God's purpose.

Neither side was wrong, but their personal convictions made having community impossible. One group needed to limit their freedom so that others wouldn't stumble.

You need to make sure that *"your freedom does not become a stumbling block"* to others. A stumbling block is any action or word that will cause other Christians to fall back into their former lifestyle—it causes them to sin.

The immature person always demands his freedom. The mature person can willingly give it up in certain situations out of deference for other people, to avoid influencing a weaker Christian to sin against his own conscience.

Your Conscience Is Important

"Live as free men, but do not use your freedom as a cover-up for evil."

1 PETER 2:16 (NIV84)

If you have a question about a moral decision you are facing and have some doubts, then you've already found your answer: Don't do it.

Whether it's right or wrong, permissible or not; if it bothers your conscience, you'd better forget about making that decision—at least for now.

A guilty conscience always tries to cover-up by making excuses. When Adam sinned in the Garden of Eden, what was the first thing he did? He ran and hid in the bushes. God knew where Adam was, and he said, "I want you to realize what you're doing. You're trying to hide from me." You can't hide from God—the cover-up won't work.

How do we try to ignore our conscience? In a word: rationalization.

Rationalization is making up an excuse in your mind for what you know is wrong in your heart. In your heart, you know which option isn't the best for your life. But in your head, you try to think of all the reasons why it's okay to ignore your heart.

Do you sometimes rationalize in your head when your heart is saying "no"?

People who argue with their hearts and their conscience are saying, "I have my rights. Nobody's going to tell me what to do." Nobody's telling you what to do! The Bible says if our heart condemns us, God doesn't need to judge it. If you can't do something in faith, forget it.

Are you open, honest, and transparent about your life? Or are you so ashamed that you don't want anyone to know what you're doing? Don't use your freedom as a cover-up; listen to what God is telling you through your conscience.

You Need Balance

*"It is senseless for you to work so hard from early morning until late at night . . .
God wants his loved ones to get their proper rest."*

PSALM 127:2 (TLB)

Some people prefer their employment over enjoyment. They are caught up in a fast-paced, unbalanced life.

Ideally, we all want to live balanced lives, but no one is living a completely balanced life. The only person who ever lived a totally balanced life was Jesus Christ. Everyone has work to do in this area of life.

The principle of balance is a law that God established in the universe at the beginning. Every part of the universe is built on this principle of balance and equilibrium. For instance, the earth is perfectly balanced, and God intended it that way. Nature is a system of ecosystems that live in balance. God has created a food chain with plants and animals that live in harmony on earth. Even nature is set up with a system of checks and balances. Your life needs that, too.

If your life is not balanced, you'll collapse. God designed the human body based on the principle of balance. When any one of your body's systems gets out of balance, that's called disease. When our systems are all in balance, we call that health. Healing is simply the recovery of balance to the body.

God is concerned that you get the right amount of rest. When your life is out of balance, you're not in God's will. Take the time to talk to God and take a step toward a balanced life.

God Became Man

"While they were there, the time came for the baby to be born, and she gave birth to her firstborn, a son . . . And Jesus grew in wisdom and stature, and in favor with God and man."

LUKE 2:6-7, 52 (NIV)

Jesus Christ was a real man, flesh and blood, bones and hair. He was a real person—not a myth or a fable.

Why would Jesus come as a human being? If God had wanted to communicate with dogs, he would have become a dog. If he wanted to communicate with birds, he would have become a bird. But God wanted to communicate with people, so he became a person.

How is Jesus like us?

He was born like us. He gave up all he had and came into the world like billions of other babies. There was no flashy entrance that could be seen by everyone in the world. Jesus arrived in the middle of the night in a stable in Bethlehem.

Jesus grew and developed and had growth spurts. Can you imagine what it would have been like to be in school with Jesus? He did not parade the fact that he was God. He was a Jew from Palestine. He was a real man who worked as a carpenter.

Although Jesus was without sin, he experienced the same pressures and temptations that we do without giving into them. This is important because it means Jesus can relate to you when you're struggling with temptations.

Jesus suffered like us. He felt pain and disappointment. He became tired and lonely. He grieved, and he cried. Jesus became what we are, so we can become what he is.

A Life of Legalism

"I no longer count on my own righteousness through obeying the law; rather, I become righteous through faith in Christ. For God's way of making us right with himself depends on faith."

PHILIPPIANS 3:9 (NLT)

Legalism takes the focus off of what God has done for you and shifts it to what you have done for God. This attitude is a trap because it acts as if you have to prove yourself to God in order to earn his love.

Legalism has two devastating consequences in your life. On one hand, it will steal your joy because you'll do everything for God out of fear or guilt. You will be constantly concerned whether you've done enough to make God happy. On the other hand, legalism may lead you to feelings of entitlement, which says, "God needs to do what I want because I've earned it."

You may even start insisting the same expectations on others, thinking they also have to prove their worth to God—and to you!

Before Paul understood God's grace, he was a legalist—a Pharisee who trusted the rules to make him right with God.

How do you know when you're a legalist? When you live by fear or entitlement and you're judgmental of other people.

How do you know when you're living by grace? When you're gracious to others. People who live by grace often find it easier to forgive, because they recognize God continues to forgive them.

The important thing to remember is that there's nothing you can do to make God love you more or less. He has done everything necessary to make you right with him.

All that's left is for you to live by faith.

Who Is Your Provider?

*"My cup overflows. Surely your goodness
and love will follow me all the days of my life."*

PSALM 23:5-6 (NIV)

Is your focus on what you can provide or on what God can provide?

Even though he was walking through difficult times, David was able to be thankful for God's goodness and love because his cup was overflowing. God was his Provider, so David had more than he needed.

As you walk through the different seasons of life, you can choose between two different attitudes. You can have a shortage mindset or a surplus mindset.

With a shortage mindset, you constantly think, "I don't have enough time. I don't have enough money. I don't have enough energy. I don't have enough contacts, opportunities, knowledge, or education." It's the sense that you're always a day late and a dollar short.

A shortage mindset focuses on your limited resources, and the result is an overwhelmed life.

A surplus mindset focuses on God's limitless resources, and the result is an overflowing life. He wants to meet all your needs—beyond what you can imagine—and he's the only one who can! Have you ever worried that the person breathing next to you is stealing your air? Of course not. You know that God created more than enough air for everybody to have all the air we need.

A surplus mindset focuses on God's unlimited resources, and the result is an overflowing life.

God has more than enough power and resources to meet all your needs *and* everybody else's needs at the same time. You don't have to worry about running short of anything.

You get to decide—will you have a shortage mindset or a surplus mindset?

Slow Down and Enjoy the Moment

"All of us should . . . enjoy what we have worked for. It is God's gift."

ECCLESIASTES 3:13 (GNT)

God has given you just enough time to do his will.

If you have more things on your schedule than you have the time to do them, it means either there are things on your list that God doesn't intend for you to do, or you're doing them in the wrong way.

We can get so busy, we don't take time to enjoy the moment. You need to learn to be content in the "now" while you're working toward your goals. The ultimate goal of life is to know God and enjoy a relationship with him. Use the talents and gifts he gave you to serve others because that builds your character for eternity.

If you're constantly busy, you're going to suffer from physical, emotional, or spiritual fatigue. Or you may have to deal with all three.

Physical fatigue can be cured by rest. But it takes more than rest to rejuvenate emotional and spiritual fatigue. If your spirit's dried up, a three-week Tahiti vacation isn't going to restore it. You'll rest your body, but you'll come back and still have the same problems you left behind. You need more than that. What you need to do is get plugged back into the power that comes when Christ is at the center of your life.

Jesus offers us an exchange program. He'll exchange your weariness for his peace and power.

Enjoy the moment, realizing that the life God has given you is a gift.

Your Work Isn't Your Worth

*"I have also learned why people work so hard to succeed;
it is because they envy the things their neighbors have."*

ECCLESIASTES 4:4 (GNT)

Does envy ever show up in your life?

You have two options in life: Either you spend all of your time trying to keep up with others, or you slow down and become content with what God has already provided for you.

We are caught in the grip of materialism when we buy things we don't need, with money we don't have, to impress people we don't even like. You need to be more realistic, rational, and logical about your spending. When will you stop and ask yourself, "Is it worth it to keep running this rat race?" You can win the rat race, but you're still a rat.

You can know that you are possessed by your possessions when you confuse the difference between your work and your worth. This is one reason many people have a hard time relaxing. It's a lie to believe what we do is the same thing as what we are. Your identity is not in what you do, but in who God made you to be.

Growing up, some of you were told, "You aren't going to amount to much." So in the back of your mind, you thought, "I'm going to show them. I'm going to prove them wrong." You work harder and harder, and no matter what you accomplish, it's never enough. When you try to relax and add balance to your life, those haunting words come back and you revert to your old way of living.

The greatest things in life aren't things. Your worth isn't in your work, it's in God's unconditional love for you.

Limit Your Labor

*"You have six days in which to do your work, but the seventh day
is a day of rest dedicated to me."*

EXODUS 20:9-10 (GNT)

You have to make a conscious decision to set aside time for other things besides work.

Decide how many hours you're going to work each week and stick to it. If you don't set a standard number of hours, you'll never take a break. Commit to your goal and hold yourself accountable to a friend.

Dedicating time to rest is so important that God put it in the Ten Commandments. It's right up there with "Don't murder, commit adultery, lie, or steal." God says to take a day off every seven days because he created you to be in a healthy rhythm of work and rest.

This principle is called the Sabbath, which literally means "a day of rest." God expects you to observe a Sabbath every seven days, and he designed it for your benefit. It doesn't matter what day you choose as your Sabbath, as long as you do it every week.

What do you do on your Sabbath? God says to rest your body, recharge your emotions, and refocus your spirit. If you don't take time off, your body will make you! You're not designed to go without rest. Sometimes the most spiritual thing you can do is take a nap.

You can recharge yourself emotionally through quietness, recreation, and relationships. It takes different things for different people. Figure out what recharging looks like for you.

You can refocus your spirit through worship. Spend time focusing on God—it will put everything else in perspective. Time with God shrinks your problems and reminds you that God is in control.

Your best requires rest.

Bring Life with Your Words

"Kind words bring life, but cruel words crush your spirit."

PROVERBS 15:4 (GNT)

Do your words "bring life" to others?

Kind words communicate the truth with tact. Tact is about being careful with how you say what you say. The way you say something determines how well it's going to be received. Even just the tone and inflection of your voice can change the meaning of a word.

If you want to get along with people in your life, the secret is tactfulness. It's the emotional balm of relationships. Well-chosen words reduce friction in conflict and make communication more effective. Tactfulness is the key to a happy home, a happy marriage, and happy relationships.

People with tact often have a lot less to retract. Tact means speaking the truth in love; it's the ability to make a point without making an enemy. Some people often confuse rudeness

with frankness. They say things like, "I just tell it like it is and let the chips fall where they may!" That's not kind or caring. You're basically saying, "I couldn't care less about you. I don't care if it hurts your feelings. All I care about is saying what I want to say."

Rude words don't bring life, they crush spirits.

Whenever you're frank with people, speak in a respectful way. When you want to be frank with someone, ask yourself: "Why am I going to say this? Am I going to say this to build them up or tear them down?" Sometimes when we think we're being frank, we're just spouting off our anger. There's no value to that.

The secret to bringing life with your words lies in being tactful and truthful at the same time.

How to Fish for People

"Jesus called out to them,
'Come, follow me, and I will show you how to fish for people!'"

MATTHEW 4:19 (NLT)

Following Jesus is about fishing for people.

Jesus didn't say, "Come, follow me, and I will show you how to hunt for people." Hunting isn't the best model for connecting people with their Creator. Hunting uses aggressive confrontation and scares off the target. Fishing is different because it's based on attraction and requires a gentle give and take.

When you fish for people, you need to think like the people in your "pond." What makes them laugh? What makes them tick? Before you share the Good News with a friend, relative, or co-worker, you first need to find common ground. You can do this by connecting through shared needs, interests, and hurts.

Did you know that ninety percent of sharing the Good News is the art of asking questions? Make a list of questions that will show you care and that will lead to more conversations with the person most on your heart.

Perhaps the best difference between fishing and hunting is this: When you hunt, the animal has no choice. In fishing, the fish gets to choose whether to pursue the bait or not.

Jesus came so that the world would have the opportunity to live eternally with God. Jesus is calling out, *"Come to me, all you who are weary and burdened, and I will give you rest"* (Matthew 11:28 NIV). And he is making his call through us.

You can't follow Jesus if you are not passionate about helping others follow him too.

Who's in your pond?

Pray for Greater Love

"May the Lord make your love for one another and for all people grow and overflow, just as our love for you overflows."

1 THESSALONIANS 3:12 (NLT)

God likes it when our prayers align with his will and have his ultimate plan in mind. The more specific the prayer, the better. These are the kind of prayers that work.

What kind of prayer aligns with God's will and has his ultimate plan in mind? Prayers that impact all of eternity: *"God, I want my friend to know you."*

How can you make that prayer more specific? Pray, *"Please remove this obstacle of fear I have that's keeping me from sharing the Good News with my friend."*

What's an even more specific prayer? Try this prayer: *"God, I want my friend to come into a relationship with you so that I can celebrate with her in heaven—but I'm afraid to tell her about you. Will you please increase my love for her so that my fear is no longer an obstacle?"*

Fear is one of the greatest obstacles we face when telling others about Jesus. We're afraid they will get offended, or even reject us. We're afraid they'll ask us really hard questions. However, when you live for God, who is love, your love grows more perfect. It's the kind of love that has no fear—and it's what motivates people to tell others about Jesus.

Why not pray for greater love rather than less fear?

If someone told you to jump into an icy pond, you wouldn't do it. Why? For starters, it'd be uncomfortable. It would also be scary and dangerous, and you could get hypothermia. But if your daughter fell in, you'd jump right in. Your selfless love for her would quickly replace your fear and motivate you to do what it takes to save her.

Love is what motivated Jesus to rescue us, so asking him to increase your love for others will always align with his will and his ultimate plan. It's a prayer he is sure to answer.

Transformation

"Don't copy the behavior and customs of this world, but let God transform you into a new person by changing the way you think."

ROMANS 12:2 (NLT)

God sent his Son because he loves us.

As followers of Jesus, we are called to follow his example by loving people as God loves us.

This means accepting other people no matter what choices they make. Acceptance isn't the same thing as approval of everything they do. God accepted you, just as you are, but he doesn't approve of every decision you make.

God calls us to love people, but not to copy their behavior. The world's value system is not our model for living.

The problem is this: We often get it reversed. We love the value system of the world and hate the people. Christians do this all the time. Instead of being different, we can be just as materialistic, just as hedonistic, and just as enmeshed in the culture. And we do all of this while judging the world and hating its people. That's backward.

For the rest of your life, you'll face great pressures to conform to the culture. This was Israel's biggest problem for thousands of years—they wanted to be like the other nations around them. However, God gave them all kinds of moral, civil, and ceremonial laws to make them different—and he did this on purpose.

One reason you may not know what God wants you to do in life is because you may be too infected with the culture. Often this happens without you realizing it. However, you can't think like the world and think like God at the same time. You have to make a choice.

Fill your mind with God's truth, and let it transform your life by changing the way you think.

Stop Passing Judgement

*"Each of us will give an account of ourselves to God.
Therefore let us stop passing judgment on one another."*

ROMANS 14:12-13 (NIV)

As followers of Jesus, we live in a constant tension.

On one hand, we want to honor God and do what he wants. On the other hand, everything in our world is directly opposed to God. Life in the Kingdom of God is at odds with the ways of the world. You are going to see many things that disagree with your values, and more importantly, with God's values. How do you respond?

Unfortunately, too many Christians respond by passing judgment on others.

You can avoid being judgmental by telling the truth with gentleness. You can tell someone that disobeying God will lead to negative consequences in a way that doesn't pass judgment on them.

You become judgmental when you take the truth and hold it over peoples' heads, in order to make yourself feel superior. We are called to tell the truth to help people, not to harm them or put them down. You can disagree with someone without being disagreeable. Even if you are right about something, being rude about it puts you in the wrong.

Being judgmental—expecting an unbeliever to act like a believer—doesn't make sense. The Bible says that people can't act the way God wants them to act until they invite God into their lives and accept his power to change their ways.

You will stop passing judgment on others when you remember that everyone is accountable to God. That means they aren't accountable to you. You aren't the judge, God is. Remember, you are accountable to stop passing judgment on others.

God's Gift to You

"Thanks be to God for his indescribable gift!"

2 CORINTHIANS 9:15 (NIV)

God has a wonderful gift for you.

God's gift to you is unlike anything you'll open this Christmas. You might get a gift that's *impersonal*, like a bunch of gift cards to your favorite places. Or, you'll get an *impractical* gift that you simply don't have any use for. Some gifts you receive might be *temporary* because they'll wear out or break before you know it. Other gifts are just going to be flat out cheap.

Thankfully, none of those adjectives apply to God's gift to you. Rather, God's gift is personal; he came to earth with you in mind. It's practical; he gives you everything you need to live a life that pleases him. It's forever; it will last throughout eternity and it will never wear out. And most importantly, it's priceless: Jesus Christ paid for it with his own life.

You can't get a gift like that from anyone but your heavenly Father. The gift of his Son, Jesus, will heal all your deepest hurts, forgive every mistake you've ever made, and help you understand the purpose for which you were put on earth. It will make you a better person, fill your life with joy, and secure your future in heaven.

Don't go another Christmas without accepting and unwrapping God's gift to you. An unopened gift, no matter how wonderful, is a worthless gift. When you fully understand how wonderful God's gift is to you—how incredible, how magnificent, and how mind-blowing it is—there is only one logical response.

Don't wait another moment to open his gift today!

Make a Commitment to God's Standard

"How can [anyone] keep his way pure?
By living according to your word."

PSALM 119:9 (NIV84)

Is your purity a priority?

There is only one way you can remain pure in a polluted world, and it's dependent on your standard for what is right and wrong. If your standard is God's Word, you will be pure. If it is anything else, you will be as impure as the world.

God says several things in his Word that aren't popular and may seem counterintuitive. You have to decide that when God says something, you're going to do it because he knows what's best for you. God loves you and his standard is in the Bible to help you. If you want to be pure in an impure world, you will need to commit to God's Word as the standard for your life.

Sexual impurity has always been a problem for humanity. The truth is,

God invented sex, and it is far more than a physical act. It is also spiritual and it has spiritual consequences. Not only that, sex has emotional, social, and legal consequences as well.

The Bible also says that sex is exclusively reserved for a husband and a wife who are committed to each other in marriage. Anything outside of that—sex before marriage, or sex outside of marriage, will have profoundly negative consequences. Sex is a gift from God, but if your ideas are different than God's Word, what will be your standard?

God has a plan for your relationships, finances, gifts, abilities, and every other area of your life. Will you be committed to purity? Will you live according to his Word?

The Danger of Pride

"In his pride the wicked man does not seek him;
in all his thoughts there is no room for God."

PSALM 10:4 (NIV)

Pride is almost as old as humanity.

The first temptation is found in Genesis 3, where Satan tells Adam and Eve that they will be like God if they decide for themselves what is right and wrong. Wanting to be like God is a good thing, but attempting to become God is rebellion.

Pride is a mask that pretends to be God.

Pride is the desire to call our own shots, and it's the cause of so much stress in our lives. Pride keeps you from seeking God and even thinking about him. We aren't God—and never will be. We are created beings. When we try to be God, we end up more like Satan, who tried the same thing.

Have you ever noticed it's easy to accept your human limitations intellectually but not emotionally? You give mental assent to the idea, but when you're faced with your own limitations—your desire to be taller

(or shorter), smarter, stronger, more talented, beautiful, or wealthy—you react with irritation, anger, and resentment.

Pride is unmasked by your limitations.

The unmasking is painful, but it also presents you with an opportunity. Have you ever wanted to have it all and do it all, only to get upset when it doesn't happen? Then, when you notice that God has blessed others with characteristics you don't have, you respond with envy, jealousy, and self-pity. There's a better way to respond.

Unmasked pride allows you to surrender to God.

Surrendering is best demonstrated in obedience, when you cooperate with your Creator. You say "Yes, Lord" to whatever he asks of you. Actually, "No, Lord" is a contradiction. You cannot claim Jesus as your Lord without laying down your pride.

Your Freedom of Choice

"I am giving you the choice between a blessing and a curse!"

DEUTERONOMY 11:26 (NLT)

The Bible is very clear that life is unfair. Earth is not heaven. It is an imperfect place, and because of sin in the world, there is injustice.

One of the reasons God allows injustice in the world is because he has given us the freedom of choice. In the story of creation, God says, "I'm going to make man in my own image." That means you, as a human being, are different from animals.

Being made in God's image means having the freedom to make moral choices. You can choose between right and wrong. In fact, every day, you make hundreds of decisions.

Animals choose only by instinct, which is based on survival. People, however, rely on more than just their instinct.

They live by their conscience, which is based on morality.

The choices we make have a real impact in the world; as there are consequences that ripple out from the decisions we make. We often make poor choices, which lead to negative effects. Why does God allow this? Because God wants you to love him by choice, not by force. God loved us first, and he's calling us to love him back.

We create problems when we choose to not do what God wants us to do.

God could take away all the injustice in the world. All he would need to do is take away our freedom of choice. But God loves us, and wants us to live in freedom. How will you love him back today?

Spend Time with Wise People

"Spend time with the wise and you will become wise,
but the friends of fools will suffer."

PROVERBS 13:20 (NCV)

Popularity is overrated.

You just need a few good friends who will build you up. Truth is, it's not easy to find good friends. It takes time and intention. But if you don't make the effort to seek out and build quality relationships, you will suffer. Foolish friends create relational havoc in your life.

You need wise friends because spiritual growth happens in community. You cannot grow when you are isolated and alone. You could move to the top of a mountain by yourself and spend your life in silence, reading books. You would grow in knowledge, but you wouldn't grow in wisdom. Smart people aren't necessarily wise. That's why many people with advanced degrees still have marriages that are falling apart.

Wisdom and love go together because wisdom shows up in relationships.

Wise friends don't always tell you what you want to hear, but they will tell you what you need to hear. Sometimes this hurts. And while no wound is pleasant, these will make you wiser. Foolish friends wound without purpose.

A wise friend wants what's best for you. That person loves you in spite of the worst in you. A foolish friend tells you what you want to hear. The wise friend loves you enough to tell you what you need to hear.

Are your friends building you up and helping you grow?

Confession

"Forgive us our sins, just as we have forgiven those who have sinned against us."

MATTHEW 6:12 (TLB)

Confession is like taking out the garbage.

It doesn't take a long time, but it keeps your house from stinking. If you don't take out the garbage in your soul every day, your soul starts to stink. Don't let sin stockpile in your life because then you'll start carrying around shame.

You weren't built to carry guilt.

Confession simply means that you own up to your wrong actions and reactions. You admit your sins. You also need to forgive everyone else who's sinned against you. Don't let the grudges build up in your life, because then you'll end up carrying resentment.

Nothing will weigh down your life like guilt and resentment.

You must understand: There is never any reason for you to walk around feeling guilty if you know the Lord.

Some people actually think they're more spiritual by feeling guilty. As a result, we regret the past, we worry about the future, and we waste today. We crucify ourselves on the cross of guilt and resentment. You don't become more spiritual by feeling guilty.

Jesus died on the cross so you don't have to carry guilt.

There is no rational reason for carrying around guilt. When you feel guilty, it should last about three seconds. That's about how long it takes to confess it and ask for forgiveness. Make this your prayer:

"Lord, is there anything in my life I need to clean out? Is there any sin? God, is there something here that I need to just admit to you? I need to confess. I don't want to carry the garbage into the rest of the day. Is there anyone whom I need to forgive? I can't handle my guilt and resentment so I'm giving all my life to you. Amen."

Always Keep Praying

"And pray in the Spirit on all occasions with all kinds of prayers and requests. With this in mind, be alert and always keep on praying for all the Lord's people."

EPHESIANS 6:18 (NIV)

Practically speaking, what does it look like to always pray?

Anyone can do it, you just need to keep a running conversation with God. You just talk to him like you'd talk with anyone else. Don't ever end it, simply keep the conversation going throughout the day by talking about whatever comes up throughout the day.

In the beginning, you have to think about prayer—you will need to make a decision and you'll need reminders to pray. After some time, you will be able to develop a habit of continuous prayer. You'll get to the point where you are talking to God without even thinking about it.

Your prayers will become like breathing. You don't think about breathing, you just do it. If you didn't breathe, you'd die. Prayer is spiritual breathing. Prayer is to your soul what breathing is to your body. Continuous prayer needs to become so natural that you don't even think about it.

Consider this: You talk to yourself all the time. You are your biggest fan! No matter what happens to you, you feel it, taste it, touch it, smell it, and hear it . . . and you talk to yourself about everything you experience.

Instead of talking to yourself, just talk to God. You don't need to use fancy words; you can just speak to him conversationally. Whatever you are interested in, talk about it with God. It's not hard to make a switch from talking to yourself to talking to God.

If you don't feel like praying, it means you're not praying about how you feel. You need to talk to God about what you are feeling, as you feel it. Tell him about your nervousness, anxiety, excitement, and frustration. God already knows everything about you, he just wants you to talk to him.

You can talk to God anywhere, anytime, about anything. Pray as the Spirit leads.

Scripture Index

GENESIS
1:1 — 322
6:22 — 84
12:2 — 312
32:24-25 — 240
32:26 — 79

EXODUS
3:4 — 317
20:9-10 — 368
34:21 — 75

DEUTERONOMY
11:2 — 41
11:26 — 377
30:19-20 — 209

1 SAMUEL
17:47 — 186

1 KINGS
19:3, 11 — 38

2 CHRONICLES
20:20 — 264
31:21 — 54

NEHEMIAH
12:27 — 351

JOB
1:21 — 192
11:13, 15-16 — 196
11:13-18 — 167
23:8-10 — 67
33:14 — 229
34:29 — 179

PSALMS
5:3 — 231
6:3-4 — 285
10:4 — 376
18:30 — 145
23:3 — 151
23:4 — 68
23:5-6 — 365
23:5 — 62
23:6 — 304
32:3 — 94
34:18 — 18
37:7 — 287
37:23-24 — 6
50:15 — 157, 244
51:12 — 273
53:2 — 14
62:8 — 107
70:5 — 270
73:26 — 70
90:12 — 194
100:5 — 130, 138
101:3 — 258
103:2 — 31
103:10, 12 — 239
103:13 — 35
103:14 — 201
119:9 — 375
119:18 — 110
119:39-42 — 113

119:45 — 297
119:104 — 71
127:2 — 362
139:16 — 11, 252
139:23-24 — 263
141:3 — 249
145:13-14 — 298
147:7 — 8

PROVERBS
2:9 — 220
3:5-7 — 216
3:5 — 156
4:23 — 69
9:9 — 290
10:9 — 83
10:10 — 330
11:13 — 336
12:16 — 227
12:26 — 72
13:20 — 378
14:8 — 20
14:23 — 347
14:29 — 74, 358
15:4 — 369
15:12 — 175
16:9 — 202
16:21 — 300
17:3 — 24
19:21 — 33
20:3 — 40
20:25 — 133
20:27 — 190
21:5 — 77, 129
23:12 — 171
25:28 — 25, 30
26:20 — 115
28:13 — 203, 267
28:26 — 134
29:8 — 126
29:11 — 109
29:25 — 116
31:8-9 — 319

ECCLESIASTES
3:1, 4 — 163
3:13 — 366
4:4 — 367
4:9 — 342
5:19 — 259
6:9 — 215
11:4 — 131, 307

ISAIAH
26:3 — 95
40:31 — 150
43:1-2 — 183
44:20 — 352
48:10 — 123
53:3 — 60
54:10 — 325
58:10-11 — 185

JEREMIAH

15:19 — 276
20:13 — 292
29:11-12 — 146
29:13 — 23

LAMENTATIONS
3:22-24 — 234
3:40-42 — 254
3:40 — 108
3:53-57 — 10

DANIEL
1:8 — 168
1:11-13 — 44
2:16 — 182
3:28 — 177

HABAKKUK
2:1 — 112
2:3 — 281
3:17-18 — 193

MATTHEW
1:21 — 348
2:1 — 350
4:19 — 370
5:5 — 314
5:18 — 55
6:12 — 379
6:33 — 96, 241
7:24 — 91
11:28-30 — 63
16:24 — 213
16:26 — 268
20:26 — 329
20:28 — 305
24:35 — 105
26:38-39, 42 — 81

MARK
6:48 — 229
9:24 — 103
10:48-49 — 233
10:51 — 234
11:22-24 — 243
11:24 — 249
12:29-30 — 349, 351
12:30 — 261
16:15 — 296

LUKE
2:6-7, 52 — 363
4:18-19 — 187
4:18 — 243
5:4-5 — 180
6:27-29 — 43, 136
8:12 — 47
8:13 — 48
8:14 — 49
8:15 — 50
9:23-24 — 148
9:62 — 265
10:37 — 228
10:41-42 — 219
11:1 — 324
11:11-13 — 206

16:10-11	161	4:20	308	3:12	371
19:5	246	6:12	338	5:11	214
23:34	225	8:9	360	5:16-18	73
JOHN		9:25-26	260	5:18	87
4:23	76	10:24	303, 301	**1 TIMOTHY**	
4:39	242	10:31	137	4:7	256
6:48, 51	114	12:27	61	4:15	58
8:31-32	232	13:1	5	6:18-19	277
8:31	106	13:3	222	6:21	158
8:32	152	13:4	159	**2 TIMOTHY**	
8:36	9	13:7	166	1:7	59
8:44	22	15:10	144	1:8	125, 199
9:4	289	15:33	88	1:12	28
10:9	101, 250	**2 CORINTHIANS**		2:21	178
11:21-23	274	1:4, 6	64	3:16	251
11:25-26	17	1:9	100	4:16-17	21
12:24	271	4:8-9	320	**TITUS**	
14:13-14	335	4:16-17	173	3:14	294
14:26	189	5:17	204	**PHILEMON**	
14:27	197	5:18	184	1:6	296
15:16	355	9:6, 8	85	**HEBREWS**	
16:24	328	9:15	374	2:1	46
17:4	310	10:5	327, 195	4:13	52, 340
20:19	118	13:11	316	10:24-25	181, 331
ACTS		**GALATIANS**		10:25	89
2:44-45	230	5:13	78	11:7	248
4:29	143	6:3	343	11:26	224
10:2	154	6:4	45	11:27	236
16:26	124	6:5	149	12:1	164
17:11	122	6:9	221	12:15	337
20:24	32, 117	**EPHESIANS**		**JAMES**	
27:20-22	345	1:4	332	1:4	141
27:24	208	2:8-9	211	1:18	66
ROMANS		3:20	279	1:22	111
1:12	56	4:17-19	334	1:25	37
1:17	306	4:22-24	147	2:14; 17-18	280
3:24	82	4:23	155	2:15-16	39
4:17	326	4:26-27	353	3:5-6	321
4:18	283	4:29	80	3:13	315
5:1	153	4:32	13, 346	3:17	51, 344
5:3	299	5:15-16	170	4:6-7	212
5:8	99	5:15-17	86, 323	4:17	139
5:10-11	12	5:15	354	5:16	188, 210
7:24-25	42	6:12	235	**1 PETER**	
8:1	120	6:17	7	1:6-7	282
8:6, 8	104	6:18	207, 380	2:2	19
8:9	245	**PHILIPPIANS**		2:9	261
8:11	90	1:6	127	2:16	361
8:28	135	1:19	333	3:8	226, 293
8:32	53, 339	2:4	262	3:10	142
8:33-34	284	2:13	162, 278	3:13-15	200
8:34	341	2:17	275	4:2	98
10:9-10	291	3:9	364	4:10	272
10:17	26	4:6-7	311	4:16	92
12:2	372	4:6	172	4:19	93
12:4-5	176	4:8	218	5:12	288
12:14	269	4:11-13	198	**2 PETER**	
12:15	102	4:19	217	3:11	119
12:18	29	**COLOSSIANS**		**1 JOHN**	
14:12-13	373	1:15	16	4:4	174
15:7	309	1:23	165	4:9	356
15:13	57	2:14	169	4:16, 18	205
1 CORINTHIANS		3:10	313	5:13	295
1:30	15	3:13	140, 257	**REVELATION**	
3:10-13	121	**1 THESSALONIANS**		2:4-5	132
4:7-8	27	2:4	34